GOING GLOBAL: KNOWLEDGE-BASED ECONOMIES FOR 21ST CENTURY NATIONS

GOING GLOBAL: KNOWLEDGE-BASED ECONOMIES FOR 21ST CENTURY NATIONS

EDITED BY

MARY STIASNY
University of London, UK

TIM GORE
University of London, UK

United Kingdom − North America − Japan
India − Malaysia − China

Emerald Group Publishing Limited
Howard House, Wagon Lane, Bingley BD16 1WA, UK

First edition 2014

Copyright © 2014 British Council

British Library Cataloguing in Publication Data
A catalogue record for this book is available from the British Library

ISBN: 978-1-78441-003-2

Printed and bound by CPI Group (UK) Ltd, Croydon, CR0 4YY

ISOQAR certified
Management System,
awarded to Emerald
for adherence to
Environmental
standard
ISO 14001:2004.

Certificate Number 1985
ISO 14001

INVESTOR IN PEOPLE

Acknowledgements

We would like to express our thanks to the British Council for their steadfast support for this publication in its third year. We would particularly like to thank Aimee Watson for her guidance through the collation, organising, and editing process. We would also like to thank the copy editors, Tony Brown and Sylvia Suddes who we think have brought a consistent style to the publication without losing the diversity of content. We have both very much enjoyed the privilege of being able to edit this important series of books.

Editors
Mary Stiasny
Pro-Director, Learning and International, Institute of Education
United Kingdom

Tim Gore
Director Global Networks and Communities, University of London
International Programmes, United Kingdom

Contents

**SECTION 3: HOW HAS INTERNATIONAL COLLABORATION
CONTRIBUTED TO INTERNATIONALISING TERTIARY
EDUCATION STRUCTURES AND SYSTEMS?**

List of Contributors

Abdul Sattar Al-Taie	Executive Director, Qatar National Research Fund, Qatar Foundation, Qatar
Alexander Bedny	First Vice-Rector, Lobachevsky State University of Nizhni Novgorod, National Research University, Russia
Alexander Grudzinskiy	Vice-Rector for International Affairs, Lobachevsky State University of Nizhni Novgorod, National Research University, Russia
Andreas Göthenberg	Executive Director, STINT Foundation, Sweden
Christopher Hill	Director Research Training and Academic Development, University of Nottingham Malaysia Campus, Malaysia
Dorothea Rüland	Secretary General, German Academic Exchange Service, Germany
Gerald Wangenge-Ouma	Director for Institutional Planning, University of Pretoria, South Africa
Hannah Ellis	Analyst, Study Portals, The Netherlands
Hans Pohl	Program Director, STINT Foundation, Sweden
Ian Willis	Head of Education Development Division and UK Director of Lahore INSPIRE partnership, University of Liverpool, UK
Jo Beall	Director of Education and Society, British Council, UK
Joanna Newman	Director, UK Higher Education International Unit, UK

John Knagg	Head of Research and Consultancy, English and Exams, British Council, UK
Jonathan Ledger	Director, Proskills Group UK and National Skills Academy, UK
José Celso Freire Junior	Head of International, São Paulo State University, Brazil
Kenneth Omeje	Professor of International Relations, United States International University, Nairobi, Kenya
Kgomotso H Moahi	Dean, Faculty of Humanities, University of Botswana, Botswana
Leandro R Tessler	Associate Professor, UNICAMP, Brazil
Lucky T Moahi	Co-ordinator, Botswana Education Hub, Ministry of Education and Skills Development, Botswana
Martin Hall	Vice-Chancellor, The University of Salford, UK
Maryam Rab	Registrar and Director for Research Innovation and Commercialisation, Fatima Jinnah Women University (FJWU), Pakistan
Mary Stiasny	Pro-Director, Learning and International, Institute of Education, United Kingdom
Nicholas NN Nsowah-Nuamah	Professor of Statistics and Rector, Kumasi Polytechnic, Ghana
Patricia G Owusu-Darko	Lecturer and Director, International Affairs and Institutional Linkages, Kumasi Polytechnic, Ghana
Peter Darroch	SciVal Consultant, Elsevier BV., The Netherlands
Rebecca Hughes	Director of International Higher Education, British Council, UK
Sue Parker	Global Director, Skills, GEMS Education Solutions, UK
Tim Gore	Director Global Networks and Communities, University of London International Programmes, United Kingdom
Yussra Jamjoom	Vice Dean of Academic Affairs, University of Business and Technology, Saudi Arabia

Foreword

I am delighted to introduce this third volume of Going Global papers, arising from the British Council's Going Global 2013 Conference. Last year's conference was held in Dubai, in the UAE, where there is a strong presence of international higher education with a growing number of international campuses. 1,300 education ministers, education policy makers and education practitioners came together to explore the theme: "Internationalising Higher Education" and this volume presents some key thinking on this important area.

The UK Government recognises the value of international collaboration within higher and vocational education. Within our globalised and interconnected world it drives growth, builds knowledge economies and enables countries to face global challenges collectively. The authors of this volume explore the ways that international collaboration has facilitated research and innovation, led to an increase in skilled knowledge workers and had an impact on the structures and systems of higher education.

A shared belief in the power of education to transform individual lives underpinned the conference in Dubai and threads through this volume. The role of education in economic growth is a central theme too. And no one can ignore education's wider cultural and social value. The papers presented illustrate the diversity of thinking and, at the same time, the shared commitment to internationalisation of education from the global education community.

The Rt. Hon David Willetts MP
Minister of State for Universities and Science,
Department for Business, Innovation and Skills, United Kingdom

Introductions: Intersections in a Connected World

The contributions brought together in this volume show both the immense value and the unrealised potential of internationalisation in higher education. There are some 10,000 institutions in the world today that are widely accepted as universities. Together, they form a vast and invaluable network of scholarship, innovation, learning and teaching, and engagement with community. Ideas, people and information flow and move across this network irrespective of nationality and language and, increasingly, through rich virtual connections. While the chapters here can only touch the edges of this universe of knowledge, they bring together in one book perspectives from five continents and 16 countries.

Three interconnected themes are clear threads that link the 22 following chapters. First, what are the benefits of international collaboration for research and innovation? Second, how is internationalisation resulting in greater global capacity in highly skilled people who understand, and can work in, the knowledge economy? And third, how are these dimensions of teaching and research affecting the ways in which individual institutions and systems of higher education are organised, and how are current transitions contributing to sustainability and new opportunities in the international sphere?

Taken together, the ways in which contributors explore these themes address some of the challenges posed by Homi Bhabha when he opened the 2012 Going Global conference. Bhabha drew attention to the 'staggering inequalities' that characterise both the distribution of knowledge and the capacity to use it across the world today, and warned of the dangers of disguising this through the 'magical thinking' of globalisation − the easy claims for frictionless movement across the wonders of a digitally connected world. The chapters brought together here follow Bhabha in mapping the contours of internationalisation today, marking out the indisputable advances and benefits and highlighting the opportunities and challenges ahead.

International Collaboration in Research and Innovation

With the exception of initiatives in research and innovation launched by global organisations such the World Bank, the United Nations and the International Monetary Fund, international collaboration is invariably a balance – and sometimes a tension – between national interests and trans-national benefits. Launching such initiatives invariably requires investment by individual institutions or from within national science budgets. The anticipated return must take into account both the global and the local benefits, particularly given the ease with which massive amounts of digital information can be transmitted across the world and the concomitant difficulties in protecting local investments in intellectual property. To complicate matters further, the 'big issues' in contemporary enquiry – climate change, global health, financial stability – require both sustained investment and, often, the surrender of narrower national interests in favour of a common good.

In practical terms, these considerations can be manifested in decisions about establishing in-country international hubs as nodes in the global network of knowledge. Two chapters in this volume nicely demonstrate the opposite ends of the spectrum of inequality that Bhabha highlighted. Qatar has the highest per-capita GDP of any country in the world (US$100,600 in 2011) and has invested heavily and consistently in using its wealth to build international networks. Abdul Sattar Al-Taie describes how the Qatar National Research Fund has now completed six cycles of funding which, together, have attracted more than 2,000 key investigators from 300 institutions and 30 countries. As he points out, this has also resulted in sustained benefits for Qatar's domestic economy. In contrast, Botswana has a GDP that is less than one fifth of Qatar's, at US$16,400 per capita. Lucky Tebalebo Moahi and Patricia G Owusu-Darko shows how Botswana has also benefited through establishing an international hub, promoting strong and beneficial partnerships, and enabling the growth of Botswana's science and innovation infrastructure. In between these extremes is South Africa; in his chapter Gerald Wangenge-Ouma argues that the 'academic core' of a university can be strengthened by reaching out to diasporic academics and re-connecting them to their home countries. The point here is that international collaboration in research and innovation can be beneficial whatever a country's circumstances and objectives.

As internationalisation develops, more sophisticated methodologies of measuring its benefits will become available – a matter of concern to policy makers in both Doha and Gaborone. GDP is notoriously deceptive as a way of measuring returns on investment, and Peter Darroch's chapter sets out some of the emerging thinking about new forms of calibration. Here, an intriguing idea is 'transitory connections': an index of the extent of an internationally mobile researcher's connection with her or his host country. On this measure, Saudi Arabia, Egypt and the United Arab Emirates have comparatively low measures of 'stickiness', at about 50 per cent. In contrast, Darroch shows that only 20 per cent of international research capacity in Turkey is transitory. While we need to be cautious about what this means, and the relationship of the measure to the value of the research that is carried out, this sort of perspective does begin to throw light on the contours of the very uneven world of international collaboration.

The combination of ever-extending practice and new forms of measuring impact will, in turn, allow more sophisticated systems research and better policy making. Alexander Grudinskiy and Alexander Bedny's 'Knowledge Tetrahedron' contributes to this by pulling out the key relationships between education, research and innovation. Their insights come from Enhancing University Research and Entrepreneurial Capacity (EURECA), an international consortium looking for universities' key competitive advantages. They show that older assumptions about the nature of knowledge transfer have left universities at a significant disadvantage in comparison with large-scale, international corporations. Similarly, Rebecca Hughes and John Hearn urge us to look beyond conventional priorities, often limited to institutional- or national-level advances, and to focus instead on a far more extensive canvas. Using the case study of the four 'Global Challenges' set by the Worldwide Universities Network, they demonstrate the benefits of network collaboration in key areas such as climate change and non-communicable diseases.

Preparing People for a Global World of Work

It would be neither feasible nor appropriate to draw a hard distinction between research and the development of a skilled global workforce for the knowledge economy. The production of new knowledge and its distribution and application through the work that people do are inseparable. Clearly, bringing together more than 2,000 key investigators and their associated research teams across more than 30 countries has established Qatar as a major centre for the development of people. At the theoretical level, Grundiskiy and Bedny's 'Knowledge Tetrahedron' sees the production and distribution of new knowledge as enabled by the combination of education, research and innovation, not their division. In like spirit, Leandro Tessler and José Celso Freire Jnr are critical of Brazil's first-generation 'Science without Borders' project in that it separates student mobility from research collaboration. Sustainability, they argue, will only be achieved if education is coupled with research and innovation – a good example of the application of the 'Knowledge Tetrahedron' in advocating the development of more effective policies and priorities.

An important strand in the contributions to this volume is the emergence of 'second-generation' concepts of transnational education. Rather than settling for unmediated exports of education and training programmes from rich economies to an uncritical periphery, strong arguments are made for contextualisation, adaptation and nuance; for much more of a partnership than a one-way flow.

Particular focus is on the local contextualisation of transnational education. Taken together, this set of chapters reflects a generation change in this history of provision – a broad consensus that the undifferentiated export of undeveloped education projects from an economically developed core to a developing world margin is no longer tenable. Christopher Hill, working through the lens of Malaysia, sees a clear need for reform to take local requirements into account. Similarly, Maryam Rab shows how a sense of ownership of educational objectives at the local level can be achieved when programmes are appropriately adjusted in her example of their implementation at Fatima Jinnah Women University in Pakistan. Meanwhile, Nicholas Nsowah-Nuamah shows the potential for localised curriculum development that is focused on in-country community benefits. This approach at Ghana's Kumasi Polytechnic shows the potential for a two-way flow in educational development – the opportunity for those studying in the north and west to learn from southern innovation and entrepreneurship.

This emerging insistence on local contextualisation is, in turn, provoking a re-examination of assumptions and opportunities by traditional 'donor' countries. In her chapter, Dorothea Rüland provides insight into the ways in which transnational education has been contextualised in Germany and is characterised by high levels of engagement and an orientation towards practice and research. Joanna Newman provides a case study of the UK's 'Outward Mobility Strategy'. This intervention has been designed, with government support, to correct the low levels of outward mobility across all of Britain's universities. These responses recognise that, in a highly connected world with a complex global economy, low levels of outward mobility will place individuals and their countries of origin at significant disadvantage in years to come.

This evolution of the form of transnational education can be better understood in the context of the shifting centre of gravity in the world economy. It is surely no accident that the three 'recipient' case studies in this collection have patterns of sustained economic growth; in 2012, Ghana's economy grew by 7.9 per cent, Malaysia's by 5.6 per cent and Pakistan's by 4.1 per cent. In contrast, the two 'donor' case studies have economies that have grown by a tenth or so of these levels: Germany by 0.6 per cent and Britain by just 0.2 per cent. Again, this reflects Bhabha's insistence that internationalisation cannot be understood outside the economic, social and cultural frameworks in which it operates. In future years, both the funding and the volume of demand for a highly skilled workforce will continue to shift to the south and the east, and new-generation approaches to provision are reflecting these underlying drivers.

In considering local nuances, language is always a key issue and, more specifically, the issue of English as a world language. Here, a paradox is at play: the more effective transnational education becomes in meeting local needs, the more important English language provision is likely to be. Both John Knagg and Yussra Jamjoom address this in their contributions. Knagg differentiates between the English language needs of students – itself an area of increasingly specialised research – and the less well understood needs of university staff (often themselves members of an international workforce) who must develop the competency to teach often highly specialised subjects in English as the medium of instruction. Jamjoom's chapter addresses the issue of international language competence in a more specific context. Writing in the context of Saudi Arabia's evolving policy on the language of instruction, which is permitting courses to be offered in English as well as Arabic, this study presents evidence from graduate employers regarding the value ascribed to English language competency.

There are also further complexities ahead as transnational education provision continues to evolve in terms of both national policies for post-compulsory education and training and in the balance between 'academic' and 'vocational' provision. Sue Parker points out that many employers find they have to re-train graduates to ensure that they have competences appropriate for today's highly demanding workplace needs. She questions the value of many academically oriented transnational programmes and asks whether international occupation standards could be used to achieve a better fit between need and provision. Jonathan Ledger's work is also focused on developing vocational utility. His aims are to find the common elements in vocational skills development to guide the emergence of national policies and strategies. He argues that, by taking an employer-focused approach, international standards can be developed.

Looking beyond the chapters in this volume and to future work, we can expect more attention to be given to the extraordinary implications of the digital 'access revolution'; the combination of ubiquitous internet access, massive and affordable digital storage and cheap, locationally aware mobile interfaces. This will continue to create huge volumes of widely available content and new and flexible options for education and training. Books such as the one in which this chapter appears, priced and distributed in ways that restrict its access to small elites, are likely to become obsolete as new knowledge requirements overwhelm older ways of doing things.

Universities' Ways of Working

How are these dimensions of teaching and research affecting the ways in which individual institutions and systems of higher education are organised? How are the transitions described in the contributions to this volume resulting in new and sustainable opportunities?

One way of teasing this aspect of internationalisation is to contrast the emphasis on individual institutions with new inter-institutional structures. Of course, individual universities' resources, identity and reputation still matter a great deal. Major international hubs − Qatar in this volume, centres such as Singapore, Hong Kong, Dubai, London and New York more generally − comprise sets of individual institutions that often have global recognition and reputation. International ranking systems such as the Times Higher Education (THE) World University Rankings and the Shanghai Jiao Tong Academic Ranking of World Universities are hugely influential, and individual universities compete fiercely for relative standing. No university can compete successfully in these tournaments of value unless they have global reach in their research and in the students they attract.

At the same time though, the primary client in the transnational arena is not cloistered within a specific institution. As Darroch shows in his chapter, contemporary high-value knowledge workers move across all boundaries and may be highly transitory, with complex institutional affiliations. And international students want the experience of difference, not of tradition and conformity. Magnus Olson's chapter outlines the results of a survey of 25,000 international students, establishing their motivation for studying abroad, the influences on their satisfaction, and what policy makers and institutions can do to improve international university exchanges. This survey shows that, while students value studying abroad, there are still substantial differences in students' experience and there is a great deal still to be done in this evolving area of provision. Old institutional identities, however venerable, are not enough.

It is perhaps for this reason that there is more interest across contributors to this volume in inter-institutional developments rather than in university-specific case studies. Where individual institutions are looked at in detail − Nsowah-Nuamah on Kumasi Polytechnic, Rab on Fatima Jinnah Women University − this is because aspects at this scale provide the context for external developments.

One way of conceptualising this interplay between structural changes within institutions and sustainable innovation at the inter-institutional level is to think of networks as tangible assets, however virtual they may be in their form. After all, the very word 'university' originates in the Medieval Latin for a society of scholars, rather than in any concept of buildings or a specific place. Whether criss-crossing early European borders with a common language in Latin, exchanging knowledge across the formative Buddhist world or forging Arabic networks of scholarship, higher education has always been about networks rather than closed and contained systems of thought. In this perspective, current and future innovations in inter-institutional networks continue a deep and definitive thread in the creation and distribution of knowledge.

Seen in this way, almost all the chapters brought together here contribute to understanding how institutions and systems are organised, and how they can be sustainable. Hughes, in her own chapter and in her contribution co-authored with John Hearn, focuses on network effects through the example of the World University Network. Ledger's research has been about acceptable sets of international standards and the ways in which they can be used more widely – a necessary condition for any network to be effective. Hans Pohl's case study takes a view across Swedish higher education as a complete system, as does Rüland's overview of approaches to internationalisation in Germany. Tessler and Freire show how the decade-long collaboration between six Brazilian universities and France's Écoles Centrales can be used as a model for more productive approaches to international collaboration in Brazil.

This focus on networks as critical assets that bind individual institutions into sustainable systems of collaboration allows the significance of specialised sub-fields such as quality assurance to be recognised. Effective networks depend on common standards of interoperability that must be maintained through appropriate protocols. In her chapter, Nadia Badrawi describes work across 18 Arab countries that allows a shared 'language' across autonomous national systems of regulations. Similarly, Rab highlights the importance of quality assurance in a rapidly evolving, internationally connected higher education system such as Pakistan's. Work such as this is a necessary condition for any effective international network, and therefore also for the success of any individual institution participating in such a network.

Overall then, 'second-generation' approaches to transnational education, along with the growing sophistication of collaboration in research and innovation, appears to be creating strong and sustainable networks between institutions. If Thomas Jefferson's neo-classical Rotunda for the University of Virginia has been a metaphor for the inward-looking 'academic village' of the past two centuries, then new and emerging images, such as the 'Knowledge Tetrahedron', are challenging these introverted concepts with new models for the network structures of the future.

Conclusion

This overview has shown that the three themes of international research collaboration, education and training for a global workforce, and systemic structure and sustainability are ineluctably inter-connected; Grundinsky and Bedny's 'Knowledge Tetrahedron' is an icon appropriate for our time. From this appreciation of our current condition, we can look forward with Rebecca Hughes in her contribution here, as she asks about the key issues in the lifetime of a child born in 2013. What will be the outcomes of present imperatives, such as mobile technologies and funding systems? How should national resources be prioritised? How can global higher education systems address increasingly uneven economic development?

Hans Pohl's overview of internationalisation in Sweden is reflective, taking stock of a changing world in which long-established institutional forms may not suffice in the future. Here, a child born in 2013 will experience a world in which the dynamics of economic growth have shifted to the east and the south, requiring very different competences to those of his or her parents' generation.

Both children will, in all likelihood, be global travellers. In opening Going Global 2012, Bhabha suggested that, rather than the impersonal concept of 'globalisation', we think in terms of a complex set of intersecting 'journeys' such as financial transactions and flows, scholarly exchanges, multinational corporate connections, and migrancy: 'a tracery of different trajectories'. Internationalisation happens where these journeys intersect, where we learn to live and work 'side by side with strangers'.

This essential, humanitarian aspect of internationalisation is captured for this volume in Kenneth Omeje's chapter, in which he describes conflict prevention and peace-building projects carried out in countries currently dealing with high levels of violence and recovery from recent conflicts.

Omeje, with Bhabha, remind us of the integrating role of the humanities in making sense of an ever more complex world. Beneath specific protocols, such as quality-assurance systems, the development of international hubs, concerns with the local adaptation of curricula structures and ways of measurement of returns on investment are core humanitarian issues. Internationalisation generates huge benefits, whether in addressing the 'grand challenges' of research or in enabling a vast workforce of highly skilled migrants. At the same time, internationalisation proceeds in the context of massive inequalities and prevalent disruption and violence. Without the reflection and analysis so evident in the chapters in this collection, we will be blinded by the deceptions of 'magical thinking'.

Chapters Reviewed

Al-Taie, Abdul Sattar: Fostering a closer relationship with the global research community through international collaborations
Badrawi, Nadia: Quality assurance in higher education: collaborating for impact in the MENA region

Darroch, Peter: Analysing research outputs to support research innovation and international collaboration

Grudzinskiy, Alexander and Bedny, Alexander: Raising innovators as a major task of leading universities

Hill, Christopher: Re-defining TNE: the challenges and opportunities of internationalisation

Hughes, Rebecca: Our universities to 2013: a case study on network effects

Hughes, Rebecca and Hearn, John: An international university network as laboratory for internationalisation: benefits, challenges and lessons learned

Jamjoom, Yussra: Going English: private higher education and graduates' employability in Saudi Arabia

Knagg, John: The changing role of English and ELT in a modern, multilingual and internationalised world

Ledger, Jonathan: Transferable models for international standards collaboration

Moahi, Lucky Tebalebo: Education cities and hubs: what is their contribution to global, national and local community agendas? A case of the Education Hub in Botswana

Newman, Joanna: The UK Higher Education Outward Mobility programme: a national strategy for increasing the proportion of UK students accessing international opportunities

Nsowah-Nuamah, Nicholas and Owusu-Darko, Patricia: The role of international collaboration in developing skilled knowledge workers — the case of Kumasi Polytechnic

Olsson, Magnus: What are the influencers that impact the international student experience?

Omeje, Kenneth: Transnational 'education-for-peace' in the era of international terrorism: capacitating universities as drivers of attitudinal change in volatile transitional societies

SECTION 1
HOW HAS INTERNATIONAL COLLABORATION FACILITATED RESEARCH AND INNOVATION?

Chapter 1.1

Editors' Introduction to Section 1

This volume brings together front-line accounts of what Martin Hall calls the 'second generation of transnational education'. He highlights for us a transition to a far more nuanced, context-sensitive approach to internationalisation characterised in this section by initiatives that genuinely promote a wider and more locally sensitive engagement in knowledge production. It is clear that the logic of a 'flat world' in Thomas Friedman's classic characterisation of our globalised world is misleading and the geography of research, innovation and the commercialisation of research is overwhelmingly concentrated on the east and west coasts of the US, central Europe and parts of East Asia, although it is true that research production in China, India and Brazil is increasing rapidly and starting to close part of the gap. In this section we see further evidence of progress in knowledge production gains in Turkey, Russia, the Middle East and the Gulf, as well as considering more general developments in knowledge production.

What is the primary role of universities in knowledge production is the question asked by Alexander Grudzinskiy and Alexander Bedny? The opening chapter in this section lays out a line of thinking that challenges the orthodoxy that universities should be major players in both research and the commercialisation of knowledge. Their main thesis is that universities should develop their principal expertise in developing innovators rather than innovation as such. Whether or not you agree with the thesis, the chapter lays out a very useful framework for analysis of the principal dimensions of a university's involvement in education, science and innovation through a 'knowledge tetrahedron'. This discussion usefully leads us into the section on knowledge production in the context of universities examining where to prioritise their resources in this respect.

The work of the Qatar National Research Fund opens the debate on new and developing sites of knowledge production, in this case, a country trying to build its capacity to produce and apply research with little or no previous history of research to build on. Clearly, building a knowledge infrastructure is a complex and multi-faceted enterprise. The chapter details the way Qatar is approaching this and stresses the role of its developing international research connectivity as being crucial in this process. Fortunately, Qatar has considerable resources from its hydrocarbon industries to invest in developing this capacity, but what resources can other regions anxious to develop their research capacity draw on? In the case of Africa, Gerald Ouma describes the way that Africa's substantial diaspora can provide just such a resource. This approach to internationalisation fully reflects the nuanced approach of second-generation internationalisation. Here, the web of relationships into funding, research capacity and academic strength is through a diaspora that maintains strong links to its home base.

Peter Darroch takes us further into regions where research capacity is benefiting from internationalisation and reflects on an increase both in quantity and quality of research output from Iran, Turkey, Egypt, Lebanon, Saudi Arabia and the United Arab Emirates. An important role is attributed to the degree of international linkages in the research, and transitory researchers who spend limited amounts of time working in the countries described, with Saudi Arabia and UAE being notable examples of this. In the context of a UK-Pakistan collaboration, Ian Willis explores the potential of emergent processes that are encouraged in a collaboration that takes time to reflect and evaluate allowing and encouraging new ideas and ways of working to emerge from this process to the great benefit of the overall collaboration.

Finally, it is fitting to end this section and lead into the following two sections with an exploration of the changing fortunes and roles of the humanities in both knowledge production and the dissemination and application of knowledge. Jo Beall argues that the humanities are an essential part of our humanity and deliver to universities and societies a vast range of benefits. Some of these are immediately functional, such as the development of higher skills, and others intimately interwoven with other forms of knowledge and awareness that help humankind chart its way through a complex world and develop and use knowledge responsibly.

Chapter 1.2

Raising Innovators as a Major Task of Leading Universities

Alexander Grudzinskiy and Alexander Bedny

Introduction

The formation of a global knowledge economy puts universities under significant new pressures, as businesses and governments raise their expectations regarding the role of universities in social and economic development in a world where the generation of knowledge is becoming a key to growth and prosperity. At the same time, the academic community develops new opportunities for the application of its intellectual potential. In addition to acting under the conditions of publicly funded academic freedom, academics start to focus on requests from business in order to compete in the global market of education, research and innovation.

In the modern world innovation is seen as a crucial response to global economic challenges, and higher education institutions (HEIs) are assumed to be the major actors in finding effective solutions to socio-economic problems. In the European Union Innovation Agenda, knowledge is increasingly seen as the new strategic production factor (Van Vaught, 2009). The creation, transfer and application of knowledge are assumed to be of prime importance for economic re-orientation and further social and economic development. In the United States, meanwhile, research universities are also considered to be nation's leaders out of the economic crisis, and are expected by those who support them and the public at large to lead the way in terms of innovation (Thorp, Goldstein, 2010).

As a consequence of this, universities around the world are seeking adequate new development models for the changing external conditions. The concept of market-oriented innovative universities based on the 'Knowledge Triangle' (Education-Research-Innovation) starts to dominate in all developed parts of the globe.

Universities in the Global Market of Innovation: Is there a Chance to Beat Corporations?

Universities have not yet fully recognised all of the opportunities for implementing their 'market-oriented' function, and most tend to concentrate efforts on the generation of income from the commercialisation of inventions made by their researchers. At the turn of the 21st century universities all over the world introduced the system of technology-transfer offices. The primary tasks of these was the evaluation of the commercialisation potential of inventions made by university researchers, their patenting, and further support. While the role of universities' innovation infrastructure is considered to be the commercialisation of inventions, the launch of new innovative products or services and the creation of university spin-off companies, the situations where universities acquire a large income from licensing a prospective technology or receive a return on equities from a rapidly developing spin-off company are very rare. Moreover, generally, such luck is fragile, because the university can receive income from licensing a new prospective technology on average for only around two years, after which the technology goes out of date. As a result, the Technology Transfer Development Programme of one of the USA's and the world's leading universities, the University of California, states that 'for the last 90 years the bulk of university revenue from technologies is earned on a small number of so-called "blockbuster" inventions and, unfortunately, it is almost impossible to predict which inventions have blockbuster potential' (UC TLP, 2012).

The second market function of universities is the commercialisation of university inventions through industry connections (i.e. through contract research and developments). In recent years, the global industry has become more active in terms of implementation of applied research at universities. In a sense, it is a more reliable and stable option for the university, as the industry knows exactly which applied scientific research it requires, and formulates objectives for university researchers. Thus, the university enters the market whether or not its researchers have any breakthrough inventions.

This form of commercialisation of inventions has a number of disadvantages for the university though. First, in contract research the university is usually not the full owner of the results of research activities. Second, businesses, acting as sponsors of research, follow their own business interests.

Contract research, in most cases, is of an applied nature and aimed at the production of new knowledge to solve specific problems for the sponsor. In addition, each industrial enterprise employs its own professional research staff and, in the case of large enterprises, entire research laboratories and centres to conduct professional research in their respective areas. Participating in contract research puts the university in the position of an assistant catching up to corporations. In this way, similar to a social and economic phenomenon of 'catching up modernisation', we can talk about universities 'catching up innovatisation' with industry. If a university wants to catch up with corporate research in a certain area, then it will likely have to concentrate the maximum internal resources on a particular area of research, which is an impossible task for a comprehensive university involved in a wide range of subject areas.

This leads us to a conclusion about the inconsistency of the situation regarding the innovative activity of universities. On the one hand, modern leading universities do their best to emphasise their innovative mission and the world's leading countries assign their universities the role of key players in knowledge production and their market application (Hagen, 2008). On the other hand, meanwhile, there are concerns that the role of universities is reduced to the 'catching up innovatisation' in respect of the high-tech sector of the economy – figuratively speaking, 'playing in the second league'.

The experience of leading countries shows that the real drivers of global innovative development are the large industrial corporations. Private-sector companies are the main source of innovation in Organisation for Economic Co-operation and Development (OECD) countries and in rapidly developing economies, driven by the need to ensure market competitiveness (OECD, 2011). The economic impact of university innovation is actively fuelled by the examples of successful innovation clusters such as the Silicon Valley, Boston and North Carolina areas in the United States or Cambridge in Great Britain. An important role in this process is played by the well-known cases of high-yielding licences for university technologies, such as the Gatorade energy drink (University of Florida), human growth hormone (University of California, San Francisco), the vaccine against hepatitis B (of the same university), the chemotherapeutic drug Taxol (University of Florida) and a number of successful world-class companies that came out of universities such as Cisco, Google, Yahoo (all three originated from Stanford University, while two of them purchased licenses from the university) and Facebook, founded by students at Harvard (though, in this case, against the university's will).

Less well known is the fact that the creation of new businesses based on university research and technology constitutes only a small fraction (about three per cent) of the total number of new companies (Lester, 2005). The same applies to university patent activity: the results of 2011 show that even in the US – a world leader in university research and innovation activities – out of approximately 224,500 patents granted, only about 4,000 were issued to the universities (AUTM, 2012; USPTO, 2012). The probability of universities deriving significant financial benefit from the activities of technology transfer is also low. The total revenue of US universities from licence sales in 2011 was only four per cent of the volume of Research and Development funding ($2.5 billion and $61 billion, respectively). Interestingly, this percentage has not changed significantly over the past decade: in 2002 it amounted to the same four per cent, but with the absolute volume of maximum funding twice as small (Lester, 2005).

A university is unable to perform the functions of major industrial corporations, while even the traditional name for small innovative enterprises created at universities – spin-outs and spin-offs – indicates that there is some 'centrifugal force' shaping the direction of the development of such companies. There is no such university in the world where the innovative component of its budget plays a decisive role, a fact that demonstrates the importance of university innovation is manifested in areas other than finance.

We should recognise that universities will not be able to beat corporations in the innovation market. This new understanding of contemporary reality has come around only recently and now it is trying to fight its way through the enthusiasm and dreams of possible economic return on university innovation development.

The realistic assessment of universities' potential in technology transfer does not mean that this function is rendered useless, or that the effort spent on its development should be curbed. The new functional model of a university – an innovative university based on the 'knowledge triangle' – became ingrained in everyday life and now it is the fundamental paradigm of university development. If we view the university technology transfer as its main contribution to the creation of an innovation economy we put leading universities into a dead-end position of 'catching up modernisation', and they will try to become something that they fundamentally can never be – commercial industrial enterprises.

Major Task of Leading Universities in the Innovation Economy: The Tetrahedron of Knowledge

So, what can universities offer for the innovation economy? What unique competitive advantage do HEIs have that will prevent other players from driving them out of the global market? In our opinion, this advantage is the historic function of the university – production of human capital, but human capital of a fundamentally new quality. Universities should give the innovation economy its main resource for development – highly qualified professional creators, skilled in innovative entrepreneurial activities, or, in other words, innovators.

While the results of academic research and innovation activities such as scientific publications and patents are not a unique product to universities, human capital is 'produced' only by universities and acts as a main factor in the successful development of an innovative economy. International experience shows that large multinational companies consider collaboration with the world's leading universities primarily as a means of selecting talented students and nurturing future employees, who should be highly educated effective professional innovators.

This idea was confirmed by the international case study based on implementation of the Russian–American Programme 'Enhancing University Research and Entrepreneurial Capacity' (EURECA). The programme was launched in 2010 to develop the Russian national research universities' ability to successfully transfer the results of university research to the economy through the experience and capabilities of US research universities. This programme is an initiative of the US-Russia Foundation for Economic Development and the Rule of Law (USRF), and is supported by the Ministry of Education and Science of Russia.

Lobachevsky State University of Nizhni Novgorod National Research University (UNN) has participated in the EURECA programme since its launch, and has implemented joint projects with the two US research universities: Purdue University and the University of Maryland. The projects are addressing the issues of international technology transfer and student innovation entrepreneurship development at UNN on the basis of the foremost experience of the leading US universities in that sphere.

This exclusive experience of international co-operation helps us to propose a new approach to the interpretation of the functional model of the university on the basis of the 'knowledge triangle'. As before, we consider fundamental and applied research and education to be the basis for the development of innovation activities at the university, but suggest changing the alignment of priorities in understanding the problems of universities' innovation activities.

Without denying the importance of the actual production of innovations at universities, we are also convinced that the most important part of their innovation infrastructure is as a 'laboratory base' for the training of entrepreneurs capable of effectively developing innovative activities in their areas of expertise. Just as the participation of students in the scientific work of the department or the laboratory is an integral part of the training of highly qualified professionals or researchers, university students' participation in the activities of technology transfer offices or small innovative enterprises is essential in effectively forming the competences of innovation entrepreneurs. Innovative university infrastructure, therefore, plays the same role in the development of a new type of professional innovator as university research laboratory does in the preparation of traditional 'Humboldtian' specialists and scientists.

Thus, we believe that the innovator, being the main 'product' of innovative universities, should be placed on top of the 'knowledge tetrahedron' – the geometric interpretation of the proposed functional model of the leading universities in the innovation economy (see Fig. 1). At the base there is the 'knowledge triangle', the corners of which stand for the three key components of the university: Education, Science and Innovation.

This 'knowledge tetrahedron' gives a clue as to what the main competitive advantage of the university is in relation to the other players in the knowledge economy. The concept of the 'knowledge triangle' involves close and effective interaction between education, research and innovation activities in a university. Each of the three edges of the triangle can be associated with certain types of the modern university's activities that reflect the interaction of education, science and innovation. In particular, on the edge that connects education and innovation there are types of university activity such as the organisation of contract training commissioned by companies, the involvement of practical trainers from business, the development of university-wide entrepreneurship training, and the preparation of theses and student business projects. The edge that connects science and education corresponds to the traditional 'Humboldtian' university lectures and practical classes, the organisation of research and practical training, and laboratory experiments. Finally, on the edge that connects science and

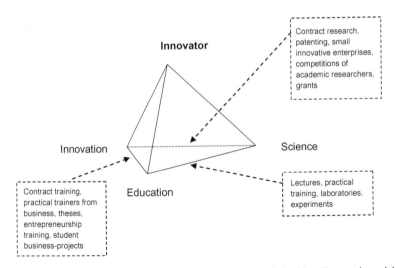

Figure 1: Knowledge tetrahedron: a functional model of leading universities.

innovation, there are activities such as contract research commissioned by industry, the patenting and licensing of scientific inventions, the creation of small innovative enterprises, competitions of academic researchers and innovators, and applications for innovation grants. Full implementation of all three key functions is equally important for the effective development of innovative modern universities and for the training of highly qualified innovators.

Conclusion

The university 'knowledge tetrahedron' is a clear interpretation of the concept of the entrepreneurial university. The main characteristic of the entrepreneurial university is a comprehensive entrepreneurial culture of employees and the development of such a culture among students (Clark, 1998). A new mentality of researchers, teachers, students and postgraduates, and a new organisational culture of the university as a whole – that's what the term 'entrepreneurial university' means.

It has been generally recognised that the creation of innovative products requires an entrepreneurial mindset that views great problems as great opportunities. An entrepreneurial approach is a necessary component of the innovation process, a special mechanism for problem solving and an effective addition to the basic methods of fundamental knowledge in the liberal arts and natural sciences (Thorp, 2010). The 'knowledge tetrahedron' clearly shows that all aspects of the activities of a modern competitive university must be imbued with the spirit and culture of entrepreneurship.

References

Association of University Technology Managers (AUTM) (2012) US Licensing Activity Survey Highlights. Retrieved from www.autm.org.

Clark, BR (1998) Creating entrepreneurial universities: organizational pathways of transformation. Issues in Higher Education. Paris: IAU Press, Pergamon, Elsevier Science.

Hagen, S (2008) From Tech Transfer to Knowledge Exchange: European Universities in the Marketplace // Wenner-Gren International Series. 2008. Vol. 84. p. 103–117.

Lester, RK (2005) Universities, Innovation, and the Competitiveness of Local Economies: summary report from the local innovation project. Cambridge, MA: Massachusetts Institute of Technology. Retrieved from http://web.mit.edu/ipc/publications/pdf/05-010.pdf.

OECD Reviews of Innovation Policy: Russian Federation. Paris: OECD Publishing, 2011. p. 261.

Thorp, H, and Goldstein, B (2010) Engines of Innovation: The Entrepreneurial University in the Twenty-First Century. The University of North Carolina Press. Chapel Hill.

The Times Higher Education (THE) World University Rankings 2012–2013. Retrieved from www.timeshighereducation.co.uk/world-university-rankings/ 2012-13/world-ranking.

Van Vaught, F (2009) The EU Innovation Agenda: Challenges for European Higher Education and Research, Higher Education Management and Policy, Vol. 21/2.

University of California Technology Licensing Program (UC TLP). Executive Summary. 19 January 2012. URL: http://regents.universityofcalifornia.edu/ regmeet/jan12/f9.pdf.

US Patent and Trademark Office (USPTO) (2012) Patenting by Organizations 2011. A Patent Technology Monitoring Team Report. Retrieved from www.uspto.gov.

Chapter 1.3

Fostering a Closer Relationship with the Global Research Community Through International Collaborations

Abdul Sattar Al-Taie

Introduction

Driven by the aim of fostering a culture of research in Qatar, Qatar National Research Fund (QNRF) was established in 2006 to advance knowledge and education by acting as a support system for researchers. It is a centre within the Research and Development establishment at the Qatar Foundation for Education, Science and Community Development (QF).

QNRF is a primary building block in the creation of a domestic research culture and a key force in generating a phased strategy as part of its thrust to create a critical mass in scientific research in Qatar. QNRF has encompassed a broad cast of characters who are engaged to play a variety of roles in building an environment that would overcome cultural, institutional and academic differences through a shared set of objectives. QNRF is preparing the people of Qatar and the region to meet the challenges of an ever-changing world and to make Qatar a leader in innovative education and research.

QNRF's vision is to become an internationally recognised institution that uses research as a catalyst for expanding and diversifying Qatar's economy, enhancing the education of its citizens and the training of its

Going Global: Knowledge-Based Economies for 21st Century Nations
Copyright © 2014 by Abdul Sattar Al-Taie
All rights of reproduction in any form reserved
ISBN: 978-1-78441-003-2

workforce, fostering improvements in health, wellbeing, environment and the security of its people and those of the region. To meet this vision, QNRF has three goals:

- to build human capital
- to address national research needs
- to raise Qatar's profile in the international research community.

A strategy for establishing and maintaining an infrastructure has enabled research to be conducted in Qatar in the form of a series of funding programmes and activities, all designed to ultimately transform Qatar from a hydrocarbon-based to a knowledge-based economy. The strategy also provides opportunities for local researchers in Qatar to establish excellent links for international collaboration, facilitating technology transfer and promoting Qatar as a global hub for research and development while creating a pool of talent and a pipeline of innovations. Capacity is based on shared academic interests rather than skill sets.

QNRF also established a set of guiding principles to ensure alignment of its programs and services with the needs of researchers and, more recently, the Qatar National Research Strategy, Qatar National Vision 2030, and thus addresses the priority needs of Qatar.

QNRF's clear, transparent and consistent programs and activities are flexible enough to accommodate research being carried out in different parts of the world, while being acceptable to the target institutions. QNRF's funding models avoid rigid financial metrics, and the participating institutions are incentivised to establish the policies and infrastructure needed to support research in Qatar.

The key to truly becoming an internationally respected research funding agency is in adapting to feedback and making changes over time in programs and policies in order to better meet the needs of Qatar's research community and Qatar's goals. QNRF is deeply committed to the process of innovation and has developed a clear framework designed to allow new ideas to take shape with policies that allow for the evolution of new programs in a dynamic environment.

Physical assets do not reflect the true value of QNRF's investments, and intellectual property (IP) and patentable technology represent a significant portion of its intangible value. One of the challenges has been in striking a balance between the researchers' expectations and meeting QNRF's objectives during the commercialisation of intellectual property. In the absence of any existing IP framework, an international model was adopted, which has proven to be robust enough to withstand the demanding legal requirements of the international research community.

QNRF's Approach — Work so Far

QNRF's funding mechanisms, which support competitively selected research, are fully integrated with a structured exploitation and commercialisation of the projects' outcome, in other words, infrastructure capable of supporting second-stage activities, such as incubation, proof-of-concept and prototypes, with the ultimate goal being to take the end product to market.

The collaboration aspect of the support system offered by QNRF is extremely important when working towards the long-term goal of building a critical mass of indigenous researchers. When this is combined with the experience of global research, development and innovation, it creates a realistic, fast-track plan to conduct world-class, collaborative scientific research in state-of-the-art facilities.

QNRF's flagship funding program, the National Priorities Research Program (NPRP), encourages both intellectual freedom (by allowing researchers to submit proposals for topics of their own design) and technical merit (through competition). Projects must outline a well-defined life-cycle, a reporting schedule and a budget; things that may be foreign to those previously undertaking basic research.

It was initially decided that NPRP research priorities would be viewed through the lens of building capabilities rather than funding specific topics. As a result, QNRF developed a non-exclusive list of suggested sample topics to motivate researchers' ideas about research areas of importance to Qatar. The funding criteria are continuously reviewed and revised, and have now been aligned with Qatar National Vision 2030 and the Qatar National Research Strategy to more closely reflect those areas considered a national priority.

To encourage knowledge transfer, the majority of the budget spent and at least half of the work done would have to be in Qatar. In addition, certain key personnel for projects would have to reside in the country. Research institutions abroad could administer up to 35 per cent of the project budgets, as it was recognised from the outset that research collaboration is a very effective way of building human capital.

It is unsafe to assume that the aims, commitments and conceptions of the funded researchers are shared. QNRF recognised early on that lack of face-to-face contact between researchers can be a critical impediment and prove problematic, leading to a lack of focus, a sense of isolation and a loss of momentum. Time delays can lead to uncertainties between team members regarding their work and, although these can be addressed to some extent by teleconferencing, it can lead to a problem when prioritising tasks. Allowing researchers to meet face to face can stimulate and motivate them, avoiding any fragmentation of the research effort and providing greater clarity.

As a result of these issues, QNRF ensures that proper funding and a quality support system allow for face time among researchers. This has resulted in the sharing of operational and research contexts and to sound conceptual underpinnings of the research and its implementation. Sometimes, interactions and communications issues can be more challenging than the research itself and so a reasonable portion of the funding is devoted to travel and attending conferences. Research teams can then have a reasonable expectation of the outcome, complement each other and develop strong bonds and, in turn, those strong relationships determine that the full potential is reached, thus maximising the chances of success while simultaneously building a culture of research.

While recognising that failure can be an outcome along the path to commercialisation, QNRF does attempt to identify concepts with market potential. Several research projects have gone on to register patents, representing the potential to generate a return on the significant investment made by QNRF in building both the human capital and the physical infrastructure of a research-friendly environment.

One example of patented technology has been the development of Wireless Sensor Networks for the Survey of Gas and Water Distribution Networks. An international collaboration between Qatar University and Politecnico di Torino has led to a new method of identifying a technological solution able to monitor the wear and deterioration of underground civil infrastructures for fluid transportation and distribution. The team has developed a device able to flow inside pipes, determining the presence of eventual fluid leakages by monitoring variations of the acoustic spectrum of the noise produced by the fluid flowing in the pipe (NPRP 08-372-2-142).

Closer to home, a project looking into the innovative use of recycled materials in construction aims to convert waste aggregate from construction projects into an asset, in order to radically cut costs while maintaining quality. The project also aims to encourage people to think in a more environmentally conscious manner by demonstrating the potential to save massive amounts of energy by not importing heavy construction materials (NPRP 4-188-2-061).

Details of many more practical examples of the outcome of QNRF's investments are available at www.qnrf.org.

One final aspect of the QNRF model is that staff development is a core component used when measuring staff productivity. Colleagues are able to question the assumptions and the work because they are unfamiliar with the context within which it was introduced. This can lead to scholarly growth as it promotes and develops greater understanding and contributes to the underlying infrastructure that supports a research culture.

QNRF's Impact

The outcomes of QNRF's efforts, and all of the projects supported, promise not only to contribute to science worldwide, but to also have a positive impact on lives around the globe.

QNRF's collaborative funding mechanisms encourage intellectual activity on a global scale. Such an investment in research and the building of human capital generates a comparative advantage for Qatar, significantly influences the next generation of scientists and represents an incalculable dividend for generations to come. While success is not guaranteed, QNRF recognises that the collective endeavours of its funded researchers may survive the countless challenges faced when engaging in international and multi-institutional collaborations.

The research carried out here not only serves the country, but also the larger regional and global community. It has enhanced the country's social, human, economic and environmental development, while fulfilling the nation's ambitions to become a global hub for research and development. New spin-offs continue to broaden the complexity of the activities of QNRF and QF's supporting infrastructure as researchers translate their work into practical, useful outcomes.

Individuals, as opposed to institutions, normally drive the sharing of resources, and tightly knit peer networks help to organise such research activities. The drive to collaborate has become a feature of contemporary research activity, stimulating output globally, enhancing academic skills and broadening perspectives. QNRF has truly acted as a catalyst in all these respects and has witnessed a trend in horizontal rather than vertical (which describes the relationship whereby junior researchers work for seniors) collaborations among peers.

By making Qatar a centre of innovative education and research in a relatively short period of time, QNRF has grown into an internationally recognised grant institution with fully operational, multimillion-dollar programmes and the foundation of a domestic research infrastructure in place.

Global issues, such as health, need more than one country to participate due to the sheer amount of resources needed; there are a limited number of researchers working in ever-increasingly specialised fields, and collaborations prove beneficial. Hence the collaboration and research funding opportunities in Qatar attract global academics. Academics tend to follow opportunities such as post-doc posts and funding as part of their career development, and contribute to building the critical mass necessary for the development, exploitation and commercialisation of innovations developed in Qatar.

Conclusion

Networking opportunities at Going Global highlighted both the intellectual and commercial rewards that original research projects can bring. It also showed that certain key constituents (i.e. those potential researchers not falling directly within the catchment of existing funding programmes) were not being catered for by QNRF's funding programmes.

To be able to reach out to this section of the research community, QNRF has now designed a series of further funding opportunities and activities that will serve to broaden the support systems it offers across all disciplines, as well as collaborations with commerce and industry with the prospect of establishing partnerships based on a more commercial footing.

The nature of collaborative partnerships is now entirely different to what it was a few decades ago (industry collaborations are different from academia in that they steer away from one-off grants and the straightforward exchange of money for research. Instead, long-term partnerships and multi-player ventures, in which all sides help direct the science, are the order of the day). Networking opportunities at Going Global offer a pathway to understanding the innovation ecosystem, developing synergies and allowing new areas of expertise to define and exploit new markets.

Going Global helps to identify who all the players are, it provides solutions to the problems and issues that need to be dealt with, and can act as an introduction to other universities working in a similar arena that we could team up with.

There is no overnight solution to innovation and, as collaborations with industry gather pace, scientists with the same spirit and the same goals — to advance research — will contribute to the pace of innovation. Collaborative work is a highly demanding extension to the academic's work and normally occurs where countries share more similarities than differences. The dazzling breakthroughs, blending of cultures and solving of global problems along the way will come to define Qatar as it evolves into a leader of global markets, as it re-examines its governance and management infrastructure, as it revisits its policies and, ultimately, designs a host of new programs, some already planned and some as yet unimagined.

Chapter 1.4

Diaspora Linkages and the Challenge of Strengthening the Academic Core in African Universities

Gerald Wangenge-Ouma

Introduction

There are increasing numbers of Africans in the academic diaspora. The estimated numbers by region are: North America, 39.16 million; Latin America, 112.65 million; Caribbean, 13.56 million; and Europe, 3.51 million (World Bank, 2012). As far as the migration of skilled Africans and professionals is concerned, Chacha's (2007) study claimed that on average 23,000 qualified academics were emigrating from Africa and, according to Shinn (2008), approximately 65,000 African-born physicians and 70,000 African-born professional nurses were working overseas in economically advanced economies by 2000. Shinn (2008) further claims that, as at 2007, there were over 300,000 highly qualified Africans in the diaspora, 30,000 of whom have PhDs. This is the context from which the questions that inform this study are derived, namely: is the migration of skilled Africans and professionals a net loss of expertise as generally portrayed in the literature and the metaphor of 'the brain drain'? Alternatively, in the context of higher education internationalisation, can linkages with the African academic diaspora play an important role in the pursuit of 'internationalisation strategies that strengthen their internal institutional and intellectual capacities, qualities, reputations and competitiveness...?' (Zeleza, 2012: 15) Overall, can the African academic diaspora play a role to advance and, in some cases, help revitalise the knowledge project in African universities?

Going Global: Knowledge-Based Economies for 21st Century Nations
Copyright © 2014 by Gerald Wangenge-Ouma
All rights of reproduction in any form reserved
ISBN: 978-1-78441-003-2

The preceding questions are important in view of some of the challenges confronting universities in Africa. For example, a recent study by Cloete, Bailey and Maassen (2011) has argued that one of the major challenges facing universities in Africa is a weak academic core, characterised mainly by weak postgraduate education and research. The reasons for this weak academic core include limited output of master's and doctoral graduates, which, other than stunting the supply of researchers and the development of the next generation of scholars, has implications for the ability of the universities in Africa to reproduce themselves as vibrant knowledge institutions. Other reasons include an 'ageing' professoriate, as is the case in South Africa where about one-fifth of academics are due to retire in less than a decade, including nearly half of the professoriate (Higher Education South Africa, 2011). Thus, does engagement with the African academic diaspora offer opportunities for strengthening the academic core of African universities? This is the primary thrust of the paper.

Based on a recently completed study[1], the paper discusses how some South African universities have engaged with the country's academic diaspora as part of their internationalisation strategies – albeit in a fragmented and un-institutionalised manner – to leverage worldwide networks of collaboration, to enhance research, to facilitate knowledge transfer and to build capacity.

Situating the South African Diaspora

Who exactly constitutes the diaspora[2] is a question that remains unsettled and is one that this paper will not attempt to resolve. However, operationally, and so that the figures below make sense, the paper adopts Zeleza's (2008: 8) description of African diasporas as including 'all those peoples dispersed from the continent in historic and contemporary times, who have constituted themselves or have been constituted into diasporas.' The focus is especially on those dispersed from the continent and, in the context of this paper, South Africa, in contemporary times, mainly during the apartheid period and the present post-apartheid period (the period after 1994 following the collapse of apartheid).

Information regarding the exact numbers of South African academics and professionals in the diaspora is scant, and what is available is on particular fields. Marks (2004) reported that at least 12,207 South African

1. This study was part of a multi-country research project funded by the Carnegie Corporation and led by Professor Paul Zeleza that explored how African universities in South Africa, Kenya and Nigeria perceive and deal with African diaspora academics in North America. The study was concluded in 2012.
2. See, for example, Braziel and Mannur (2003), Butler (2001), Zeleza (2004, 2008), among others, for discussions on the various understandings of the diaspora as a social formation.

health workers, including an estimated 21 per cent of doctors produced in the country, were practising abroad at that time. In 2005, more than 13,000 South African-trained physicians were working in OECD countries, of which about 7,718 were in the United Kingdom, 2,215 in the United States, 1,877 in Canada and 1,022 in New Zealand. More recent data from Canada indicates that there were 2,193 South African physicians in that country in 2009 (Crush and Chikanda, 2012).

Crush (2011) has recently compiled the following data (obtained from the Global Migrant Origin Database) on the distribution of the South African diaspora:

Table 1: Regional distribution of South African diaspora, 2007.

Region	Number	Per cent
NORTH		
Europe	243,716	40.0
North America	108,221	18.0
Australasia	105,721	18.0
Sub-total	457,658	76.0
SOUTH		
Africa	302,764	20.0
Asia	14,042	2.0
Middle East	9,500	1.5
Latin America	2,305	0.5
Sub-total	328,613	24.0
TOTAL	786,721	

Source: Crush, J (2011).

Table 2: Major countries of South African diaspora, 2007.

Country	Number
United Kingdom	142,416
Australia	104,120
United States	70,465
Canada	37,681
Germany	34,674
New Zealand	26,069
Netherlands	11,286
Portugal	11,197

Source: Crush, J (2011).

Read together, the data in the two tables shows that even though South Africans migrate to virtually all parts of the world (Table 1), they are concentrated in about three countries: the United Kingdom, Australia and the USA (Table 2).

The State of the Academic Core in South African Universities

As argued by Castells (1998), Cloete, Bailey and Maassen (2011), Etzkowitz and Leydesdorff (1997) and others, universities in the knowledge economy are considered to be key institutions for the production of high-level skills and knowledge. However, for universities to be able to produce high-level knowledge and skills, and to effectively play their role as strategic actors in society, the nature, strength, size and continuity of their academic core or academic heartland (Clark, 1998) is critical (Cloete, Bailey and Maassen, 2011). As pointed out by Clark (1998) and Cloete, Bailey and Maassen (2011), the academic core or heartland:

> '... is where traditional academic values and activities such as teaching, research and training of the next generation of academics occur... [It entails] the basic handling of knowledge through teaching via academic degree programmes, research output and the production of doctorates (those who, in the future, will be responsible for carrying out the core knowledge activities).' (Cloete, Bailey and Maassen, 2011: 23)

Simply put, the academic core is the key distinguishing feature of a university. Various indicators can be used to assess the strength of a university's academic core. These include the extent of knowledge outputs by academic staff, percentage of academic staff with doctorates, shape of student enrolments and staff-to-student ratios, among other indicators. Various studies (for example, Ajayi, Goma and Johnson, 1996; Langa, 2011; Cloete, Bailey and Maassen, 2011) have concluded that the academic core of many African universities is weak, characterised, *inter alia*, by low research productivity, low qualifications (many academic staff do not have doctorates) and weak postgraduate education.

Recent analysis by the Centre for Higher Education Trust (CHET) (www.chet.org.za/resources/open-data-differentiated-south-africa-higher-education-system) on the shape of student enrolments, permanent academic staff with doctorates and levels of knowledge outputs, as evidenced by publications in South Africa's 23 public universities, provides important insights into the nature and strength of the academic core of these institutions.

In terms of the shape of student enrolments, CHET's analysis shows that between 2008 and 2010, 14 of South Africa's 23 public universities had an annual average postgraduate student population of less than 20 per cent. Stellenbosch University had the highest postgraduate student population with an aggregate of 37 per cent. Some universities, such as Mangosuthu University of Technology and Vaal University of Technology, had an aggregate postgraduate student population of just about 1 per cent. The picture is worse when it comes to doctoral enrolments – eight universities had 0 per cent doctoral enrolments, while, with five per cent, the University of Cape Town had the highest doctoral enrolments. Thus, enrolment data shows that the South African university system is largely an undergraduate system, with low master's and doctoral enrolments, a situation that has significant implications for the development of South Africa's next generation of scholars and the sustainability of these universities as vibrant knowledge institutions.

In terms of the percentage of permanent academic staff with doctorates, only four (the University of Cape Town, Stellenbosch, Rhodes and Witwatersrand) of the 23 universities have more than half of their staff with doctorates. Overall, 65 per cent of permanent academics in the South African higher education system did not have doctorates.

A comparison of the knowledge outputs[3] of permanent academic staff shows the same significant variations as those observed with regard to the shape of student enrolments and the percentage of permanent academic staff with doctorates. Academics in only three universities (University of Cape Town, Stellenbosch and Rhodes) had at least one publication unit per annum. The average publication units for academics with doctorates are significantly higher than the general aggregates, which suggest that the doctorate is an important prerequisite for a successful research career.

The mapping above of the academic core of South African universities is not intended to suggest that the South African academic diaspora would be 'fixers' for the generally weak academic core at most of these universities. It is, rather, intended to show the opportunities available for engagement with the diaspora in terms of collaborative research, co-authorships and joint supervision of postgraduate students, among other possibilities.

---

3. In South Africa, publication units are counted by considering the number of authors per output. For example, a journal article with four authors will accrue 0.25 publication units per author. Therefore, publication units do not refer to number of publications.

Any Role for the Diaspora?

Several initiatives have been implemented in South Africa to enhance collaborations with South African diaspora academics. These include the South African Network of Skills Abroad (SANSA), the Economic Research Southern Africa (ERSA) Diaspora Fund and the University of the Witwatersrand's Faculty of Health Sciences (Wit's FHS) Alumni Diaspora Programme.

SANSA was formed in 1998 with the aim of establishing links between highly skilled people located both abroad and in South Africa. The network is not restricted to South Africans or people of South African origin, though it is primarily directed at them. Basically, the initiative was meant to encourage the transfer of skills, especially in the fields of science and technology, by the South African diaspora and other skilled individuals abroad, while not necessarily returning to or settling in the country (Marks, 2004; Benton, 2007).

The ERSA Diaspora Fund was established in 2009 to encourage the growing number of South African economists based at leading international institutions into a continued and extended association with South Africa. The intention was to minimise a net loss of South African academics working abroad (ERSA Report, 2010). And lastly, the Wit's FHS Alumni Diaspora Programme was formed in 2010 to tap into the expertise of alumni who held high positions in the diaspora, especially in the USA, Canada, Europe and Australia. This programme facilitates research collaboration and other forms of academic engagements with diaspora alumni.

It is significant that the primary focus of these initiatives is not the permanent return of skilled diaspora, but to productively engage with them from wherever they are settled. It is a strategy that allows South Africa not only to benefit from the expertise of its 'citizens' now living abroad, but also tap into the diaspora's useful networks and other forms of capital at their disposal.

Forms of Engagement

Engagements with the diaspora in South African universities can be described in several ways, namely, formal versus informal engagements, individualised versus institutional engagements and demand-driven versus supply-driven forms of engagement. Whereas formal engagements operated within university norms governing research collaborations, and often involved memoranda of understanding, informal engagements were generally characterised by personal relationships and previous collaborations before one of the parties emigrated. Informal engagements were further characterised by occasional co-authorships, and invitations to speak at conferences and to act as external examiners, among other forms of collaboration. A good example of formalised engagements is the appointment of diaspora academics as adjunct or honorary professors. Although not always the case, most individualised engagements tended to be informal while institutional engagements were highly formalised.

As with any demand-driven initiatives, engagements with the diaspora that are demand-driven address a particular need, and tend to be a part of broader institutional processes — be it mentoring students, capacity building, improving research outputs or addressing skills shortages. Even though some supply-driven engagements may fit into broader institutional goals, they are mainly driven by the interests of the diaspora academic; for example, an alumni on holiday who wants to visit his alma mater for sentimental reasons or to connect with former colleagues and ends up giving a lecture on a topic of his interest. Another example is where diaspora academics strategically cultivate collaborations with local institutions in order to advance their own research interests that might not be of benefit to the local institutions.

One of the most common ways in which the South African academic diaspora were engaged with local universities was through invitations to give lectures and short courses. This happened either within the framework of initiatives such as ERSA and the Wit's FHS Alumni Diaspora Programme or in the context of what might be described as 'holiday engagements' (supply-driven engagements). Whereas the former was structured and part of a clearly defined programme, the latter was conducted mainly on an ad-hoc basis by diaspora academics on holiday in the country or visiting for other purposes.

Co-authorship is increasingly becoming a popular form of engagement with the South African academic diaspora. A recent study by Mouton (2012) shows that co-authorships between South African and overseas scholars have increased significantly since 1996. For instance, co-authored papers appearing in ISI [Institute of Scientific Information] journals increased from 22 in 1996 to 39 in 2007 at the University of the Western Cape, while those of the University of the North West increased from 30 to 57, and the University of Pretoria's from 220 to 251 over the same time period. The University of Cape Town, often ranked the most pre-eminent in Africa, has the highest number of co-authorships with overseas scholars — 285 ISI papers in 2007 (Mouton, 2012).

Mouton (2012) argues that collaboration with overseas scholars is one of the main reasons for the increasing impact and visibility of South African research. Even though the data on co-authorship is not disaggregated to identify the quantity of publications co-authored with the South

Africa-born academic diaspora, interviews with academics confirmed that some of these were co-authored with South African academics in the diaspora.

The appointment of the South Africa-born academic diaspora as adjunct or honorary professors and as research chairs could be described as the more formalised and institutionalised form of engagement with the diaspora. Diaspora adjunct or honorary professors are a very important resource to local universities. They tend to be high-profile academics, leaders in their fields of specialisation. They contribute to the universities in various ways, namely by teaching courses, co-supervising postgraduate students, and mentoring and supporting their faculty in their respective local universities. They also undertake joint research and co-author papers with local colleagues. As already mentioned, papers co-authored with overseas scholars have had a significant impact in making South African research more visible (Mouton, 2012). Equally important are the opportunities these scholars make available to students and staff in South African universities. These opportunities include, inter alia, receiving South African graduate students in laboratories or training programmes, making available conference and research funding opportunities, and scholarship, internship and sabbatical opportunities.

Another benefit that these diaspora academics and professionals bring to local institutions is reputation. Given the present competitive context in which universities find themselves, they are, as Van Vught (2008: 167) has pointed out, enticed 'to represent themselves in the best possible ways. They underline their self-acclaimed qualities hoping that by emphasising these, they will be able to convince the clients of their attractiveness'. Therefore, in this competitive context, an association with these leading scholars provides local universities with important social capital, which they exploit to their benefit.

Conclusion

The key argument in this paper is that the highly skilled diaspora are an important component of global intellectual resources that can be tapped into by African universities to enhance their missions and as part of their internationalisation strategies. As has been shown in this analysis, there exist multiple possibilities for African universities to productively engage with the diaspora. These engagements have the potential to contribute to the enhancement of research, postgraduate education and capacity building, among other benefits.

Even though there is some evidence of engagement between the academic diaspora and some South African universities, these engagements remain largely individualised and fragmented, and do not constitute part of an institutional strategy. The lack of an institutional strategy was partly as a result of the lack of acknowledgement by key departments within universities (alumni, international and research offices) that the country's academic diaspora are a key constituency that could play an important role in advancing the missions of local universities.

References

Ajayi, JFA, Goma, LKH and Johnson, GA (1996) *The African Experience with Higher Education*. Accra: Association of African Universities.

Benton, S (2007) *Harness Africa's Diaspora*. Retrieved on 15 May, 2012 from http:// southafrica.info/abroad/dispora-150607.htm.

Braziel, JE and Mannur, A (ed.) (2003) *Theorising diaspora: a reader*. Oxford: Blackwell Publishing.

Butler, KD (2001) Defining diaspora, refining discourse. *Diaspora: a journal of transnational studies* (10)2: Pp. 189–219.

Castells, M (1998) Possibilities for Development in the Information Age. Paper prepared for the United Nations Research Institute for Social Development, Geneva, 22–24 March.

Chacha, A (2007) *Brain Drain in Africa: From an African Perspective*. Retrieved on 20 May, 2012 from www.afrikanet.info/index.php.

Clark, BR (1998) *Creating Entrepreneurial Universities: Organisational Pathways of Transformations*. Oxford: Pergamon.

Cloete, N, Bailey, T and Maassen, P (2011) *Universities and economic development in Africa: pact, academic core and co-ordination*. Wynberg: CHET.

Crush, J (2011) Diasporas of the South: Situating the African Diaspora in Africa. In: Plaza, S and Ratha, D (Eds) Diaspora for development in Africa. World Bank: Washington, DC.

Crush, J and Chikanda, A (2012) *The Disengagement of the South African Medical Diaspora*. Southern African Migration Programme, Migration Policy Series No. 58.

ERSA Report (2010) *Economic Research Southern Africa Activity April 2009–March 2010*. ERSA annual report.

Etzkowitz, H and Leydesdorff, LA (1997) *Universities and the global knowledge economy: a triple helix of university-industry-government relations*. London: Pinter.

Juma, C and Agwara, H (2006) Africa in the global knowledge economy: strategic options. *International Journal of Technology and Globalisation*, (2) 3/4: Pp. 218–231.

Langa, PV (2011) Scientific capital and engagement in African universities: the case of the social sciences at Makerere University. Paper prepared for the Higher Education and Advocacy Network in Africa (HERANA).

Marks, J (2004) *Expatriate professionals as an entry point into global knowledge-intensive value chains: South Africa*. World Bank: Washington DC.

Mouton, J (2012) Measuring differentiation in knowledge production at South African Universities. Presentation to the Ministerial Committee on University Funding, 8 July 2012. Pretoria.

Shinn, DH (2008) *Brain drain and migration in sub-Saharan Africa: making the best of a dilemma*. Unpublished manuscript.

Van Vught, F (2008) Mission, diversity and reputation in higher education. *Higher Education Policy* (21), Pp. 151–174.

World Bank (2012) *African Diaspora*. Retrieved 26 April 2012 from http://sitere sources.worldbank.org/INTDIASPORA/Resources/AFR_Diaspora_FAQ.pdf.

Zeleza, PT (2004) The academic diaspora in the United States and Africa: the challenges of productive engagement. *Comparative Studies of South Asia, Africa and the Middle East* (24) 1: Pp. 261–275.

Zeleza, PT (2008) The challenges of studying the African diasporas. *African Sociological Review* (12) 2: Pp. 4–21.

Zeleza, PT (2012) Internationalisation in higher education: opportunities and challenges for the knowledge project in the global south. Keynote address, conference organised by the Southern African Regional Universities Association, the International Association of Universities and Universidade Eduardo Mondlane. Maputo, Mozambique, 21–22 March 2012.

Chapter 1.5

Analysing Research Outputs to Support Research Innovation and International Collaboration

Peter Darroch of Elsevier B.V.

Introduction

In the global knowledge economy, fostering world-leading research and innovation is critical to securing future economic stability and growth. The changing global research landscape means there is an increasing demand for greater interdisciplinary and trans-boundary research collaboration in order to facilitate creative thinking and address the global challenges of today's world. Furthermore, there is a growing need for greater transparency in research, the explanation of the 'impact' of research (for example, from a social or economic perspective) and also the demonstration of the return on investment from research. It is generally accepted that international and cross-sector collaborations are effective strategies for promoting research and innovation, and the positive correlation between these types of collaborative activities and research impact, as measured by citations, has been demonstrated (International Comparative Performance of the UK Research Base, 2011; The Royal Society, 2011). Publication and citation analyses such as co-authorships can also provide unique views of research collaboration networks, brain circulation and global talent migration.

Our aim was to investigate similarities and differences between the research activities of Iran, Egypt, Lebanon, Saudi Arabia and the United Arab Emirates, as well as Turkey. To achieve this, we performed a case study into the levels of international collaboration, international mobility

Going Global: Knowledge-Based Economies for 21st Century Nations
Copyright © 2014 by Peter Darroch
All rights of reproduction in any form reserved
ISBN: 978-1-78441-003-2

of researchers (so-called 'brain circulation') and citation analyses using the SciVal suite of tools (www.info.scival.com).

Research Productivity and International Collaboration Rates

Searching the abstract and citation database Scopus (www.elsevier.com/online-tools/scopus) for the selected countries and analysing the affiliation country of the authors on each article allowed analysis of the publication volume as well as of the publications involving collaborations with international partners. Figure 1 illustrates how the publication output levels of each country have increased over the period 1996–2011, with Turkey and Iran showing the most dramatic increases. However, looking more recently at the five-year period from 2007–2011, the greatest increase in output levels are demonstrated for Saudi Arabia (3.3-fold increase) and Iran (2.4-fold increase).

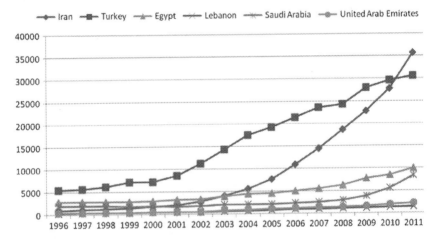

Figure 1: Analysis of publication volume from Iran, Turkey, Egypt, Lebanon, Saudi Arabia and the United Arab Emirates for the period 1996–2011.[1]

Figure 2 shows the trend in number of publications involving international co-authors for each country between 1996 and 2011. While all countries show significant increases in the absolute number of international co-authorships over the time period, it is clear that Iran, Turkey, Egypt

---

1. The increases in values observed post-2002 are partly due to the growth in coverage of the Scopus database.

and Saudi Arabia produce significantly more publications involving international collaborations. Furthermore, if we look at the five-year period between 2007 and 2011, the rate of increase differs significantly between the selected countries, with Turkey showing a 1.4-fold increase compared to Saudi Arabia where we see a 5.7-fold increase in international co-authorships over the same period.

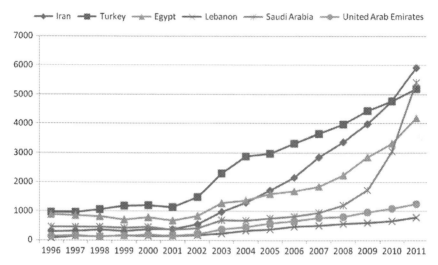

Figure 2: Analysis of publication volume involving international co-authors from Iran, Turkey, Egypt, Lebanon, Saudi Arabia and the United Arab Emirates for the period 1996–2011[2].

It has been previously observed that Saudi Arabia demonstrated an outward-looking collaborative orientation (Halevi and Moed, 2011). Extending this analysis to the other countries in the study (see Table 1) as a percentage of the total output of each country in 2011, international colla-borations represent around 16 percent of the total output of Iran and Turkey in comparison to the other nations, where international collaborations occur in around half of the publications from 2011. This would suggest a more international or 'outward' collaborative orientation for Egypt, Lebanon and the United Arab Emirates compared to a more 'inward' orientation for Iran and Turkey. Looking at the most frequent collaborating countries, similari-ties are clearly seen with the United States and United Kingdom featuring heavily for all countries. There are many factors that contribute to the

---

2. The increases in values observed post-2002 are partly due to the growth in coverage of the Scopus database.

collaborative profiles of each country, but examples could include the disciplinary research profile, the relative research standing of the collaborative nations, historical and cultural ties, and geographical proximity.

Table 1: The percentage of the total output involving international collaborations for Iran, Turkey, Egypt, Lebanon, Saudi Arabia and United Arab Emirates, and apparent collaborative orientation in 2011.

	Publications involving international collaboration %	Collaborative orientation	Most frequent collaborative countries
Iran	16.6	National	United States, Canada, United Kingdom, Malaysia
Turkey	17.0	National	United States, Germany, United Kingdom, Italy
Egypt	41.9	International	Saudi Arabia, United States, Germany, United Kingdom
Lebanon	56.9	International	France, United States, Canada, United Kingdom
Saudi Arabia	64.6	International	Egypt, United States, United Kingdom, India
United Arab Emirates	56.5	International	United States, United Kingdom, Canada, Australia

International Mobility of Researchers ('Brain Circulation')

Applying the novel approach of using researcher affiliations listed in research outputs, showcased in the report published for the Department of Business Innovation and Skills in 2011 (International Comparative Performance of the UK Research Base, 2011), we were able to map international researcher mobility over the period 1996–2011 for the United Arab Emirates (UAE), Saudi Arabia, Egypt and Turkey. Figure 3 shows the 'brain circulation' map for the UAE as an example of this type of analysis. This analysis looks at 'brain circulation' from many perspectives, such as in terms of mobility classes (migratory and transitory) and relative productivity and seniority, in order to extensively map the mobility patterns of the country and some of the resultant effects of this mobility.

Analysis of these migration streams for the UAE reveal that 13.3 percent of the scientists stayed within the UAE during the 15-year study period (stay-at-home researchers), 58.6 percent were visiting (or transitory) researchers (travelling in or out of the UAE for a period of less than two years), 17.8 percent moved to and 10.3 percent left the UAE; summing up to a net inflow of 7.5 percent. Furthermore, it is also of note that the 47.5 percent of researchers representing a group of mainly non-UAE researchers who stay in the UAE for under two years are the most productive group, with a relative productivity (relative to the UAE country average) of 1.3. In contrast, the group of stay-at-home researchers are the least productive, with a relative productivity of 0.49.

Overall, the analysis suggests that the UAE attracts a large number of short-term researchers from abroad (transitory, mainly non-UAE) who are also highly productive, with this group representing over 47 percent of UAE researchers. This reveals that the UAE research base is constantly being refreshed and suggests that the UAE is an attractive place to conduct research for these foreign researchers. Indeed, it would be of interest to investigate further the potential role that foreign universities with campuses in the UAE play in these migratory patterns.

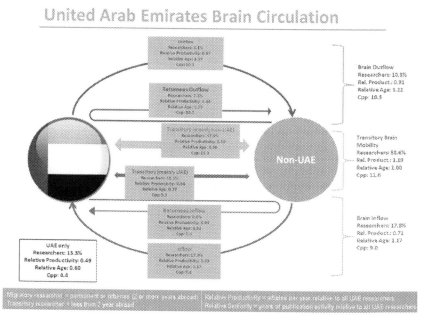

Figure 3: Brain circulation map for United Arab Emirates for the period 1996–2011.

Table 2 shows the parameters from the brain circulation analyses for the United Arab Emirates, Saudi Arabia, Egypt and Turkey in order to compare the different profiles of these countries with regards to international mobility. While all countries demonstrate net brain inflow, it is significant to note that Saudi Arabia and the United Arab Emirates show the greatest levels of foreign transitory researchers and overall transitory researcher migration. While Egypt also shows significant levels of transitory researcher migration, only 25.8 percent of the total researchers represent foreigners moving to Egypt to conduct their research as opposed to the almost 50 percent shown for Saudi Arabia and the United Arab Emirates. In contrast, Turkey shows the lowest levels of transitory researcher mobility, with almost 73 percent of researchers representing 'stay-at-home' researchers.

Table 2: Brain circulation analysis for Saudi Arabia, Egypt, United Arab Emirates and Turkey for the period 1996–2011.

	Not internationally mobile (%)	Transitory foreigner migration (%)	Overall transitory researcher migration (%)	Researcher outflow (%)	Researcher inflow (%)	Net researcher migration (%)
Saudi Arabia	19.7	48.3	60.8	7.4	12.1	4.7
Egypt	39.7	25.8	43.7	8.1	8.4	0.3
United Arab Emirates	13.3	47.5	58.6	10.3	17.8	7.5
Turkey	72.8	10.1	21.3	1.9	4.0	2.1

Significantly, if we then look at the relative productivity (Table 3) of each of the migratory groups, it is clear that transitory researchers represent the most productive research group and 'stay-at-home' researchers the least productive research group for all of the countries analysed. It is also worth noting that, apart from Saudi Arabia, the researcher outflow groups are generally slightly more productive than the inflow groups.

Table 3: Relative productivity of migratory groups for Saudi Arabia, Egypt, United Arab Emirates and Turkey for the period 1996–2011.

	Not internationally mobile	Researcher outflow	Researcher inflow	Transitory researchers
Saudi Arabia	0.45	0.67	0.71	1.26
Egypt	0.5	0.84	0.79	1.46
United Arab Emirates	0.49	0.91	0.71	1.19
Turkey	0.74	1.01	0.98	1.69

Table 4 shows the most productive institution and the dominant disciplines represented in the research output of each country. Similarities in the disciplinary focus of each country are immediately observed, with Engineering and Medicine representing an area of focus for all countries and Chemistry plus Physics and Astronomy also featuring heavily. This demonstrates an apparent disciplinary focus for the countries as a whole, which mirrors the similarities observed with the most frequent collaborating countries detailed in Table 1.

Table 4: Analysis of the most productive institutions and the dominant disciplines represented in 2011 for Iran, Turkey, Egypt, Lebanon, Saudi Arabia and United Arab Emirates.

	Most productive institution 2011	Dominant disciplines by volume of publications
Iran	Daneshgahe Azad Elsami	Engineering, Medicine, Chemistry, Materials Science
Turkey	Gazi Universitesi	Medicine, Engineering, Agricultural and Biological Sciences, Physics and Astronomy
Egypt	Cairo University	Medicine, Engineering, Chemistry, Physics and Astronomy
Lebanon	American University of Beirut	Medicine, Engineering, Computer Science, Biochemistry, Genetics and Molecular Biology
Saudi Arabia	King Saud University	Medicine, Engineering, Chemistry, Physics and Astronomy
United Arab Emirates	United Arab Emirates University	Engineering, Computer Science, Medicine, Mathematics

Citation Analyses

In addition to looking at productivity, international collaborations and 'brain circulation' analyses, it is also possible to perform analyses based on citations as 'proxy' indicators of the quality of the research output of the countries of interest.

Over the period 1996−2011, all countries have enjoyed an increase in their volume of publications, as shown in Figure 1. Using the Field Weighted Citation Impact (FWCI), which looks at the ratio of citations received relative to the expected world average for the subject field, publication type and publication year, we are able to gain a view of the relative change in the quality of the outputs from each country over the period 1996−2011. Figure 4 shows the FWCI for each of the countries in the study, and it can be seen that while all countries have enjoyed an increase in the FWCI over the period 1996−2011, the relative quality of the publications from each country as measured by citations generally remains below the world average. However, it should be noted that the FWCI for Saudi Arabia was equal to the world average in 2011, with Lebanon and the United Arab Emirates also having a FWCI over 0.9 in 2011. Of significance is the rate of increase in FWCI observed for Saudi Arabia since 2007, with an increase from 0.75 to 1.0. This is the greatest increase of all the countries in the study.

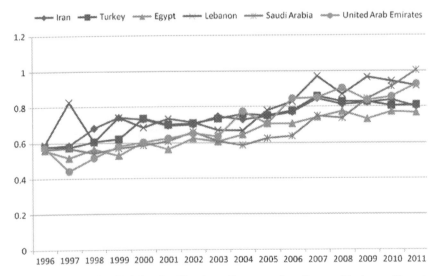

Figure 4: Field Weighted Citation Impact for Iran, Turkey, Egypt, Lebanon, Saudi Arabia and United Arab Emirates for the period 1996−2011. The fluctuation observed in the FWCI is mainly due to smaller numbers of publications being analysed.

As noted, the correlation between publications involving international collaboration and an increase in citation impact has been demonstrated previously (International Comparative Performance of the UK Research Base, 2011). This effect is also observed for all countries analysed in this study. Figure 5 shows the relative citation gain achieved for internationally co-authored articles compared to articles involving national co-authors over five-year rolling periods from 1996. It can be seen that all countries gain a benefit in citation impact through international collaborations, with the biggest gains being enjoyed by researchers in Turkey and the United Arab Emirates (both now enjoying around a two-fold boost in citation rates). Of note, however, is the significant decline in relative citation gain for internationally co-authored articles observed for Saudi Arabia and, in particular, Lebanon over the same time period. It is possible that this is a reflection of the increasing levels of international collaboration occuring in these countries, with around half of all papers involving international part-ners in 2011. This appears to reflect significant gains at the early stages of internationalisation of the research in these countries, which has decreased as more publications overall have involved international partners.

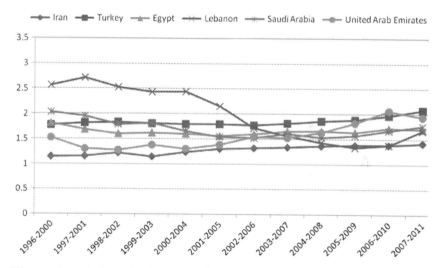

Figure 5: Relative citation gain for internationally co-authored articles compared to nationally co-authored articles within five-year rolling windows from 1996–2011. A value of 1 represents the average for nationally co-authored articles.

Concluding Remarks

The case study has analysed the research activities of Iran, Egypt, Lebanon, Saudi Arabia and the United Arab Emirates across the areas of publication volume, citation analyses as a 'proxy' indicator of the quality of the research outputs and international collaboration rates. Furthermore, we have also presented a novel researcher mobility analysis for Saudi Arabia, Egypt, the UAE and Turkey.

All countries in the study have shown an increase in the volume of research outputs as well as an increase in the number of research outputs involving international co-authors over the time period analysed. Indeed, we see that around half of all publications from Egypt, Lebanon, Saudi Arabia and the UAE involved international co-authors in 2011. It is of interest to note that while Iran and Turkey produce the largest volume of outputs, they have the most 'inward' or 'national' collaborative orientation of all the countries analysed.

Furthermore, it can also be seen that all countries in the study have enjoyed a relative citation gain from their international partnerships and an increase in their FWCI over the time period. Saudi Arabia, the UAE and Lebanon have shown the most significant increases in FWCI over the period analysed and, while all countries citation impact is observed to be below world average, it is of note that Saudi Arabia's FWCI in 2011 was equal to the world average in 2011 and on a significant upward trend.

The researcher mobility analysis or 'brain circulation' maps for Saudi Arabia, Egypt, the UAE and Turkey revealed that transitory researchers represent the most productive researchers and stay-at-home researchers the least productive researchers in all countries. Furthermore, it revealed that Turkey has the lowest proportion of these transitory researchers with over 70 percent of the researchers in Turkey not being internationally mobile. This correlates with the low proportion (17 percent) of the total publications being produced by researchers in Turkey involving international co-authors in 2011. It is of note that the analyses conducted also reveal that Turkey has received the greatest citation gain of all the countries analysed from internationally co-authored articles over the recent past.

It would be of interest to investigate more fully the potential reasons for the apparent similarities and differences observed in this case study. For example, looking at the countries from the perspectives of culture, language or the underlying policy landscape could bring new elements to light, but this was out of the scope of this study.

In conclusion, the global research landscape is fluid, dynamic and intensely competitive. It is also becoming more collaborative, interdisciplinary, international and interconnected. The analyses presented have shown some of the many ways through which we can provide insight and knowledge to support adaptation to the changing research landscape, and how publication and citation analyses can support planning and strategy. We believe that this information can help nations and institutions to continue to grow and thrive in the rapidly changing global research landscape.

References

International Comparative Performance of the UK Research Base (2011) from www.snowballmetrics.com/wp-content/uploads/11-p123-international-comparative-performance-uk-research-base-2011.pdf

The Royal Society (2011) *Knowledge, Networks and Nations — Global scientific collaboration in the 21st century* from http://royalsociety.org/policy/reports/ knowledge-networks-nations/

Halevi, G and Moed, H F (2011) *Country Trends: Emerging scientific networks. Research Trends* (www.researchtrends.com), 24, 5–6.

Chapter 1.6

Ripples of Influence: How One Leads to Another in Successful Collaborations

Ian Willis

Introduction

It is the goal of most international collaborations to build capacity in some way, to work together for mutual advantage and to achieve goals that could not have been achieved acting alone (Huxham, 2003). Collaborative endeavours are usually framed by institutional agreements and funding arrangements, which provide the necessary supporting structures. Acting within these supporting structures, individuals, through their own initiative and action, shape the project.

This paper examines the actions of staff involved in our collaboration and specifically looks at how the unplanned or emergent actions of one partner group influenced and impelled a response from the other partner and, in turn, encouraged further responses. Termed 'ripples of influence', these actions significantly enriched the collaboration and helped it to reach its goals. The key point is that the actual path was unexpected and depended on an action—influence—response cycle.

No doubt this will resonate with those involved in other international collaborations. We are concerned with how we can foster emergence, the possibilities for unplanned ideas and practices to emerge from collaborative working, and how to support active engagement and professional dialogues in order to produce changes to teaching practice in a developing country.

Each collaboration will have its own story with its own patterns; in telling our story we aim to draw out the critical factors that can be generalised and supported theoretically. We will examine the conditions that set up

Going Global: Knowledge-Based Economies for 21st Century Nations
ISBN: 978-1-78441-003-2

possibilities for emergent responses, the specific actions and motivations of local staff, the responses of the international partners and the tangible outcomes.

We propose a model for collaborative working in higher education that draws attention to the conditions necessary for productive responses to emerge, the overarching structures, the role of professional dialogues and the quality of individual engagement in order to improve practice (Walsh and Kahn, 2010).

The Setting

Ensuring quality higher education provision is a worldwide challenge that involves a synthesis of international ideas research and practice and sensitivity to local context. It also requires systems and structures that support local initiatives to enhance the student experience. Along with many developing countries, Pakistan is striving to improve learning and teaching throughout the higher education sector.

This paper outlines a project that aims to enhance learning and teaching in medical education in the Punjab, a province of 80 million people. It is supported by the British Council through the International Strategic Partnerships in Research and Education (INSPIRE) programme. In a collaborative partnership, staff from the University of Liverpool (UoL) in the UK and from the University of Health Sciences (UHS) in Lahore have worked together to design, deliver and accredit a Master's in Health Professionals Education (MHPE). This programme is available to staff in any of UHS's 40 affiliated medical and dental colleges in the Punjab and so has the potential to have a significant impact in the field of medical education where there is limited opportunity to gain a master's-level qualification while remaining at home and at work. In addition, the collaboration has developed introductory teaching courses, run workshops and fostered local research projects in medical education.

Creating Conditions for Emergence: How did it All Happen?

Our collaboration is based on international input to encourage innovative ways of learning and teaching in medical education – the first ripple of influence. In the MHPE we used an active learning and contructivist approach, where learners are expected to synthesise concepts of learning and their existing experience in order to create new understandings appropriate to their context (Murphy, 1997). In their first assignment the medical educators undertaking the programme were required to critically reflect on their own practice and their teaching context. As a result of this assignment and associated dialogues, several local educators voluntarily started to make changes to their teaching practices.

In general terms, medical education in Pakistan can be characterised as traditional in the sense of being lecturer-centred, didactic, exam-centred and slow to change (Khan, 2013). This overall claim masks a desire for change among many teaching staff and a willingness to innovate, where innovate can mean making quite significant changes to practice, notwithstanding a traditional setting. So, we return to the question of how and why these educators were motivated to make changes to their practice at this time.

Events in the 'ripples of influence' interactions can be understood through the notion of emergence in complexity science. Emergence is seen as behaviour or actions arising from the interactions of participants and is often unpredictable in advance, 'constructed through interaction and dialogue' and the resultant outcomes are emergent (Tosey, 2002 p18). In this interpretation, it is more than the actions of individuals that are at play but phenomena are viewed as 'mutually dependent, mutually constitutive and actually *emerge together* in dynamic structures' (Fenwick, 2012 p144). In order to understand the conditions of emergence, we need to examine the actors, their motivations, actions and outcomes, along with the context, *and* pay attention to the interactions within the system as a whole (Davis & Sumara, 2009). This takes our focus beyond just the individuals involved and their context and focuses additionally on the nature of their interactions; in our case the 'ripples of influence' that permeated our collaboration and led to innovations in practice that were emergent and unplanned.

Innovations to Practice: What Happened?

Before examining in more detail the quality of interactions that led to unplanned outcomes, it is worth documenting what has been achieved. Local staff have initiated some excellent projects that are bringing change in medical education in the Punjab, including:

- metacognition in physiology postgraduates using a Metacognitive Assessment Inventory
- study skills in physiology undergraduates using the Approaches and Study Skills Inventory
- the impact of student study methodology workshops in enhancing learning and performance
- the impact of Objective Structured Practical Examinations on undergraduate medical students' approach to learning

- the implementation of a formal mentorship programme to enhance the student experience, both personal and professional, in an undergraduate dental education programme
- the introduction of a 'three-in-one' model of active learning in tutorials
- student-led peer learning and peer feedback
- the use of learning outcomes in anatomy lectures
- learning advantages and disadvantages in the use of simulated bodies in dissection, rather than cadavers.

Evidence of Impact

In seeking to develop the critical underpinning factors for success, it is not sufficient just to tell localised good-results stories, compelling as these might be. It is also important to provide evidence of impact and of wider interest. So far, there have been three presentations at international conferences, including one sponsored attendance, one peer-reviewed local journal article, one peer-reviewed international article, six abstracts for conference presentations and two papers for international publication in process. This is over a relatively short period of time and with staff who had no prior experience of qualitative research in medical education. Therefore, we argue that if the right conditions are consciously developed then this type of result will be replicable in comparable settings.

Ideas for these projects and their implementation led to discussions with UoL staff that can be characterised as professional dialogues: effective communication involving criticality, trust and negotiation in order to improve professional practice (Sachs, 2003; Walsh & Kahn, 2010). We argue that interpersonal relationships are central to professional dialogues and that consciously engaging in these professional dialogues is one of the critical factors in our 'ripples of influence' cycle, and can be applied and generalised to other similar international collaborations.

Understanding the Reasons for Staff Engagement: Why did it Happen?

Continuing the 'ripples of influence' theme, these ideas for innovation encouraged the international staff to set up an introduction to research in medical education workshops, as well as researching the emerging process.

Researching the Process

A research project was designed in order to understand more about the factors that encouraged staff at UHS to voluntarily engage in change projects in their own learning and teaching practice. An action research approach was used, as the UoL and UHS staff were researching their own practice and using each other as critical friends. (McNiff, 2013), while standard ethical approval and practice were followed. A total of ten interviews were conducted, audio taped and transcribed. Data was analysed using a Thematic Analysis approach, which recognises that some data will be generated in direct response to the interview schedule questions and some data will arise as a result of the unique interactions in each interview (Braun & Clarke, 2006).

Active Engagement from Local Staff

Innovative teaching does not just arrive unchanged in a new setting; it requires adaptation to local conditions, but the wheel does need to be re-invented to suit the local context (Trowler, 2004). Critically, what is also required is a group of local enthusiasts and their active engagement. Here, engagement is simply taken to mean individuals' commitment to the project as a whole and to their own particular projects (Archer, 2003).

The local staff exhibited high levels of personal commitment and commitment to their own learning:

> 'I have to have something that I can improve my teaching.
> I want to learn, this is a great opportunity and there is some-
> one coming from abroad and this is a great opportunity that
> I may not be able to ever have it again while sitting comforta-
> bly in my own homeland.'

The opportunity to learn while remaining at home and at work was mentioned several times, along with the value of international input: 'The three main attractions were for my personal growth, that it was in collaboration [with UoL] and that it was in Lahore.'

It is worth adding that these staff did not mention time as a barrier to their engagement and the additional work that implies, despite the fact that they are all already sufficiently busy:

> 'It was internal motivation, although I had to do a lot of
> work; I feel happy when I am learning something and I am
> teaching. I was overworked; I am a mother, I am a teacher,
> I am a clinician, I am a private practitioner and now I am
> involved myself as well in this medical education, but it's
> happiness, I feel happy.'

These staff were self-selected to take on the extra work of innovating in their own practice, contributing to the new teaching programmes and, for most of them, to undertake their own research projects. This was a considerable commitment, sustained by the opportunity to advance projects of their own interest and to learn 'at home' with international input.

Importance of Personal Relationships

There are a number of principles that underpin the development of collaborative endeavours, one of which is the importance of personal relationships. Without a basis for trust and healthy inter-personal connections between people, strategic alliances [collaborations] will not have a solid foundation on which to stand (Gadja, 2004 p69). This was neatly echoed by one of the local staff: "Collaboration is just a big relationship, more formalised, lots of paperwork, but it boils down to people interacting with each other".

It was a consistent theme throughout the interviews that the relationships that developed were important to all: 'We have developed wonderful relationships among all of us. Being honest to the other person ... being committed, helping each other, sharing things.' Key terms were passion, commitment, compatibility, shared values, sincerity 'which matters in all human relations' and 'being responsive to each other according to the needs of each other, whenever you are in need of the other then the relationship will also grow more'. These manifest qualities were the basis for developing effective professional dialogues or communication:

> 'It is also remarkable we have had so much communication and the quality of communication is very important, it has a strong emotional and rapport-building component and this was unitised in facilitating the learning. If you only stick with the practical components we wouldn't have opened up. The emotional component builds a bridge for knowledge to transfer, hopefully bilaterally, so you exchange knowledge.'

Communication must be purposeful; in collaborations it is important to articulate shared goals (these are often pre-determined) and to create the space for people to advance their own projects or goals (these are often unknown in advance and emergent).

Place of Research

The local staff exhibited high levels of professional drive to improve their own practice and in the longer term to influence change in their institutions: 'I need to know what is going on, I need to do it [research]'; 'I really need to know how my students learn'; 'Only research and things that are published, evidence, will influence people.' It was a general goal of the INSPIRE project to foster locally based research but the particular projects were entirely determined by the local staff, and so again were emergent.

It is worth noting that most of those interviewed reported that they had supportive contexts, and received support from their managers or from their colleagues. This is not universally the case in the Pakistani higher education system, which, as elsewhere, can be resistant to change.

Summary

Based on our research and experience of working together, we argue that successful collaborations are likely to exhibit similar underlying factors of active engagement from local staff, i.e. high levels of personal commitment and strong interpersonal relationships leading to productive professional dialogues. In addition to this, we would include ensuring that research is built into the process in order to provide credible evidence.

These factors have led to a situation where our shared commitments and strong interpersonal relationships have created a space for emergent activity based on the projects of the local staff supported and encouraged by the international partners. This action−influence−response cycle or 'ripples of influence' can be represented as below (Figure 1):

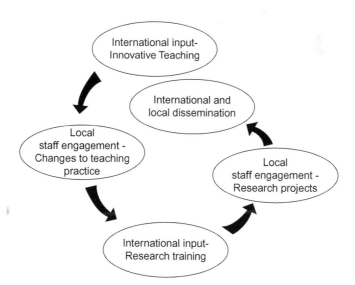

Figure 1: Action-influence-response cycle.

Wider Application: What are the Implications for Others?

While we have attended to factors 'within' the project, the overall context
is also crucially important. In this case, the project was framed by an overarching collaboration between the universities involved and the British
Council, the influence that UHS has in medical education throughout
the Punjab and the requirement of the Pakistan Medical and Dental
Council that medical universities and colleges set up departments of medical education. Thus, in general terms we were operating within a supportive
context or, expressed another way, it is important to shape projects to take
advantage of prevailing contextual factors.

We propose a model for collaboration that involves attending to key
process factors and monitoring both outcomes and the process itself. These
key process factors are:

- project design that fosters conditions for unplanned actions to emerge
  within the pre-planned project aims
- professional dialogues
- engaged collaborators.

These factors create the conditions for 'ripples of influence': the interactions that build productive capacity. Following from this are more tangible
outcomes:

- personal projects
- collaboration goals
- research-based evidence.

Project Design and Emergence

International collaborations are well placed to provide the structures to
meet the goal of enhancing education provision. In making applications
to funding bodies, collaborative projects often have to state in advance
quite specific outcomes against which the project will be evaluated.
Clearly, this is important in order to be accountable for funds received.
However, project design must also be sufficiently flexible to not only
allow for, but to actively encourage, emergent ideas and initiatives that
necessarily cannot be foreseen in detail at the point of framing the collaboration and determining its outcomes. This can be achieved by building
in evaluative processes that, as well as having an overall audit and
accountability orientation, also support ongoing critical review and
enhancement as the project develops, drawing on ideas from ppreciative

inquiry and developmental evaluation (Cooperrider, Whitney, & Stavros, 2003; Gamble, 2008).

It is not only the project that needs to have flexible structures; those involved must also be flexible in order for there to be the personal capacity to develop a 'ripples of influence' cycle. Being alert to the importance of this responsiveness and asking questions about flexibility and responsiveness are ways to foster emergence and comparable 'ripples of influence' in other collaborations.

Professional Dialogues

In collaborations, Gajda (2004) asserts that attending to personal factors is as important as procedural issues. Collaborations depend on 'positive personal relations and effective emotional connections between partners', (p 69). These are prerequisites for the development of trust in professional dialogues.

Professional dialogue includes the notions of trust in communication and mutual negotiation of goals and processes: key constituents of genuine collaboration. Walsh and Kahn (2010) suggest the project can seek data on its own processes by asking questions such as:

- to what extent are those involved contributing to a holistic process rather than working separately with their work being joined up later?
- what strategies are in place to promote the exchange of ideas, aims and resources?

To these project-level questions we can add 'personal-level' questions about the development of social networks, cross-cultural learning and the enjoyment of working together (Willis 2012). These ideas are mirrored in the key principles for research partnerships that include joint decision-making, building trust, sharing responsibly, sharing information and building networks (Barrett et al., 2011).

The quality of personal relationships, manifest in professional dialogues, is central to successful collaboration. It may be expressed in different ways in different collaborations but attending to 'the personal' can be part of any collaboration's research and evaluation.

Engagement

Collaborations need to build in the space for those involved to meet their own interests and projects or to draw in those whose own interests and projects fit together with the collaboration's aims. Archer (2003) describes this as the opportunity for individuals to exercise their own agency and to advance projects that are important to them. Personal attributes are vital for realising goals in international collaborations (Gajda, 2004), while commitment, energy and determination are essential personal qualities (Walsh and Kahn, 2010). Therefore, in order to engage those involved in the collaboration there must be space for individuals to fulfil their own projects and those involved must have the potential to demonstrate essential personal qualities. Again, being alert to different individuals' interests and aims can be built into a collaboration's evaluation processes.

Evidence and Research

While we have paid attention to the importance of process-type factors, such as emergence, dialogue and engagement, these will have limited interest unless they can be shown to lead to useful outcomes. In this case, we have created local research projects in medical education and dissemination in local and international settings. As a result, research and publication are essential components in meeting collaboration goals and in better understanding the process involved. In addition, research and publication often meet individual goals and so foster increased engagement.

In Summary

The experience of the UoL−UHS collaboration illustrates some important concepts that can be usefully generalised to other international collaborations. We have drawn attention to the place of emergence and the centrality of personal factors. We have also stressed the importance of the generation of research evidence as part of the process and as an outcome in itself. While there must always be local variations, there are commonalities in approach that illustrate ways of working that can be applied in many settings.

Acknowledgements and Thanks To

Dr Janet Strivens, Dr Arif Khawaja, Dr Noreen Akmal, Dr Alia Bashir, Dr Faraz Bokhari, Dr Noora Hassan, Dr Kiren Malik, Dr Nazish Nabeel, Dr Shaila Tahir, Dr Gulfreen Waheed, Dr Raza Yunous, and Zainab Zahra.

References

Archer, M (2003). *Structure, agency and the internal conversation.* Cambridge: Cambridge University Press.

Barrett, AM, Crossley, M, & Dachi, HA (2011). International collaboration and research capacity building: Learning from the EdQual experience. *Comparative Education, 47*(1), 25–43.

Braun, V, & Clarke, V (2006). Using thematic analysis in psychology. *Qualitative Research in Psychology, 3,* 77–101.

Cooperrider, DL, Whitney, D, & Stavros, JM (2003). *Appreciative inquiry handbook: The first in a series of AI workbooks for leaders of change.* USA: Lakeshore Communications Inc. and Berrett-Koehler Publishers, Inc.

Davis, B, & Sumara, D (2009). Complexity as a theory of education. *TCI (Transnational Curriculum Inquiry), 5*(2), 33–44.

Fenwick, T (2012). Complexity science and professional learning for collaboration: A critical reconsideration of possibilities and limitations. *Journal of Education and Work, 25*(1), 141–162.

Gajda, R (2004). Utilizing collaboration theory to evaluate strategic alliances. *American Journal of Evaluation, 25*(1), 65–77.

Gamble, JAA (2008). *A developmental evaluation primer* JW McConnell Family Foundation.

Huxham, C (2003). Theorizing collaboration practice. *Public Management Review, 5*(3), 401–423.

Khan, JS (2013). *The relationship of awards of various components of MBBS final professional examination and the effectiveness of each in the evaluation process.* (PhD, University of Health Sciences, Lahore, Pakistan).

McNiff, J (2013). *Action research: Principles and practice.* London: Routledge.

Murphy, E (1997). Constructivism: From philosophy to practice. Retrieved September, 2013, from http://eric.ed.gov/?id = ED444966

Sachs, J (2003). *The activist teaching profession* Open University Press Buckingham.

Tosey, P (2002). *Teaching at the edge of chaos: Enhancement in a messy and unpredictable world* LTSN Generic Centre, HE Academy.

Trowler, P (2004). Reinventing the university: Visions and hallucinations. *Proceedings of the Rhodes Centenary Celebration Conference: Reinventing the University,* University of Rhodes.

Walsh, L, & Kahn, P (2010). *Collaborative working in higher education: The social academy.* London: Routledge.

Willis, I (2012). Collaborative reach: A model for international collaborations through engaging different levels within partner institutions. *Education: Connecting the Future World. Going Global 2012,* London.

Chapter 1.7

21st Century Nations: What Place for the Humanities?

Jo Beall

Introduction

The study of languages, literature, art and history is as old as scholarship itself. In the 19th century, the social sciences, too, became very much part of our effort to understand the world. For centuries, such studies have nurtured critical thought and promoted intellectual development in a way that has moulded, challenged and invigorated nations worldwide. And in today's globalised world, the humanities (including social sciences) have an ever-more important role to play in building knowledge economies through international collaboration.

The Role of Humanities in a Globalised World

In his introduction to the 2012 Going Global conference in London, Professor Homi Bhabha of Harvard University spoke of the importance of understanding a central 21st-century paradox: that in a globalising world we live as neighbours with people who are often strangers. Professor Bhabha pointed out that the humanities' important contribution to the world today is to its very *humanity*, to the humane understanding of other cultures and people. He argued that the integrative potential of the humanities, and the

Going Global: Knowledge-Based Economies for 21st Century Nations
Copyright © 2014 by Jo Beall
All rights of reproduction in any form reserved
ISBN: 978-1-78441-003-2

way they impart knowledge, are key in laying the foundations for a truly global civil society.[1]

Yet, in her 2010 book *Not For Profit: Why Democracy Needs the Humanities,* the celebrated philosopher Martha Nussbaum argues that education has gone awry in the United States and abroad, with educational institutions seeing the need to teach students to be economically productive rather than to think critically and to become knowledgeable and thoughtful citizens as their primary goal. This she refers to as a silent crisis. Are the humanities and social sciences in crisis? It is the case that in many parts of the world, policy makers increasingly have to justify why the humanities and social sciences are relevant, not just something to be stripped away in order to stay competitive in a global market. STEM subjects (science, technology, engineering and mathematics/medicine) are often seen as more relevant, whether towards securing a sustainable global future or in purely market terms. Cuts in funding for the humanities suggest that research viewed as having greater utilitarian value is given preference. This is happening in the United States, but is it the case internationally?

The humanities often face a decline during economic downturns — and the most recent recession is no exception. The 2008 financial crisis has compounded the situation, as its impact was felt in both industrialised and emerging economies, and recovery remains fragile. In the midst of all this, in countries across the Middle East and North Africa (MENA), the so-called Arab Spring has led to calls for democracy, social justice and a new way of life. Regions undergoing social and political upheaval, the lingering international economic crisis and the demands of globalisation all call for the analytical skills, social enrichment and new ideas that the humanities can foster. If the humanities have a crucial role to play in the 21st-century economy, polity and society, are we seeing the commitment to the humanities necessary for them to make a critical contribution to international collaboration and positive social change?

In the UK, the humanities and social sciences have not faced the same fate as described by Martha Nussbaum for the US. Research funding has been maintained to a degree and humanities courses are being well sustained through the introduction of student fees. In her book *The Value of the Humanities,* Helen Small of Oxford University argues that the notion of a crisis of the humanities is somewhat extreme and that scholars of the humanities have been their own worst enemies, often exercising a tone of critical grievance and hyperbolic overstatement, which in turn undermines

---

1. Homi Bhabha, *Education: connecting the future world.* Opening Speech, Going Global. 13 March 2012. London, UK. http://ihe.britishcouncil.org/going-global/sessions/education-connecting-future-world

a better public conversation incorporating humanistic forms of thinking. What she shares with Nussbaum is a concern when such forms of thinking get downgraded.[2]

The Wider Value of the Humanities

However, there is a growing tendency to view studies in the humanities simply as having utilitarian economic value, emphasising their efficacy in the context of interdisciplinary approaches to problem solving. There is no doubt that the humanities bring benefit in increasing understanding, raising skills levels, encouraging innovation and responding to the ethical dimension of technological and scientific change. The creative industries themselves generate income, consumer products and valuable intellectual property, while broader study and research in the humanities leads to the acquisition of the sorts of high-level skills essential for a knowledge-based economy. A recent Oxford University report analysing the career destinations of 11,000 humanities graduates highlights the striking consistency with which they have had successful careers in sectors driving economic growth.[3]

Innovation is a driving force of raised productivity, and an ability to generate new ideas is at the core of arts and humanities activity. Professor Geoffrey Crossick, formerly Vice-Chancellor of the University of London and now Director of the Cultural Value Project at the Arts and Humanities Research Council in the UK, has argued that in the future profits will not be made out of new technology, but from creative content. As creative arts and technology draw ever closer together, it is *content* that will attract people, produced by industries dominated by graduates and driven by new ideas from research and a vibrant cultural sector.[4] The nature of humanities studies – of critical questioning, of challenge – is an important factor here. *Leading the World*, an Arts and Humanities Research Council report on the impact of the arts, affirms that: 'The critical capacity of the arts and humanities to challenge conventional assumptions is an essential asset if innovation is to thrive.'[5] The report goes on to point out that this capacity is combined with a sense of the historical context and cultural

---

2. Helen Small (2013) *The Value of the Humanities*. Oxford University Press: Oxford, UK.
3. Philip Kreager (2013) *Humanities Graduates and the British Economy: The Hidden Impact.* University of Oxford: Oxford, UK.
4. Geoffrey Crossick (2011) 'The arts and humanities in the new higher education environment', Open lecture at the University of Kent, March 2011.
5. AHRC (2009) *Leading the World: The Economic Impact of UK Arts and Humanities Research.* Arts and Humanities Research Council: London, UK.

setting in which society and the economy function. To this we may add the ethical dimension that studies in the humanities contribute to technological change.

Innovation in science and technology is crucial, but it sometimes has unintended consequences. Research in the humanities and social sciences gives us the equipment to deal with social and ethical issues that new inventions might create. As the economist Christina Paxson put it: 'We need humanists to help us respond to the social and ethical dimensions of technological change ... to help us filter [changes], calibrate them and, where necessary, correct them.'[6] There may be ethical questions attendant on an advance in genetics, or issues regarding competition for resources following a new invention. When programmes for HIV/AIDS antiretroviral drugs are introduced in developing countries, we need to know if people will take them, and how they will take them – the issue is not simply about the science of the medicine. The humanities, here, are justified in relation to making science more effective – a perspective that must be expanded. The humanities and sciences are not two separate cultures, but are co-dependent, interlinked. As Professor Bhabha put it, we who are championing the humanities should not see ourselves as participating in 'some great campus civil war against the sciences or professional schools', but rather in a 'collaborative conversation ... which makes it very clear that it is only if and when we come together, from the sciences, business, the professional schools, the social sciences, medicine and law, we can create a global civil society that treats ourselves, our own people and others with civility, generosity, real intellectual inquisitiveness.'[7]

The humanities are also justified in functional terms in relation to the skills and competencies people need in the 21st century, often referred to as 21st-century skills. Today, creative and critical ways of thinking, together with collaborative and communication skills, are important both in the workplace and for living in the world. It is just such a skill set which humanities graduates develop over the course of their degrees. Employers value these transferrable skills, which demonstrate a flexibility in approach and a capacity for critical evaluation – Oxford University research analysing humanities graduates' careers found that the financial and legal sectors, in particular, drew on humanities degree subjects in employing their

6. Christina Paxson (2013) 'The Economic Case for Saving the Humanities'. New Republic, 20 August 2013. www.newrepublic.com/article/114392/christina-paxson-president-brown-humanities-can-save-us

7. Homi Bhabha, *Education: connecting the future world*. Opening Speech, Going Global. 13 March 2012. London, UK. http://ihe.britishcouncil.org/going-global/sessions/education-connecting-future-world

workforce, valuing graduates' literate, critical and communication skills.[8] Speakers at the Going Global 2013 conference repeatedly highlighted the importance of integrating the needs of commerce and industry with what education systems can deliver. This includes the important contribution made by the humanities and social sciences, which impart language and intercultural fluency, critical thinking and analytical skills. Professor Santiago Iñiguez de Onzoño, President of Instituto Empressa (IE) University and Dean of IE Business School in Madrid, Spain, speaking during Going Global 2013 commented that management is about leading people, about developing a vision for the future: 'The skills that are required to become a good successful manager are not acquired through management courses but through the humanities courses ... We spread the humanities across our curriculum in our executive MBA with Brown University so that our students become cosmopolitan citizens, well-rounded graduates.'[9] Thus there is a persuasive argument for the utility of the humanities in the workplace, as Professor Onzoño demonstrates. However, our commitment to the humanities must go beyond a purely functional argument.

The Role of the Humanities in Society

In addition to economic benefits, the humanities also have an important role to play in polity and society. Martha Nussbaum argues that, historically, the humanities have been central to education because they have been seen as essential for creating competent democratic citizens. A preoccupation with regarding education solely in terms of being economically productive, rather than as a path to thinking critically and knowledgeably, produces citizens who are no longer able to criticise authority, to censure bad government. In studying the humanities, we learn how to think creatively and critically, to ask questions and to reason. And as Professor Martin Hall, Vice-Chancellor of the University of Salford, made clear during the humanities panel discussion at Going Global 2013, without the ability the humanities give to think more deeply, to analyse what is happening behind the scenes and to speak critically of government policies, we are simply not going to understand what is going on in our multicultural world of intersecting global journeys. A grounding in the humanities not only leads to greater awareness and

---

8. Philip Kreager (2013) *Humanities Graduates and the British Economy: The Hidden Impact.* University of Oxford: Oxford, UK. p. 31

9. Santiago Iniguez de Onzono (2013) Position statement at '21ˢᵗ century Nations: No Place for the Humanities?' Going Global 2013 conference. Dubai, United Arab Emirates. http://ihe.britishcouncil.org/going-global/sessions/21st-century-humanities

deeper understanding of how our lives are being run, but to further public engagement. The recent 2013 Oxford University study of humanities graduates indicated extensive involvement in civil-society organisations and related activities. And on a wider political level, it is arguable that more involvement in the humanities is a step to overcoming social ennui and political apathy, especially among young people.

What of the intrinsic worth of the humanities, of studying them for their own sake? In his opening address to the Going Global 2013 humanities panel, Professor Michael Worton, Vice-Provost of University College London, pointed to how the humanities help us deal with difficult issues of social change and cultural difference and allow us to grapple with important questions about tolerance – constant, complex processes in a globalised world. The arts and humanities are essential in promoting the mutual understanding needed for living peacefully with religious and cultural diversity. In his book, *Education's End: Why Our Colleges and Universities Have Given Up on the Meaning of Life,* Professor Anthony Kronman of Yale Law School talks of the humanities as the best way of addressing problems we have facing us today. A good grounding in the humanities helps us hone our answers to the tough questions that the modern world throws at us. In a context of greed, irresponsibility and fraud – which is how Professor Kronman describes the financial meltdown – he says: 'We never have needed more than we need now to re-examine what we care about, what we value.'[10] In other words, what it means to be human.

The arts and humanities help us understand our own lives, give us insight into the way communal identities hold together – they fire our imaginations and help unearth the complexities of the human experience. This gives the humanities an international dimension, as a vehicle for cross-cultural understanding, a means of overcoming the paradox Professor Bhabha identified – that of people living as neighbours with strangers in a globalising world. The humanities and social sciences contribute enormously to our intellectual and cultural wellbeing, to our understanding of both our own cultural heritage and that of others. Research of other cultures and societies encourages more awareness and flexibility in international-relations policies, and helps challenge widely held misconceptions and cultural assumptions.

The British Council is closely involved in this interplay of the humanities and cultural relations – in fact, the humanities is as close as you can get to cultural relations. In 2012, jointly with the Centre of Islamic Studies at Cambridge University, we published *Building a Shared Future,* which looked to bridge the gap between academic expertise and public knowledge

---

10. Anthony Kronman (2007) *Education's End: Why Our Colleges and Universities Have Given Up on the Meaning of Life.* Yale University Press: New Haven, CT.

of cross-cultural relations engaging Islam. One of the research areas addressed was how an exchange of knowledge could help outline a common sense of identity between Muslim and non-Muslim societies. The report went on to say that knowledge was not enough, that an understanding of difference should encourage individuals to progress from sympathy to empathy, and then beyond to responsibility: 'Transcending difference is based on a fundamental ability to see oneself in others, to perceive one's reflection in difference and to recognise that there is nothing whatsoever natural about one's own way.'[11] We continue to support and develop programmes that build international links and value the humanities as essential contributors to global prosperity, security and stability. And the humanities continue to be an issue that the 'Going Global' conference highlights, fostering an evolving debate around the subject each year.

The Humanities and International Collaboration

'Going Global 2013' robustly demonstrated that the role of international collaboration is absolutely critical to peace and prosperity in our global world. Meeting the challenges of 21st-century nations means fostering international research links, innovative communications technologies, and cross-sectorial partnerships, such as the UK–India Education and Research Initiative (UKIERI), aimed at enhancing educational links between India and the UK, or Development Partnerships in Higher Education (DelPHE). In Rwanda, for example, DelPHE has facilitated a partnership between the Kigali Institute of Education and the University of Nottingham from the UK, to develop formal and informal ways of promoting community cohesion as a means to citizenship education and enhancing peace. The future lies in such initiatives, and in institutions that cross-pollinate disciplines, such as the IE Business School in Madrid, where humanities courses are spread throughout the management curriculum. As its Dean, Professor Santiago Iñiguez de Onzoño puts it: 'Let's mix both the humanities and the sciences, and let's work in the interstices of disciplines.'[12] *The Heart of the Matter*, a report by the American Academy's

11. British Council and Centre of Islamic Studies (2012) *Building a Shared Future: Religion, Politics and the Public Sphere*. British Council and HRH Prince Alwaleed Bin Talal Centre of Islamic Studies, University of Cambridge. www.britishcouncil.org/new/PageFiles/16695/ReligionPoliticsPublicSphere.pdf

12. Santiago Iñiguez de Onzoño (2013) Position statement at '21st-century Nations: No Place for the Humanities?' Going Global 2013 conference. Dubai, United Arab Emirates. http://ihe.britishcouncil.org/going-global/sessions/21st-century-humanities

Commission on the Humanities and Social Sciences, identifies three national goals for economic and intellectual wellbeing: to equip Americans with 21st-century skills; to foster a society that is innovative, competitive and strong; and to equip the nation for leadership in an interconnected world. The report emphasises that these goals cannot be achieved by science alone, but 'recognises the urgent need to support the next generation of humanists and social scientists. And it reaffirms the connections between the humanities and social sciences, and the physical and biological sciences'.[13] These connections and collaborations — this recognition of the importance of the humanities — is a global issue.

Conclusions

Where are we going on this front? The question of the future of the humanities was the focus of much discussion at the Going Global 2013 conference. As the initial euphoria after the Arab Spring gives way to frustration with the slow pace of change, anger at reversion to authoritarian rule, increasing religious conflict and a questioning of the relevance of democracy to local culture, the place becomes ever more important for studies that promote understanding of fellow citizens, encourage civic participation and expand the skills needed to build peace and create a place for more countries across the world. An academic from Egypt, asking a question during the Going Global 2013 humanities panel highlighted the contemporary importance of the humanities in MENA countries. He said there had been a paradigm shift in awareness, that many of the younger generation were reconsidering their academic choices because they felt a need to understand democracy, their own history, Islam, issues of human rights and gender, what a good constitution should be — and that the humanities showed the way. The ongoing economic crisis, coupled with record high youth unemployment, underlines the need for an education that builds 21st-century skills and helps create a body of imaginative thinkers and problem solvers.

In many emerging powers, it is recognised that the nurturing of participative citizens, equipped to question government, understand and prevent conflict and social unrest, and help produce accountable institutions, is crucial. It is perhaps no surprise, therefore, that in South Africa the Minister of Higher Education and Training commissioned an investigation into the state of the humanities in the country, drawing on insights and experiences

---

13. American Academy for Arts and Sciences (2013) *The Heart of the Matter: The Humanities and Social Sciences for a Vibrant, Competitive, and Secure Nation.* The Commission on the Humanities and Social Sciences. www.humanitiescommission.org/_pdf/hss_report.pdf

from India and China as much as from Europe and the United States.[14] In India, a survey of higher education stakeholders undertaken by a researcher for the British Council found widespread agreement that a focus on the humanities, social sciences and arts is vital for the future growth and development of Indian society and culture. Despite many challenges, including a disproportionate focus on science and technology, there are indications that the social sciences, arts and humanities are moving back into Indian higher education institutions, student demand and government strategy. For example, there is a re-emergence of the humanities and social sciences in the government of India's 12th five-year plan (2012−17) and several key higher education institutions are predicting an expansion in the provision and need for humanities courses.[15]

Across the globe we need individuals who understand people with backgrounds different from their own, who can empathise with different cultural viewpoints, who speak foreign languages and demonstrate respect for others. Above all, we need a global mindset that encompasses careful, creative, critical thought, one moulded not by the humanities alone, but enriched by interdisciplinary connection. Change is a constant in our lives. New technologies and a globalising world put it at the core. If we do not bring new ideas and strategies to dealing with 21st-century challenges, from climate disruption and competition for resources to issues growing out of medical research and religious and cultural diversity, we will lose our way. Without humanities research and studies, we cannot even begin to understand the challenges the new century presents, or the complex social issues we need to grapple with. There are no easy answers. But we know that we need good public policy, thoughtful public debate, open institutions and a vibrant, innovative society to make this brave new world work. For centuries, the arts, humanities and social sciences have studied languages, religions and the ways different cultures interact and integrate. They have instilled citizens with the capacity for reflection, critical thought, personal and social awareness. Bring all that up to the sciences, so that the humanities and sciences are not seen as polar opposites, but engage in a collaborative conversation, and we have a way forward to a secure, thriving global civil society.

14. Republic of South Africa (2011) *Report Commissioned by the Minister of Higher Education and Training for the Charter for Humanities and Social Sciences.* Department of Higher Education and Training, Republic of South Africa. www.info.gov.za/view/Download FileAction?id = 150166

15. Lynne Heslop (2013) *An analytical report on the future of the British Council's work in higher education in India.* British Council, unpublished.

References

AHRC (2009) *Leading the World: The Economic Impact of UK Arts and Humanities Research*. Arts and Humanities Research Council: London, UK.

American Academy for Arts and Sciences (2013) *The Heart of the Matter: The Humanities and Social Sciences for a Vibrant, Competitive, and Secure Nation*. The Commission on the Humanities and Social Sciences. www.humanities commission.org/_pdf/hss_report.pdf

Bhabha, Homi (2012) *Education: connecting the future world*. Opening Speech, Going Global. 13 March 2012. London, UK. http://ihe.britishcouncil.org/going-global/sessions/education-connecting-future-world

British Council and the Centre of Islamic Studies (2012) *Building a Shared Future: Religion, Politics and the Public Sphere*. British Council and HRH Prince Alwaleed Bin Talal, the Centre of Islamic Studies, University of Cambridge. www.britishcouncil.org/new/PageFiles/16695/ReligionPoliticsPublicSphere.pdf

Crossick, Geoffrey (2011) 'The arts and humanities in the new higher education environment', Opening lecture at the University of Kent, March 2011.

de Onzoño, Santiago Iñiguez (2013) Position statement at '21st-century Nations: No Place for the Humanities?' Going Global 2013 conference. Dubai, United Arab Emirates. http://ihe.britishcouncil.org/going-global/sessions/21st-century-humanities

Heslop, Lynne (2013) *An analytical report on the future of the British Council's work in higher education in India*. May 2013. British Council, unpublished.

Kreager, Philip (2013) *Humanities Graduates and the British Economy: The Hidden Impact*. University of Oxford: Oxford, UK. p 31.

Kronman, Anthony (2007) *Education's End: Why Our Colleges and Universities Have Given Up on the Meaning of Life*. Yale University Press: New Haven, CT.

Paxson, Christina (2013) 'The Economic Case for Saving the Humanities'. New Republic, 20 August 2013. www.newrepublic.com/article/114392/christina-paxson-president-brown-humanities-can-save-us

Republic of South Africa (2011) *Report Commissioned by the Minister of Higher Education and Training for the Charter for Humanities and Social Sciences*. Department of Higher Education and Training, Republic of South Africa. www.info.gov.za/view/DownloadFileAction?id=150166

Small, Helen (2013) *The Value of the Humanities*. Oxford University Press: Oxford, UK.

SECTION 2
HOW HAS INTERNATIONAL COLLABORATION LED TO AN INCREASE IN SKILLED KNOWLEDGE WORKERS?

Chapter 2.1

Editors' Introduction to Section 2

Continuing the theme of what Martin Hall calls the 'second generation of transnational education', section 2 of this volume, arising from the Going Global Conference in 2013, takes as its theme the question 'How has international collaboration led to an increase in the global capacity of skilled knowledge workers?' The papers in this section focus on different contexts and arise from a variety of jurisdictions, and therefore enable us to have a greater understanding of the theme of the section, and contribute to the whole volume's message.

Jonathan Ledger's paper focuses particularly on the transferable skills model provided by Proskills UK Group and the National Skills Academy. These institutions have worked in partnership on a range of vocational skills-based projects in several countries. By moving towards a set of international standards we see not only skills development but also increased cultural awareness.

Rebecca Hughes helps us understand the importance of establishing a network in order to enable and support good communications, but also knowledge sharing, experimentation and risk-taking, as well as the provision of a source of trusted expertise and current information for knowledge workers with universities and in policy-making contexts.

Hannah Ellis's paper explores the Student Experience Exchange (STeXX) project in the Netherlands. This aims to collect the views of international students about their experiences of studying abroad, and provides us with knowledge about what students consider to be the positive benefits, such as the job prospects, of studying overseas.

Developing skills in the English language in what John Knagg calls a 'multilingual and internationalised higher education world' is seen by Yussra Jamjoom as essential to graduate employability. The papers by Jamjoom and Knagg are complementary, and while Jamjoom's paper focuses primarily on Saudi Arabia, Knagg's more generic focus uses case studies to explore the experiences of a variety of students ranging from the English language learner to the English language teacher. They both highlight the importance for international professionals and academics to become skilled English language learners.

Nicholas Nsowah-Nuawah's focus on Ghana's need for skilled knowledge workers uses Kumasi Polytechnic as his case study, and demonstrates how international collaboration and partnership working has supported the internal development of the polytechnic and enabled the realisation of the mandate they have been given by government to develop a highly skilled workforce.

This focus on skills development is echoed by Sue Parker in her paper discussing how far higher education can realistically affect and contribute to such skills development. While retaining its traditional form, she challenges us to explore with her whether university education can be truly compatible with higher skills development.

And finally in this section, Joanna Newman sets out the importance of encouraging and enabling UK students to study abroad — as so many students from other countries already do. In an increasingly globalised labour market, the skills learned from studying abroad can only enhance students' prospects. This fittingly concludes this section, and leads us into the final section, with its concentrated focus on internationalised higher education.

Chapter 2.2

Transferable Models for International Standards Collaboration

Jonathan Ledger

Background

This paper builds on the themes of Going Global 2013 by combining inter-national standards and international collaboration through a transferable and yet simple vocational skills model that has been proved to work in multiple countries, in order to positively impact governments, employers, training-provision suppliers and learners.

The Proskills UK Group and its National Skills Academy have worked in partnership on a number of vocational skills-based projects in a mix of countries, including Kazakhstan, Ukraine and Egypt. Each of these countries has sought to establish a vocational skills system with strong links to industry and, in most cases, developed by industry, but which still links into the national qualifications structure so that it is nationally recognised.

Through this broad mix of international collaborations, Proskills has set out to create a transferable vocational skills model that can be applied in many countries and scaled according to local requirements. In this paper we will set out a number of case studies that identified the common strands of activity between similar projects across different nations, and how these were then used to shape new collaborations.

Going Global: Knowledge-Based Economies for 21st Century Nations
Copyright © 2014 by Jonathan Ledger
All rights of reproduction in any form reserved
ISBN: 978-1-78441-003-2

Main Aims:

- identify common elements in social and economic development that provide a nurturing environment for vocational skills strategies to develop
- make best use of existing vocational skills systems to create a transferable model applicable to each country, using a common platform
- create a vocational skills system and strategy definition that allows for all stages of skills requirements, from outline competence to full qualifications, woven into a national qualifications framework
- develop and implement a common framework of delivery and trainer support that contains high-quality training provision and skills assessment

Industrial Context

Government skills policy that engages employers and is developed around employer-stated need creates a strong basis on which to build and roll out any new skills system. Employer engagement has proved critical in building a swell of user demand from the outset to make any resulting international occupational standards and training delivery successfully applicable and of benefit to business. In addition, an employer-led framework has proved to create a stronger delivery platform and a higher-quality output of skills and competence.

Experiential Example 1: Kazakhstan

In Kazakhstan, the education syllabus has for many years been set by academics appointed by the Ministry of Education and does not include a large element of vocational skills capability. Over the years, this has resulted in a widening gap between the education content and delivery methodology within the technical colleges when compared with what is actually required by industry today and in the future.

A meeting with a steel-producing company revealed their clear view that local colleges providing new employees are estimated to be at least ten to 15 years behind in educational content and taught skills compared to what the company needs right now. So wide is the gap that the company has now developed on-site training facilities to teach new employees the skills needed. Indeed, the company expressed frustration that they are not able to influence the syllabus more, especially where technical colleges are the only feeder colleges for their business. There seems to be the will, but no mechanism, to make this happen.

The same employer said they are having to create their own skills standards based on business need, with their frustration being that it does not meet international standards. As a global employer, they often move senior staff around the globe to further enhance their experience. In doing so, the employer is having to provide expensive upgrades in employee training, and usually once the employee has relocated because it is only after the move is complete that any skills deficiency becomes apparent. It then follows that there is a period of time where the newly stationed employee is not contributing to the business in the way intended and so this is an additional, often unrecognised, cost.

When discussing employer links with the technical colleges, it becomes clear that these do not exist. Three technical colleges said that they would like to have employer links but they have not yet been able to secure a working framework in which to make employer partnerships work. Many technical colleges said they cannot afford up-to-date equipment and many of the training staff have outdated skills unfit for industry in current times.

One technical college visited in Astana has managed to forge links with a global employer. This has proved to be successful, as the company has supplied the latest tools, products and technical expertise to the college, as well as hands-on training to college staff to ensure the correct skills are being passed on to students. But this example of collaboration seems to be unique rather than the norm.

Experiential Example 2: Egypt

A partnership with a trade body in Egypt has revealed a similar ambition to have employer collaboration at the heart of trade bodies' skills activity, but they suffer a similar situation in that employers do not shape the curriculum, nor is the vocational skills element given national recognition compared with academic qualifications delivered by schools and colleges. Colleges also cited outdated equipment and technical expertise as problematic areas. The lack of employer participation in the education system and process has given rise to poor work practices, often dangerous to the employee, which perpetuates a lack of ambition to make the systemic changes required to ensure that industry has the skills it needs to be sustainable in the future.

A Collaborative Framework for Sustainable Change

International skills system differences have shown that there are common threads of activity that can be delivered to create a self-sustaining skills system and provide what employers and industry needs. Our experience has shown that many countries are looking at developed skills systems across the world and are trying to replicate these in a much shorter period of time, often without taking into account the local social and economic environments and cultures. The adoption and direct replication of the UK skills system in another country, for example, just does not work as it lacks the local context and fails to take into account local demands.

The UK has been developing its vocational skills system for at least 25 years, and still today constant adjustments are made to meet business and economic need. And yet, through all the changes, one process remains constant, regardless of whether there is government funding or not, or changes in innovative technology use, a change in the education structure or the infrastructure that enables the skills system to operate. This process, which we have used across many nations and which can be scaled according to in-country needs, is detailed in Figure 1.

Using this process, we have been able to work with international partners to build skills strategies, processes and content that meet their need, but also work towards or already achieve international standards.

It is designed to be simple and logical and unaffected by changing country environments. It takes the local but essential elements of industry

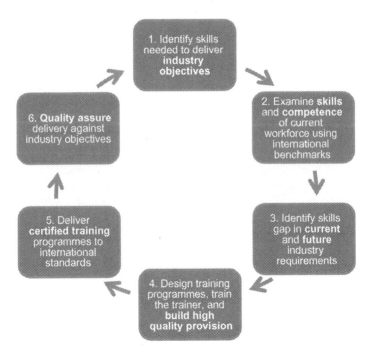

Figure 1: Consistent skills development process.

requirements and links them with the best international practices in terms of skills benchmarking and training delivery in an iterative process that can be as big and complex as the country desires. However, to achieve success in this requires strong collaborative approaches with international partners.

The process can be used in part or as a whole system: from initial employer-focused research into business needs through to development of national occupational standards and on to training and skills delivery. The skills development process internationalises standards through collaborative partnership. Each of the key stages in the process link to the one before and the one after, but can also stand in their own independent right.

This skills development process is based on local industry needs and objectives and sets out a skills strategy that is achievable against the in-county context, as it is shaped based on the local social-economic market. Making a robust assessment of the current skills of employees against the local standard, as well as the international standard (and the expected future requirement), can often be a painful process, especially where skills are proven to be lower than expected or desired. But this part of the process demonstrates that any skills or competence gaps are an opportunity for the business to improve its productivity. Often, the most difficult part of the process is building appropriate training provision to help fill any skills gaps. This is where the employers and training providers must collaborate and work on developing skills programmes that meet industry needs, but also provide sustainable demand-led programmes that are cost effective for the colleges to deliver. Stimulus for the inclusion of any programme into the national qualifications structure will start with programmes that are proven to work with industry.

International Collaboration Impact

Ukraine

An employers' association in Ukraine wanted to raise the skills levels of employees and create a common set of standards to demonstrate employee competence and generally raise the skills bar. Using the skills development process they have developed a robust future-proof skills strategy that provides an operational framework for a self-sustaining skills organisation. Built into the skills strategy are a plethora of essential skills standards for employees to work towards and achieve. Indeed, progress has been swift, with many standards initiated from those that already exist around the globe and then developed further to suit the local in-country and industry need. Feedback from the employers' association clearly demonstrates that the international collaboration has been a major factor in helping them to achieve their ambitions. But it goes further than this: staff from Ukraine have worked with our teams in the UK to build their occupational standards' writing skills and, even further, their processes and methodologies for the robust teaching and assessment of skills in the workplace.

This is a clear example of harnessing international best practice using a common skills development framework, but remaining flexible enough to fit the local context. For the first time, the employers' association has been able to articulate the skills required, define the skills standards, create appropriate training courses to develop the skills of the training and assessment staff and, finally, to certificate this in a way that is industry-acceptable and comparable to the existing national qualifications structure.

Kazakhstan

Going back to the experiential example 1 for Kazakhstan, the Mining Association has adopted the same skills development process. A series of in-country support workshops has provided the local team with much-needed knowledge and skills in order to self-create an appropriate employer-led skills system. The Mining Association is now developing appropriate occupational standards based on international best practices and is engaging much more with technical colleges to create an improved skills partnership. The beneficiaries of this are not only the students, who gain more appropriate skills, but also the employers, who spend less on unnecessary duplication of training, and the government, which now does not have to try to manage a system that cannot keep up with industrial and societal demand to create a more productive, inspirational, safe and competent workforce. Our research has shown that five out of the eight employers we have been working with have now begun supporting technical colleges with expertise and equipment, and that collaboration and partnership with UK-based training providers and colleges has helped to enhance the teaching capability of the colleges.

Egypt

In Egypt international collaboration on workplace skills standards has enabled two employer training pilots (ETPs) in different industries to develop individual skills strategies that meet industry requirements using the same skills development process. One ETP has used the skills development process to conduct initial research with employers to understand their needs and what a skills organisation would need to do in order to make employer ambitions a reality. This has gone further in that it has provided the framework for industry-wide standards and training programme development. The number of employers engaged in this process has risen from zero to almost 400, potentially positively affecting approximately 3,750 employees, all in less than one year.

The other ETP has, through its international collaboration around skills programmes, taken a leap forward and developed careers information programmes. It has also created a competition for schools sponsored by employers and linked to the standard curriculum content. As part of the competition, students learn all about an industry and its supply chain, and the hope is that this experience demonstrates that a career in the industry is worth a real look. Linked to the careers information and support from employers, it provides a conduit of aspirational careers advice, bringing youngsters into the industry.

As well as having a positive impact on businesses and employees, in its first year ten schools and 300 students interacted with industry in a way they had never done before. This has been achieved using a fun and informative programme and by enabling students to see a side of industry never seen before. Employer in-kind and cash sponsorship has been gained using international partners. Those companies based in the UK, but which also have bases in Egypt, have been influenced remotely to offer a high level of local support. They do this by providing services to the programme such as mentoring and industry tours, but they also sponsor prizes for the competition or even cash to pay for the resources required to run the programme. It is worth remembering that this is a UK-developed programme, reshaped and re-contextualised to be delivered in Egypt; sponsored by UK-based companies operating in Egypt, but delivered and owned by Egyptian industry.

Creating Return on Collaborative Investment

Throughout the course of our international partnership activity, Proskills has implemented return on investment (ROI) processes that measure the impact of these programmes. Results have demonstrated between 6:1 and 12:1 returns on skills system development. ROI has been measured using three different formats and in partnership with employers and partners involved in skills delivery.

Demonstrating return on investment requires simple success measures to be agreed and implemented at the outset of the activity and then measured consistently throughout the programme. Measures can be anything in terms of the performance of the individual or the business, but the essential thing is that the measures are real, business-focused and, most importantly, easy to measure. There is no point having a measure in place that takes three days to analyse.

The transferable model of vocational skills has created:

- innovative employer skills development and engagement strategies
- robust and high-quality cross-sector and niche skills provision and competence assessment frameworks that give almost instant positive impact to employers and learners, and thus the countries' wider economy
- measurable impact, boosting learner output by raising skills levels without degradation in quality.

The transferable model also has a profound impact on the way that partners across countries work collaboratively in developing programmes, allowing governments to work closely with employers and employer-representing organisations, along with a broad mix of private and public education partners, to leverage employer co-investment and demand. It has also helped the providers of training to re-focus their energies in terms of delivering the right training and skills for industry today and tomorrow.

Of course, the impact is not just in the development of an appropriate skills system, but also in the cultural development of all the partners involved in the process. Speaking purely from the Proskills perspective, international standards development has increased our awareness of cultural differences – sometimes majorly and sometimes subtly. And isn't that what it is all about at the end of the day?

Chapter 2.3

Our Universities to 2013: A Case Study on Network Effects

Rebecca Hughes

Introduction

In this chapter, I report on a round table on the internationalisation of higher education that ran two months after the British Council's 2013 Going Global conference (GG13). I link the details of this meeting to a presentation I made at this event on university networks and internationalisation, and also report on the key themes that emerged at the day-long 'horizon scanning' event.

During GG13 I participated in a panel on the role of international university networks with a contribution entitled 'Developing higher education networks: theory, practice, impacts'. The panel was part of the strand of presentations on 'Developing skilled knowledge workers: the role of international collaboration'. In the panel, I made three main points. First, a flourishing knowledge economy needs to be based on good communication flow between stakeholders inside and outside the higher education sector. This is not always straightforward, and in my role as Pro-Vice-Chancellor at Sheffield with responsibility for external relations as well as internationalisation, I was frequently told that a university is culturally mysterious to outsiders and difficult to communicate with — something of a 'black box'. A group of universities in a network with a recognisable structure and consistent governance has the potential to provide a set of points of contact and a framework for information to pass between different stakeholders. The day described here is one instance of this. Second, I suggested that collaboration between universities, as well as competition, is crucial to

Going Global: Knowledge-Based Economies for 21st Century Nations
Copyright © 2014 by Rebecca Hughes
All rights of reproduction in any form reserved
ISBN: 978-1-78441-003-2

knowledge sharing, experimentation and the promotion of some risk taking. University networks can provide an environment of trust for peer-to-peer dissemination of practical steps and 'what works', particularly among administrative staff and young, mobile researchers. Third, networks that are built around research-intensive institutions can provide a source of trusted expertise and up-to-date information for people such as policy makers and leaders of organisations beyond the university sector. Research-led institutions are also potential sources of insights into the skills and knowledge that emerging technologies will require from both graduates and the younger academic. An international group of similar institutions can become a source of information about the current state of knowledge on a subject, provide cross-border comparisons and assist in some 'futurology' for planners more generally. Long-standing international networks, I argued in my presentation, are a good place to see these effects at work. As a member of staff at a Worldwide Universities Network (WUN) university, I used this group of 19 research universities in six continents as the point of reference for the discussions. The round table I describe in this chapter is also a direct output of the WUN 'Global Challenge' on Globalisation of Higher Education and Research (GHEAR).

The GHEAR Washington Round Table: Summary of the Day[1]

The Washington WUN/GHEAR Round Table set out to bring together researchers in higher education, university leaders, and, crucially, influential stakeholders and thought leaders from beyond the WUN network. The event took place on 20 May 2013, prior to the WUN Annual General Meeting. The location of the event in Washington was seen as a good opportunity to bring external perspectives of experts and stakeholders to help inform the future direction of the GHEAR 'Global Challenge'. As well as a meeting of internal experts and interested parties, the symposium was intended to showcase the network and hold a mirror up to it, capturing and building on the perspectives and opinions of those outside the WUN and, indeed, outside the academy.

The audience included representatives from embassies, the British Council, the American Council for Education, the World Bank and the US Department for Education. The US Department for Education's Deputy Assistant Secretary for International and Foreign Language Education

---

1. Sincere thanks to Heather Lonsdale, Research Assistant, University of Sheffield for organisational support and note-taking, and to the WUN co-ordinators group and administration for support.

took to the lectern to pledge his government's interest in, and support for, the work of WUN.

The event was intended to be horizon scanning and to prompt imaginative and philosophically informed debate, as well as practical sharing of data and some analysis of what the 'hot topics' for the sector will be. We took the anchor point of discussions to be the life of a child born in 2013, i.e. one that might be of an age to enter an undergraduate programme in 2030. The day was framed around three main questions:

- what are the effects to come of drivers such as demographics, local capacity, funding regimes, mobile technologies and Massive Open Online Courses (MOOCs)?
- where should national resources be allocated to support research excellence, economic growth and equity of access?
- how can the HE system support scientific, economic and intellectual development in developing as well as developed nations?

These issues were addressed by two keynote speakers and through a structured day-long debate and networking lunch with the expert audience. There were also video inputs providing the perspectives of students across the network and the opportunity for the 50-plus participants to provide further written responses after each section.

The Keynotes

Dr Aims McGuinness, National Centre for Higher Education Management Systems (NCHEMS), Boulder, Colorado

'Globally competitive but locally disengaged: is this the future for universities? Implications for students, institutions and states thinking forward to 2030'

This was a snapshot-in-time representation of the US HE system and provided a polemical depiction of some of the issues facing HE. McGuinness painted a picture of a nation failing to marry educational provision with national and state-level requirements. He proposed, using NCHEMS data, that US universities are failing to keep pace with the nation's need for skilled graduates and that universities are failing to meet the needs of changing demographics of students, in terms of age, race and mode of attendance. He noted a tendency for research to have little connection with city, regional or national research needs and criticised universities as being too focused on globalisation, to the detriment of the needs of local communities and local or regional economic growth.

Dr Jo Beall, British Council, Director of Education and Society

'Adaptations and innovations universities and the HE sector need to make to prepare for the 2030 landscape'

This presentation was based on the British Council's 2012 report on trends in transnational education and the impact of demographic changes globally (*The shape of things to come: higher education global trends and emerging opportunities to 2020*). In addition, Beall brought the lens of an expert in international development to bear on issues of equity and access, particularly in relation to 'North-South' collaborations, and raised questions about the preparedness of established HE institutions to adapt to, and capitalise on, the tectonic shifts that the data contained in the British Council's survey would potentially bring about. In relation to research, this data showed that international collaborations have doubled in a ten-year period and that China will soon match the US in terms of this measure. Multilateral collaborations and publications, including major research players and smaller nations, had very high impact in terms of citations. Asked what would change in terms of international research impact in the timeframe of the report, academics predicted China, the US and India being the top players and significantly diminishing impact for the current top-ranked countries, which were reported as currently being a different trio: the US, UK and Germany.

What the Day Contributed to the Questions Posed

Here, I return to the three areas that the workshop set out to explore, and expand on them in relation to the main points made by the speakers and the expert audience on the day.

- *What are the effects to come of drivers such as demographics, local capacity, funding regimes, mobile technologies and MOOCs?*

As noted above, Jo Beall presented findings and analyses particularly relevant to demographic change, researcher mobility and international collaborations, and transnational education (TNE). Beall linked these to a broader discussion of the international drivers that would affect institutions in the timeframe in question and how aspects such as TNE were evolving and could be affected by disruptive technologies such as MOOCs. For countries such as the UK and other Anglophone HE systems, used to being net recipients of international students, the predicted slowing of student mobility would potentially affect them quite markedly. Like McGuinness, Beall suggested that academic communities and students are changing and will have to change further in response to these drivers. The rise of recognised scientific activity, international co-authorship in emerging parts of the world and the embracing of English for publication and for teaching are also shifting the balance dramatically away from 'the old order'.

Both speakers saw new technologies as having the potential to be very influential in terms of reaching new student cohorts. McGuinness predicted a changing student profile that would require different modes of delivery. These students, he proposed, would in very large numbers be 'non-traditional' in terms of age, income, educational preparedness, race/ethnicity and willingness/availability to study at set times of day. He noted that the system would need to respond to this type of student more effectively if the US was going to meet the challenge of tertiary numbers that had been set for it (60 per cent of the working population with a tertiary-level certificate by 2020).

Comments from the floor and in the ensuing debate built on the contributions of the two speakers, in some cases challenging them and in others offering possible ways forward. In terms of funding regimes and communication with stakeholders outside the academy, for instance, the question of the role of the private sector was raised. Why, one participant suggested, were universities being singled out for criticism in relation to local engagement when, for instance, they were simply acting like any other major business or large organisation? Audience contributions also noted the hard facts of the high costs of teaching large numbers in traditional mode, the difficulty of balancing research and teaching, and the 'sunk costs' of research equipment, which underpin global competitiveness in science but cannot be paid for by income from local 'good works'. One speaker challenged the notion that new technologies were actually an advance for the student and provoked further debate by suggesting that old-style lecture notes had become 'new technology' via PowerPoint but not any better instruments of instruction. Others suggested that the key to unblocking some of this was to look at the incentives given to individual academics – if promotion rewarded local engagement or teaching innovatively with new technologies academics would do it.

- *Where should national resources be allocated to support research excellence, economic growth and equity of access?*

The nub of McGuiness's position in relation to the question of funding regimes, focus and capacity was summarised in his slide on the situation in the US higher education sector:

- The nation as a whole and individual states are:
  - failing to educate the next generation workforce
  - failing to link R&D capacity to regional innovation/economic development.

- Global competition and market forces are drawing the public universities away from addressing state and regional priorities.
- States' lack of capacity for leadership and policy levers (finance and accountability) to link the nation's higher education capacity to state/regional priorities.

Beall focused more on the impact of international trends on institutions and individual academics, but the implication of her data was that new powerhouses of research will emerge and − noting that very few academics surveyed were proposing to physically remove themselves to these emerging new research hubs − new and innovative means of tapping into these resources would need to be found. She suggested that academics should note the high impact of publications with multiple international authors and that funding to encourage multilateral collaborations including smaller nations would be helpful.

McGuinness made the case for a profound tension between resources focused on local needs − whether teaching or research − and those assigned to pursuing global reputation and rankings. This topic was further developed from the floor during the ensuing debate and was the area with the greatest number of written comments from the participants. One participant felt that the tension could be resolved by allocating different sections of a university's activity to each domain, with teaching and learning being predominantly the instrument for local engagement, leaving the research element to focus on global reach. Another suggested that the global/local binary was not as stark as had been suggested, making the point that cities and regions are also in the process of becoming globally connected and internationally competitive, as are companies and small and medium enterprises (SMEs). Local students can be educated for this globally connected world without much conflict, they thought. The point was also made that not all universities should have the same 'mission' or the same balance of activities and that the discussion seemed to imply too much a 'one size fits all' definition of universities.

The nature of an academic in the future, and in particular expectations about the balance between teaching and research in academic staff, was seen by many as closely related to balancing global and local activities. In addition to creating the right incentives, linked to a precise 'mission', one participant asked: '...is the current preparation, structure and expectations for academic staff/faculty still fit for purpose?', while another thought a 'hot topic' would be the future of the academic profession. These questions also resonated with the issue of new modes of delivery and the role of private providers and/or online courses in future − what would academics be spending their time on if large numbers of students were taking their education in new ways and what would be valued and rewarded among the new generation of academic?

- *How can the HE system support scientific, economic and intellectual development in developing as well as developed nations?*

From different perspectives (one in-country on a state-by-state analysis and one looking at North–South disparities), both keynote speakers pointed to the issue of access and inclusion. Who are the major beneficiaries of higher education currently, they asked, and what would it take to expand these benefits to more able students, whatever their race or background? Factors such as new technologies and branch campuses *could* be instruments to address this, but neither speaker was optimistic about such instruments of distance delivery – yet – being linked to a broader ethical or practical goals and local impact in the host country.

Beall argued that TNE needed to evolve into its 'third stage' – more aligned to local in-country needs, focused on the quality of the student experience and on deeper engagement with local institutions and needs.

Comments from the participants in this area included the fact that universities should not simply transplant their degrees to other locations but develop 'transnational degrees' specifically for these locations; one participant offered a view that universities are 'too autonomous' to respond organically by themselves to these issues; while another noted the lack of attention being paid to the huge potential for growth in African universities in the timeframe in question.

Discussion and Conclusion

This event took place before the faltering beginnings of a global financial recovery and the debates were therefore particularly focused on the role of universities in helping their graduates gain employment and what contribution a university can make to the economy. The major challenges set to universities were for them to be: 'developing a globally competitive workforce (Human Capital Development) ... [and] a globally competitive, innovation-based economy that will employ this workforce,' (McGuinness, 2013) and promoting 'real learning, deeper engagement, research collaboration and institutional development in their international engagement.' (Beall, 2013).

These topics, though clearly significant for the development of the sector and its resourcing and rationale, are very far from the day-to-day concerns of most academics. Finding ways to bridge this gap would be a step forward for those beyond academia who look to these 'black boxes' for assistance or who are part of the 'active and frustrated' (McGuinness, 2013) private sector. There are few forums for this debate to take place. The WUN event was distinguished by being multilateral, open, with a highly informed and personally engaged set of people. Difficult or threatening topics could be aired (that universities are 'too autonomous', that they will need to become 'unbundled', that they are failing to meet societies' needs, that students will make them change or vote with their feet), yet were responded to with rationality and evidence, courtesy and further challenge or curiosity. The conventions of academic debate and 'safe spaces' for ideas to be voiced and challenged are perhaps the biggest gifts from universities to their societies and more should be made of this. Due to the existence of a group of universities with some shared values and interests across very different cultures and continents, I suggest, we were able at the event described here to bring together students, young researchers, policy makers and university leaders in a discussion about shared futures. A focused, fruitful, multi-perspective event like this is the kind of thing that a university network is able to catalyse.

Overall, these discussions combined to provide a better understanding of the role of universities as organisations with several sometimes conflicting roles and identities: thought leaders, crucibles of innovation and new knowledge, conservative anchor institutions and, crucially, consumers and producers of the skilled knowledge workforce of the future.

I end with a comment from one of the participants, which could be the starting point for the WUN 'Global Challenge' work in relation to these debates:

> 'We are clearly uniquely positioned to be the thought leaders on the challenge of combining global competition with local engagement. What do we need to do as a global academy to influence government and policy? How do we develop leadership capacity in this domain?'

References and Resources

Beall, J (2013) 'Adaptations and innovations universities and the HE sector need to make to prepare for the 2030 landscape'. Keynote talk at the Worldwide Universities Network Round Table for the Global Challenge on Higher Education and Research, 20 May 2013.

McGuinness, A (2013) 'Globally competitive but locally disengaged: is this the future for universities?' Keynote talk at the Worldwide Universities Network Round Table for the Global Challenge on Higher Education and Research, 20 May 2013.

Worldwide Universities Network site: www.wun.ac.uk/

Information on GHEAR Washington round table: www.wun.ac.uk/events/ghear-our-universities-2030-forging-collaborations-and-unlocking-excellence-generation-born-today

Chapter 2.4

What are the Influencers that Impact the International Student Experience and How does an International Experience Affect Students' Job Prospects?

Hannah Ellis

Introduction – the STeXX Project

STeXX, the Student Experience Exchange platform, was established by StudyPortals in 2011 with the aim of learning more about international student satisfaction in Europe. It is an online platform that allows students to review their international study experience. StudyPortals has collected 25,000 reviews from international students, asking each one to give comments about what they liked and disliked about their experience of studying abroad. We can draw on the results of this survey to discover trends in what international students consider to be most significant when studying abroad – the aspects that can make their time abroad even better or, indeed, those which can make it an unhappy experience. It allows us to draw conclusions about what international students see as important to their study abroad experience, as well as what they consider to be the benefits of having studied abroad, such as improved job prospects when they graduate.

The aim of the STeXX project was to better understand the experiences of students studying abroad on three levels: why students aim to study abroad, what influences their satisfaction, and what policy and decision makers at institutional, national and international levels can learn in order

Going Global: Knowledge-Based Economies for 21st Century Nations
Copyright © 2014 by Hannah Ellis
All rights of reproduction in any form reserved
ISBN: 978-1-78441-003-2

to improve international university exchanges. While mainly focusing on European institutions, the lessons learnt, as well as the methodology developed, have implications for higher education on a global level – and can be easily transferred to the wider international education field.

The results of the survey demonstrate that international students are, overall, very satisfied with their study abroad experience. Two thirds of those surveyed rated their experience with a nine or ten out of ten when asked if they would recommend it to their friends. This response shows that studying abroad is, overall, considered to be a very positive experience. However, by analysing the areas that international students comment on most frequently, it is possible to pinpoint those areas that international students are less happy with, and therefore recognise where universities can make improvements to their services and teaching processes (Graph 1).

As well as drawing general conclusions about what international students find important, we can also be more specific about what students comment on most often, according to country of origin, destination and study level, among other criteria. The more we discover about what affects the study abroad experience, the more we can help students have an outstanding time studying abroad in every respect through working together with universities and policy makers to improve the standard of international exchanges. With these findings in mind, we are able to provide institutional, national and international decision makers with concrete recommendations on how to improve their (national) higher education systems and, as a result, increase international student satisfaction.

There are striking differences between what students comment on in different countries; for instance, international students in the UK comment more often than average on the high academic reputation and the educational standard of their universities, whereas students in Spain comment more frequently on the atmosphere in their host city. However, it is

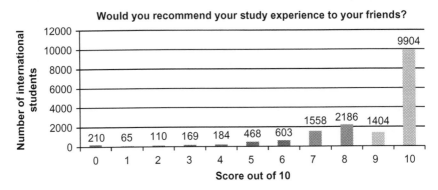

Graph 1: Number of respondents by satisfaction rating.

interesting to note that students across the board appreciate a high level of education – in countries with traditionally well-regarded university systems, students comment positively about the level of teaching and education, but students also commented when they felt that the level of education was too low, or below the level they had expected. They often drew comparisons with what the level was like in their home universities – they wished to have an equally high level of education regardless of the other aspects of their international experience such as free-time activities and the city in which they were staying.

It is interesting to note that there are some differences in what students want when the results are broken down into different groups of students for comparison – as an example, international students are slightly less interested in academic aspects of studying than domestic students. The most interesting results come when we compare different countries – for example, British students who have studied in another European country show their awareness of the importance of international experience; they are far less preoccupied by academic concerns, but instead comment on the chance to discover new cultures and languages. They recognise the benefits that come with improving soft skills such as communication and cultural understanding. European students studying in the UK, however, are more concerned with academic and pastoral aspects at their university than the European average. They also comment less on city and culture than their peers who have studied elsewhere. This shows that students going to the UK specifically go for the well-regarded and high level of education, whereas British students are more interested in gaining other skills useful in the workplace.

The satisfaction with different aspects of studying abroad also varies in other ways, depending on the country – for instance, students in Norway, Sweden and Finland make more comments than average on the cultural aspects that come with living so far north, and highly appreciate the beautiful, wild landscapes of these countries. Students studying in Spain and Italy mention more aspects of city and culture than their peers studying elsewhere, whereas students in Germany and the Netherlands are more focused on the quality of education and the job prospects at the end of it. Indeed, in these two countries, students more commonly comment on the benefits of studying abroad from a career perspective. Students in Germany also find the cost of living cheaper than elsewhere, though those in the Netherlands find it slightly more expensive. It will be interesting to see the extent to which international student satisfaction in the UK is affected by the rising cost of tuition – there is currently not enough information available to make any concrete conclusions.

The results of the STeXX survey show that though on the whole students are very happy with their international exchanges, there are areas that can be improved. There seem to be huge differences between institutions and countries in aspects such as the availability of courses in English, or the support given by the international office.

Positive and Negative Influences on International Student Satisfaction

The three biggest positive influencers of international student satisfaction are the city atmosphere, looks and size; the quality and attitude of the host university's teaching staff or tutors; and the approachability and friendliness of the locals in the host city. Other factors that influence students' satisfaction are the host university's reputation and international services office, the availability of social activities, and learning about new cultures and languages.

The local people can play a huge part in how well students settle in to their new environment. The more friendly and open they are, the more likely it is that students will enjoy and make the most of their experience. They will also be able to learn more about the cultural differences and language through a process of immersion. Students who are stuck in the 'Erasmus bubble' often complain that they were not able to meet so many local students and so missed out on really getting to know the culture of their new country.

Although there are numerous positive reasons to recommend a certain course or university for studying abroad, the results of the study also highlighted the aspects of studying abroad with which international students are unhappy. The biggest of these is a lack of adequate organisation and support at the student's host university. Moving to a new country is a huge challenge, and international students greatly appreciate any help they receive in settling in. They complain that they have to complete complicated administrative procedures and do not receive help finding accommodation. These are both relatively easy to remedy – universities must ensure that they have a well-equipped and helpful international office.

What do Students Want from their International Experience?

Through a thorough analysis of what students commented upon, we were able to draw some conclusions about the biggest things that influence their satisfaction. Students decide to study abroad for a wide variety of reasons: sometimes it is part of their study programme from the beginning, they may find a particular course they wish to study is not available in their home country, often it is to improve their soft skills or CV profile, learn a new language, gain international experience, save money on expensive tuition in their home country, or just because they think they need a change from their old routines. Knowing what influences students to go abroad in the first place is vital to providing them with what they need to make the most out of their experience. As an example, we know from the STeXX survey that many students go abroad with the intention of improving their English language skills, but that a low level of teachers' English is a reason why many students complain. Universities and institutions can use this information to improve their provisions for teaching and practising English, through offering English language training to staff, English language courses for students and allowing the students enough chances to improve their language in an academic and social environment.

Although there is a traditional perception of an exchange abroad as being an 'academic holiday', the results of the STeXX survey would seem to indicate the opposite. Students comment much more frequently on their host city and the academic aspects than about their social life (at 24 per cent and 22 per cent of comments compared to 13 per cent respectively). Particularly noteworthy is the fact that almost a quarter of negative comments are about academics – students really do care about the quality of their tuition when studying abroad. The biggest negative aspects are the level of instruction being lower than they expected, and poor-quality teaching. In order to encourage international education, it is vital that universities pitch the levels of their classes high enough. International students do sometimes initially have problems with the language of instruction, but this does mean that the level of content needs to be lowered.

Students who study abroad often wish to take advantage of programmes that they cannot study in their home countries. They also use the opportunity to study at a university that has a particularly well-regarded department for their subject. Students recognise that international mobility can give them a head start in the job market because of the expertise they can develop during this time via educational access to subject specialists perhaps unavailable in their home country. Students also often comment on the different teaching and learning processes in their host country being an excellent way to improve and develop their practical and soft skills. Through studying their subjects in practical as well as theoretical ways, they are sent out to the jobs market with more transferable skills than those students who have studied from a purely theoretical perspective.

Students see their experience abroad as an additional asset when applying for jobs: one Slovakian student studying in Sweden said: 'Dalarna University has a great selection of high-quality courses, which are truly interesting and, considering the educational system in Sweden, actually teach you a lot. The environment in the heart of traditional Sweden makes your stay there very enjoyable and unforgettable. Sweden is a country with general higher standards and I believe that my studies there improved my chances of having better job opportunities in the future.'

International experience allows students to gain more varied experiences than if they stay in their home countries. Being thrown in at the deep end of a new environment and having to adapt to their new life there not only means that they must learn to be self-sufficient and independent, but they must also improve their organisation skills and resilience. They will usually have at least some time spent in an environment where they do not speak the native language to a high level – this means they must rapidly improve their problem-solving skills and mental flexibility. Without this, they may be stuck and find that it is very difficult fitting into their new community. If they are unable to communicate in any respect with those around them (although at the university, they will usually be able to revert to using English as a lingua franca), they will quickly find themselves isolated and lonely.

International Study and Finding a Job

International experience is beneficial in the jobs market, as workers who understand the dynamics of international markets and the cultural differences between countries are a great asset. Internationally minded students are more likely to wish to work in an international environment, in their home country or abroad. Workers who can offer an insight into other cultures and national outlooks bring advantages to international trade. According to a 2011 (Quacquarelli Symonds[1]) survey, 60 per cent of 10,000 employers surveyed worldwide said that they see international experience as a valuable asset. This student studying in Germany commented on why they thought the experience was of benefit: 'I think German is a big plus in the business world (I got my current job because of it) and abroad studies are a huge advantage in general; you meet new people, learn about cultural differences and this helps a lot to relativise.'

International experience is useful in the jobs market due to the increased cultural awareness and communication skills (particularly those involved in improved language skills) that students develop during their time abroad. Students recognise this among the reasons that they give for recommending their experience to others. This Mexican student who studied in Austria cites the skills he gained on his year abroad as the reason for him now being in employment: 'I had the opportunity to work in a bigger company

1. p. 21, Molony, J, Sowter, B and Potts, D (2011) QS Global Employer Survey Report 2011: How Employers Value an International Study Experience. Retrieved September 2013 at http://content.qs.com/qs/qs-global-employer-survey-2011.pdf

that works globally because of my international experience and the practise of other language. Now, I have a good job.'

Experience abroad can not only give international students access to diverse courses and study opportunities; learning in a different environment gives students a chance to view things from a different perspective. It also means that they are more flexible in their attitudes, outlooks and working skills. Having to adapt to (sometimes very different) ways of doing things makes them more flexible when working − their experience of different methods and outlooks means that they can adapt quickly and accept that there may be several different ways of solving a problem. Studying abroad is very useful for improving soft skills such as communication, language ability and interpersonal awareness. Students meet new people from all corners of the world and are encouraged to make friends in a new environment. This allows them to develop skills for relating to other people − something that will later be very useful in a networking or business environment. This Romanian student studying in Ireland gave their experience a ten out of ten and said: 'Having the chance to study abroad is the best way to adapt in a multicultural environment and to improve many of your personal and professional skills that will be very helpful for your future career such as, communication and language skills, punctuality, creativity and it will most likely give you energy to strive for your dreams. You will find well trained staff willing to help you and the cultural experience abroad will surely enrich your character and personality'.

As well as improving soft skills, time spent studying abroad can also offer great academic benefits. Students who study their subject from a different perspective, or use different ways of learning (such as practical versus theoretical), will gain a much more developed and in-depth knowledge of their subject area. This can certainly be seen as an advantage when students are graduating, because a different way of seeing or doing things adds to mental flexibility.

How can Policy Makers and Universities Use this Information?

Policy and decision makers can learn greatly from the results of the STeXX survey results. One important factor is learning to listen to students, finding out what they need when they study abroad and doing all in their power to make the experience enjoyable, productive and meaningful. This will not only benefit students − happy students are more motivated to learn − it will also have an impact on the universities the students have attended. Students who have enjoyed their experiences are more likely to recommend their university to prospective students. Our study uses a modern method of scoring satisfaction called Net Promoter Score (NPS) to rate how likely students are to recommend their experience. The NPS is calculated by taking students' score out of ten, treating a score of 9-10 as a 'promoter' (likely to recommend their experience), 7-8 as a 'passive' (satisfied overall, but unlikely to actively promote it), and below 6 as a 'detractor' (likely to discourage others from trying the experience). The percentage of detractors is subtracted from the number of promoters, giving a score between −100 and +100. Anything above zero is considered to be a positive rating. Our data shows that exchange students in Europe are very satisfied overall, with an NPS of +56.

On a global level, our project has been designed to make student feedback accessible for students worldwide. Based on enthusiastic and encouraging shared experiences, more students will be motivated to study abroad. This promotes the internationalisation of universities in a virtuous circle; the more students talk about studying abroad, the more will start studying abroad. This will facilitate mobility flows between countries while further improving national higher education systems. The more students comment upon their experience, the more universities and policy makers can improve the areas most in need of improvement. This will in turn lead to more students.

It is vital for universities to work together to streamline international co-operation. Students should be aided in making the transition between universities and countries as easy as possible. Moving to a new country already involves many challenges − settling into a brand-new environment, often a long way from home, finding a new place to live, getting used to cultural differences − and so universities' international offices should endeavour to make their processes as simple as possible to enable students to make the most of their experience without going through unnecessary administration processes. The more universities are successful in co-operating, the more likely it is that students will want to undertake international exchanges. This will then have a filtering effect into the jobs market, improving international knowledge in the jobs market and making the mobility of skilled workers easier.

There are still many steps that can be taken to increase the number of students undertaking mobility periods abroad, some bigger than others. One of the biggest, and most important, is increasing the awareness of the benefits of time abroad across a wider community − to students, employers and governments. It is also vital to highlight to students that there is adequate funding available. Many students are greatly influenced by the cost of studying abroad − it accounts for 15 per cent of the negative comments in our survey.

An international experience is incredibly useful in the jobs market, marking students out as having better communication and often language skills than their peers who have not studied abroad. Time abroad improves international co-operation and understanding within Europe, and also equips students with valuable skills for the jobs market. It is vital that this opportunity is available to as many students as possible, and is made to be straightforward for those students who choose to go. Because of this, it is necessary for universities and government policy makers to continue funding and supporting international mobility schemes in order to improve the international workforce in the future.

References

ACA (2006) Perceptions of European Higher Education in Third Countries. Brussels.

Beyer, H (1998) Contextual Design: Defining Customer-Centered Systems. San Francisco: Morgan Kaufmann.

Ellis, H and van Aart, J (2013) Key influencers of international student satisfaction (2013 report), Eindhoven

ESN (2008) ESN Survey 2008 'Exchanging Cultures'. Brussels: Erasmus Student Network AISBL.

ESN (2009) Problems of Recognition In Making Erasmus. Brussels: Erasmus Student Network AISBL.

ESU (2010) Bologna at the finish line: an account of ten years of European higher education reform. Brussels: The European Students' Union.

ET2020 (2009) Council conclusions of 12 May 2009 on a strategic framework for European co-operation in education and training ('ET 2020').

EUA (2010) Trends 2010: a decade of change in European Higher Education. Brussels: European University Association.

Leuven/Louvain-la-Neuve Communiqué (2009) The Bologna Process 2020 – The European Higher Education Area in the new decade. Communiqué of the Conference of European Ministers Responsible for Higher Education.

Molony, J, Sowter, B and Potts, D (2011) QS Global Employer Survey Report 2011: How Employers Value an International Study Experience. Retrieved September 2013 at http://content.qs.com/qs/qs-global-employer-survey-2011.pdf

Netpop Research (2011) Social Animals US 2011. San Fransisco.

Reichheld, FF (2003) The one number you need to grow. *Harvard Business Review*, *81*(12), Pp. 46−54.

Satmetrix (2011) 2011 European Net Promoter Industry Benchmarks.

StudyPortals (2013) MastersPortal.eu. Retrieved August 2013, www.mastersportal.eu

Chapter 2.5

Going English: Private Higher Education and Graduates' Employability in Saudi Arabia

Yussra Jamjoom

Introduction

In the current era of the knowledge economy, and information and technology, nations seek all possible means to become globally connected and subsequently flourish and survive. The higher education sector has been an integral actor in this globalisation era. The use of the English language for instruction in higher education in non-English-speaking countries is one of the implications of globalisation on higher education. Higher education institutions have also been involved in certain activities in response to the demand in the global market for employable graduates.

This chapter discusses the impact of using English language as the medium of instruction in higher education institutions in a non-English-speaking country (Saudi Arabia) on graduates' employability. To a large extent, the discussion in this paper centres on Saudi Arabia as a representative of a non-English-speaking country.

This chapter comprises four sections. The section that follows this introduction briefly discusses the 'internationalisation' of higher education and the situation of the English language worldwide and in Saudi Arabia. This is followed by a discussion on the impact of the English language on the employability skills of graduates. The paper concludes with some recommendations for policy makers, employers and higher education institutions that use the English language as a medium for instruction.

Going Global: Knowledge-Based Economies for 21st Century Nations
Copyright © 2014 by Yussra Jamjoom
All rights of reproduction in any form reserved
ISBN: 978-1-78441-003-2

The Internationalisation of Higher Education and the English Language

The internationalisation of higher education is a complex and a multi-faceted topic (Qiang, 2002). Higher education institutions approach internationalisation in different ways. Some higher education institutions introduce the concept of internationalisation by integrating intercultural dimensions into the curriculum, extra-curricular activities and research. Through these modes of internationalisation, higher education institutions expose their students to global culture without having the students leave their home countries (Hénard et al., 2012). The other form of internationalisation is achieved through overseas campuses, distance learning and joint programmes (OECD, 2004). Another significant means of achieving internationalisation of higher education institutions is the use of the English language for instruction. It can be argued that using the English language for instruction facilitates the internationalisation process of higher education institutions. For example, Coleman (2006; pp. 4–6) suggests several reasons that motivate higher education institutions and governments to move towards using English as the medium of instruction:

> 'Content and language integrated learning (CLIL), internationalisation, student exchange, teaching and research materials, staff mobility and the marker in international students.'

Based on the economic and technological development of the west, primarily that of the United States, the role of the English language in the globalisation era has been discussed frequently. The English language is no longer reserved for the elite, but its acquisition has become a basic, important skill in a globalised economy. Crystal (2003) demonstrates the worldwide growth of the English language and its global impact. In his book *English as a Global Language*, he reveals that 85 per cent of international organisations use English as the official medium of communication, and 85 per cent of the world film market is in English. English is now the language of science, medicine and technology. According to him, more than 80 per cent of scientific papers are first published in English (Crystal, 2003). There is also a belief that the use of the English language has expedited the globalisation process. David Graddol remarks: 'English is at the centre of many globalisation mechanisms', (Graddol, 1997, p. 45). Therefore, the English language has definitely become the lingua franca and a necessity for those who are involved in, or aspire to be in, the globalised economy.

Transnationalisation and the extension of traditional markets mandate the use of a common language. However, many nations still have reservations about the widespread use of the English language and perceive it as a threat to their own languages, cultures and identity. In Saudi Arabia, Arabic is the official language. The significance of the Arabic language in this state can be better understood in light of its long-established educational traditions and religious customs (Jamjoom, 2012).

Until recently, Arabic was the only medium of instruction at all educational levels, including higher education, with the exception of King Fahd University for Petroleum and Minerals (KFUPM), which is a public university and all recently developed private higher education institutions. Aware of the global importance of the English language and under mounting pressure from the USA, the Saudi government recently embarked on making reforms in its educational system to prepare children for developing greater linguistic competence in English (Al-Essa, 2009). It can be argued that political and economic pressures have been more influential in the fight against the spread of the English language in the education system in the Saudi Arabia.

It is worth indicating that private higher education institutions in Saudi Arabia are not branches of international universities. In other words, the use of the English language is not a requirement of a foreign university, but the choice of a domestic university. In past decades, English-speaking countries like the UK, USA and Australia have established branches of their universities worldwide, teaching their home curricula to students in the host country. This is the case in the United Arab Emirates (UAE), where foreign universities are permitted to establish campuses; however, in Saudi Arabia foreign universities are not given sanction to provide private higher education (Jamjoom, 2012).

While Arabic is the official language in Saudi Arabia, English is the principal language used in most private multinational organisations. The use of the English language is also becoming more customary due to the increased involvement of the Saudi government with other countries, particularly after becoming a member of the World Trade Organisation that encourages foreign investment. It is worth noting that in the past English was not crucial for employment since the public sector was the automatic career destination for university graduates. However, the situation has changed dramatically. The public sector has been saturated, and the private sector has now become the only option for most graduates.

In the past, private organisations depended on expatriates who used the English language to run the business and communicate with other employees. Thus, the English language has been the lingua franca for communication between employees belonging to different nationalities. Recently, however, the 'Saudisation' policy has forced the private sector to recruit more nationals and reduce its long-standing reliance on expatriates. In turn, this has led to growing concerns among employers in the private sector regarding graduates' employability skills. This is particularly true for multinational or global companies who will pay a high price if they fail to maintain effective communication across their branches. New research shows that aptitude in English is a major skill that most graduates lack (Ghaban et al., 2002; Jamjoom, 2012). The following section discusses the impact of using the English language in higher education institutions on graduates' employability in Saudi Arabia.

Graduates' Employability and the English Language in Saudi Arabia

Graduates' employability is a debated subject, as it has different implications for different people (Harvey, 2001; Little, 2001). The most commonly used definition of graduates' employability is that of Yorke (2006), according to which employability is defined in the following manner:

> 'A set of achievements, skills, knowledge and personal attributes that make the individual more likely to secure and be successful in their chosen occupation(s), for the benefits of themselves, the workforce, the community and the economy.' (p. 6)

In this study, graduates' employability is defined as graduates' 'work-readiness' (Mason et al., 2003). All available studies that investigate employers' needs of skills emphasise the importance of the employability/transferable skills of employers (Archer and Davison, 2008; Overtoom, 2000; Robinson et al., 2007). Employability skills are 'generic in nature rather than job specific and cut across all industry, businesses, job levels, from the entry-level worker to the senior most position.' (Singh and Singh; 2008, p. 16) Examples of employability skills include communication skills, problem-solving skills, interpersonal skills and self-management (McLaughlin, 1995). According to Jamjoom's 2012 study, all stakeholders who were interviewed considered the English language to be an important skill, if not the most necessary skill, for employment. A study conducted by Klein (2007) suggests a positive effect of individuals' language proficiency on their wages and professional careers. Although no study has thus far been conducted to examine the economic return of proficiency in the English language for graduates in the Saudi context, it is obvious that all those who hold high positions are competent in the English language. All stakeholders interviewed in the study by Jamjoom (2012) agreed that graduates of higher education institutions that use English language as the medium of instruction are better valued and preferred in the market. While it might be argued that English is not needed in contexts where it is not the official language, graduates' competence in English provides them with broader employment opportunities. Graduates who are competent in English are not constrained to work in the local market. A faculty member from a higher education institution in Saudi Arabia commented:

> 'Though Arabic is the local language, if thousands of students graduating from business majors only speak the business language in Arabic, will those students be prepared for the market? This is the paradox, we are opening doors for external market, but we are not graduating students who are ready for this market. Where will students work if they lack the English language which is needed in every single business enterprise?' (Jamjoom, 2012, p. 203)

Scholars such as Coleman (2006) and Graddol (1997) have discussed the benefits of using English as a medium of instruction. Among the advantages discussed by Coleman (2006), there is the concept of content and language integrated learning (CLIL) in which students learn English while learning another subject. This arguably provides effective opportunities for students to actively practise their new language skills without requiring extra time in the curriculum. A number of studies agree that the most obvious benefit of using English as a medium of instruction is simply that it enhances students' proficiency in English (Chang, 2010; Dupuy, 2000).

Coleman (2006) and Chang (2010) contend that there are no comprehensive studies on the effectiveness of using English as a medium for instruction and that its impact on learning is not well defined. However, according to Jamjoom (2012), using the English language as a medium of instruction enhances the quality of education imparted in higher education institutions, which could have an impact of graduates' knowledge. In her study, students, graduates and faculty members who were interviewed indicated that the quality of educational materials is better in higher education institutions where the English language is the medium of instruction. The absence of the English language in higher education institutions is found to limit the access of instructors and students to educational materials. This might be attributed to the fact that most researches and publications are available in English. In addition, there seems to be an efficiency issue with translating textbooks from English to other languages. The speed of translation might not match the speed of publication. Thus, this could cause the information in translated textbooks to become out of date. In addition, accuracy in translation is not always achieved and this could have an impact on students' understanding of the subject matter (Jamjoom, 2012). As a result, students and instructors who work in higher education institutions where English is the medium of instruction are considered more privileged.

Proficiency in the English language might be the most obvious payoff for using English language as the medium of instruction in higher education institutions, but its impact on other soft skills should not be underestimated. Employers, particularly in non-English speaking countries, might be less explicit regarding their needs relating to other soft skills; maybe it is to a large extent found in graduates who are competent in the English language. While it may be questioned whether English proficiency is needed in the local labour market, employers' link English proficiency to good communication skills and self-confidence, which are all important skills in a globalised economy (Jamjoom, 2012).

Perhaps the benefits that higher education institutions accrue when they make English the language of instruction are not limited to enabling students to gain proficiency in the English language. For example, the wider access to up-to-date educational resources (discussed earlier), which higher education institutions obtain when they make English the language of instruction, could have a positive impact on the confidence level of students. The accessibility to information students have because of the English language might give them confidence in the knowledge they gain. This is not to say that proficiency in the English language in itself, if possessed by graduates, is not sufficient to enhance their confidence level; possessing this skill makes graduates feel superior over those who do not speak the language.

Among the benefits of employing the English language in higher education discussed by Coleman (2006) is that it facilitates students' participation in exchange programmes. In Jamjoom's (2012) study, higher education institutions that use English language as a medium of instruction have better chances to collaborate with other global institutions and involve their students in exchange programmes than those who use the local language for instruction. In the study conducted by The International Research Foundation (TIRF), collaboration skill was found to be an important skill for global corporations and has been found to be enhanced by plurilingual skills (TIRF, 2009).

The use of the English language as a medium of instruction is also found to provide higher education institutions with the opportunity to invite important international politicians and influential business and industrial leaders (Jamjoom, 2012). Again, the impact of such activities by higher education institutions on graduates' employability skills must not be overlooked.

It is obvious how the use of English language for instruction in higher education institutions could have a great impact on students' employability skills. That said, to use the English language as a medium for instruction in a non-English-speaking country might not be an easy task. According to Jamjoom (2012), the use of English language as a medium of instruction has increased the difficulties for providers of higher education in terms of recruiting faculty members, as new teachers need to be highly competent not only in the subject they teach, but also in the language of instruction. This is becoming a particularly pressing issue in view of the rapid expansion of higher education in the country and in the neighbouring Gulf Co-operation Council (GCC) states. It is postulated that the socio-religious status quo in Saudi Arabia causes some discomfort to many Westerners, and that this is likely to have a significant impact on the ability of private higher education institutions to attract good foreign instructors.

Although Saudi Arabia is generally viewed as an attractive place for Muslim instructors who might value being close to the holy places of their religion, this is certainly not the case for non-Muslim Arabs or faculty members from Western countries. Even after the modernisation of Saudi Arabia, people still prefer to settle in other Gulf states, which are relatively more open and permit them to lead similar lifestyles to those they would have enjoyed in their own countries. For many of the reasons stated above, it is a huge challenge for higher education institutions in Saudi Arabia to recruit local faculty members who are competent in the English language. In most cases, new faculty members are required to make an oral presentation before they are hired; thus, speaking is the only English language skill that is assessed. This leads to the question of the extent to which these faculty members are actually able to develop and cultivate students' skills in the English language. In other words, are they sufficiently competent to assess students' work? If they are, to what extent should they pay attention to students' proficiency in English while assessing their work in other non-English subjects? These questions might be important, particularly because some employers find that graduates from English-speaking institutions are not competent in all English language skills (Jamjoom, 2012); employers often find that English language writing skills are not up to the requisite standard.

Another challenge that could stand against the growth of the English language in a non-English-speaking country like Saudi Arabia is that there are still some who are firmly against the use of the English language in institutions. According to Jamjoom (2012), there are some who find the use of the English language for instruction in higher education to be a threat to their language and identity. There are others who are, in fact, calling for the 'Arabising' of subjects such as medicine and science in the public sector, which currently use Western textbooks (Al-Awsat, 2004). Moreover, Alsehli (2009) argues that there should be differentiation between the value of learning a foreign language and using it in teaching across all subjects. He claims that language is not the only reason for the recent deterioration in the quality of graduates and encourages policy makers to consider alternative reasons as well.

Conclusion and Recommendations

Evidently, there has been significant growth in the use of the English language globally and in Saudi Arabia, which demonstrates the states' response to the global economy and the progressive role it aims to play at this level. Despite the existing socio-religious resistance against any Western influence, the English language, like in many other countries, continues to gain prevalence. It is considered an essential factor in employability and as the gateway for participation in the global economy.

This paper highlighted the positive relationship between the use of the English language in higher education institutions and graduates' employability skills. In addition to the fact that employing English as the medium of instruction enhances graduates' proficiency in the English language, which is a highly required skill by all employers, it appears to indirectly enhance the development of other soft skills.

When the English language is used as the medium of instruction, it provides higher education institutions with better opportunities to involve their institutions in internationalisation activities (e.g. collaborate with other institutions, access international resources, invite international guest speakers, etc.). The impact of all of these aspects on graduates' proficiency in the English language and other soft skills (self-confidence, intercultural awareness and tolerance) should not be overlooked and warrants further research.

Nevertheless, the use of the English language in higher education institutions in a context where English is not the local language is replete with challenges. In such contexts, higher education institutions face difficulties in recruiting qualified faculty members, particularly as the local market lacks those who are suitably qualified and fluent in English, and labour regulations have made it increasingly difficult to recruit expatriates. The following are some key recommendations for policy makers, providers of English language teaching and employers.

While focusing on English language education, a balance must be established between the need for advancement and the long-standing local cultural traditions that form the fabric of society. Thus, the local native language should not be given less attention in favour of English. Further, the teaching of both the local language and English should not be limited to grammar; both languages have other essential and enriching aspects, which students must be taught.

Policy makers must be cautious in terms of establishing English as the main language of instruction in higher education. Teaching in a foreign language requires that faculty members and students possess a high level of competence and skill in that particular language. Moreover, further studies must be conducted on the impact of using English as a medium of instruction to assist in weighing the gains against the losses.

Higher education institutions should seriously consider introducing learning centres to provide support in increasing students' competency in the English language. Such centres could also assist students to better comprehend subjects taught predominately in English.

There is a definite need for more collaboration between employers and educators with regard to the English language. In particular, employers should provide greater clarity on their precise requirements for the requisite level of language skills. Critical examination indicates a number of factors: is speaking English a necessary job skill across the globe or is it something that many employers seek for prestige, or in the belief that graduates who speak English are somehow smarter? How much English is really needed and for which jobs? The answers to these simple questions could have a significant impact on educational policy. Undoubtedly, English proficiency is a necessary skill for certain jobs in international business and finance, but the job skills of non-English-speaking Saudi Arabians should not be overlooked either.

Lastly, employers must contribute to the development of English language skills directly in the workplace by training new applicants and providing tailored instruction for existing staff. The labour market itself must also fully participate in gaining the requisite skills. In any event, the responsibility for development in this area should not be the sole remit of the education system.

References

Al-Essa, A (2009) Education Reform in Saudi Arabia: Between the absence of political vision, the apprehension of religious culture and the inability of educational administration. Lebanon: Dar Al Saqi.

Archer, W, and Davison, J (2008) Graduate Employability. The Council for Industry and Higher Education.

Chang, Y-Y (2010) 'English-medium instruction for subject courses in tertiary education: Reactions from Taiwanese undergradute students'. Taiwan International ESP Journal, 2 (1), Pp. 55–84.

Coleman, JA (2006) 'English-medium teaching in European higher education'. Language Teaching, 39 (01), Pp. 1–14.

Crystal, D, (2003) English as a Global Language (second edition). Cambridge: Cambridge University Press.

Dupuy, B (2000) 'Content-based instruction: can it help ease the transtition from beginning to advanced foreign langauge classes?' Foreign Language Annals, 33 (2), Pp. 205–223.

Ghaban, M et al. (2002) Unemployment: reasons and remedies. Madinah, Kingdom of Saudi Arabia: Ministry of Interior.

Graddol, D (1997) 'The future of English?: A guide to forecasting the popularity of the English language in the 21st century'. London: The British Council.

Harvey, L (2001) 'Defining and measuring employability'. Quality in higher education, 7 (2), Pp. 97—109.

Hénard, F, Diamond, L and Roseveare, D (2012) Approaches to internationalisation and their implications for strategic management and institutional practice: a guide for higher education instituions. OECD Higher Education Program/ IMHE. Paris.

Jamjoom, Y (2012) Understanding private higher education in Saudi Arabia: Emergence, development, and perception. Institute of Education, University of London, Unpublished PhD thesis.

Klein, C (2007) The valuation of plurilingual competencies in an open European labour market. International Journal of Multilingualism, 4(4), Pp. 262—281.

Little, B (2001) 'Reading between the lines of graduate employment'. Quality in Higher Education, 7 (2), Pp. 121—129.

Mason, G, Williams, G, Cranmer, S and Guile, D (2003) 'How much does higher education enhance the employability of graduates?'. [Online]. Higher Education Funding Council of England (HEFCE). Available at: www.hefce.ac.uk/pubs/ rdreports/2003/rd13_03/. [Last accessed 23-9-2013].

McLaughlin, M (1995) Employability skills profile: what are employers looking for? ERIC Clearinghouse on Counseling and Student Services.

Organisation for Economic Co-operation and Development (2004) Internationalisation and trade in higher education: opportunities and challenges. OECD, Paris.

Overtoom, C (2000) Employability skills: an update. ERIC Clearinghouse.

Qiang, Z (2003) Internationalization of higher education: towards a conceptual framework. Policy Futures in Education, 1(2), Pp. 248—270.

Robinson, JS, Garton, BL, and Vaughn, PR (2007) Becoming employable: a look at graduates' and supervisors' perceptions of the skills needed for employability. NACTA Journal, 51(2), Pp. 19—26.

Singh, G and Singh, S (2008) Malaysian graduates' employability skills. UNITAR E-JOURNAL. 4(1), Pp. 15—45.

Chapter 2.6

The Changing Role of English and ELT in a Modern, Multilingual and Internationalised World

John Knagg

Introduction

Research and experience show the relevance of English to individuals' participation in globalised society. The nature of internationalised higher education (HE) is changing and these changes impact on the role of English and of ELT (English Language Teaching). New demands are appearing from different stakeholders – policy makers at government and university level, researchers, teachers and students. A more comprehensive model of English and other languages in international HE is needed that allows stakeholders to identify appropriate action to ensure the right policy decisions are taken and the right language skills developed. We aim to achieve a higher level of understanding of the role of English and ELT, and to disseminate that understanding so that good decisions can be taken at all levels.

The Size and Nature of the HE English Learning Sector

The size of English learning and teaching activity in higher education globally is difficult to ascertain with any degree of certainty. Internal British Council research suggests that there are some one billion learners of English in mainstream education (i.e. primary, secondary, tertiary) worldwide. However, a very large proportion of this takes place in primary and

Going Global: Knowledge-Based Economies for 21st Century Nations
Copyright © 2014 by John Knagg
All rights of reproduction in any form reserved
ISBN: 978-1-78441-003-2

secondary, and a much smaller volume in HE. Moreover, it is easier to estimate numbers of learners and teachers in primary and secondary education as the size is usually a function of national educational policy. Governments and other educational authorities impose policies regarding the teaching of languages, and while the policy often delegates the choice of language to be taught to local or institutional level, in the majority of cases globally the first choice of modern foreign language to be studied is English (see ESLC). Year on year changes will also be affected by national policy, as more governments recognise the status of English as a global lingua franca in more domains and respond, whether correctly or not, with policy decisions such as increasing the amount of English teaching especially at primary level (Rixon 2013). Thus, we can expect a substantial majority of children to come out of the school system with a good number of hours of English classes. What this means in terms of learning outcomes – that is levels of English attained – is under-researched and highly variable from context to context, with the best comparative indicators being the European Survey of Language Competences (ESLC).

The situation regarding English learners in the HE sector, on the other hand, is rarely driven by government policy and more often a function of institutional policy and individual student needs and resources. It is clear that many more HE students learn English now than was the case 20 or 40 years ago. Long gone are the days when the majority of English teaching in universities was directed at students on English Major courses. There is not space to go into the well-rehearsed reasons for this, such as the globalisation of English, the increasing number of domains in which it is used as a lingua franca and the perceived potential social and economic benefit of competence in English for the individual. Learning English is increasingly an option in addition to content studies. Different HE learners in a range of social contexts and subject to different institutional expectations will adopt differing approaches. Major factors which affect their decisions include institutional obligations to take certain courses, the lack of availability of courses, and the level and type of competence already achieved balanced against the perception of the level and type of competence that is or will be desired in their academic, working and social life.

Recent British Council estimates of the number of English learners in HE institutes globally have varied from under 30 to over 50 million. One difficulty of counting HE English learners is that large proportions of learners in some contexts do learn English but not in their own HE institute. Instead they learn in a distinct – often private sector – institute or increasingly via a variety of self-access and online options.

The complexity of the English learning picture in higher education institutions (HEIs) has increased as a result of a number of forces: first, by the move from English learners being predominantly English Major students or similar to being predominantly students majoring in non-English or non-foreign language-related disciplines; second, by the increase in student mobility to English-medium courses in majority English-speaking countries; third, by the increase in English-medium instruction in non-majority English-speaking countries; and fourth, by increased demand for specialised English learning by academic staff of universities as well as by students.

Towards a Taxonomy of English Learning in HE

To make sense of this complexity we have developed the following simple taxonomy of English learner types in HE. Within this taxonomy, each type of English learner is seen to have different needs in terms of desired learning outcomes. The taxonomy is aimed at bringing some clarity to a situation in which very different types of English learner, and therefore of English teaching in universities, are referred to as if they were the same.

The initial simple model proposed, which is not exhaustive and might be expanded, adapted or simplified for different purposes, separates learners along a number of dimensions.

- Is English a central part of the learner's HE studies, or an additional element?
- Is the learning content delivered in English medium to some extent or not?
- Is any English-medium instruction within a majority English-speaking country?
- Is the learner a HE student or an HE teacher/academic?

Model of English Learner Types in Higher Education Contexts

A – Ana. The Traditional 'English for Academic Purposes' (EAP) Learner

Ana is leaving home to take an English-medium course at university in a majority English-speaking country (the UK, USA, etc.).

Ana is what we might call a traditional EAP learner. She will need to learn specialist English terms related to her discipline. She might also need to learn academic skills that are specific to the academic culture that she will be joining. This might include listening (e.g. getting information from lectures), speaking (e.g. participating in group discussions), reading (e.g. getting information and arguments from texts) and writing (e.g. writing assignments and dissertations). Each of these is likely to follow conventions that are different from those she is used to in her home academic environment. She may also need help in operating in the new culture outside the academic environment; for example, in social settings. The amount of learning and the amount of time she needs to spend depends on her proficiency level in each of these areas.

B – Ben. The Modern EAP Learner

Ben is staying in his home country, but will be taking an English-medium university course.

Ben is what we might call a modern EAP learner. He will be following an English-medium course, but will stay in his own (non-English speaking) country. This is because many universities around the world are starting English-medium courses, and also because many universities from the UK, USA, etc., are offering online, blended or face-to-face courses in other countries. Most of Ben's needs will be similar to Ana's. He will need the specialist terminology and study skills. If he is following a course validated in another country, then, like Ana, he might need to learn about the different academic conventions. However, he may not require wider cultural knowledge and new social skills, as he will not be living within a new culture.

C – Cleo. The Standard English Learner

Cleo is taking a university course in her home country in her local language. She needs to improve her English so that she can pass the English exam that the university requires, or to improve her employability.

We can call Cleo a standard English learner in HE. She is not an EAP learner, as she has no plans to study in English medium. She may need to improve her general English, or ESP (English for Specific Purposes, such as English for medics, English for the oil and gas industry, or reading manuals in English for technical staff). If there is a requirement to pass a particular exam (e.g. IELTS, FCE, TOEFL) then she may want to follow a specific course to prepare her for the requirements of that examination.

D – Dan. The EMI Teacher

Dan is an EMI teacher – a university teacher of, say, business studies or chemistry in his home country who now needs to teach some of his courses in English medium.

Dan needs a special EAP course to develop his teaching skills in English. He will be required to undertake some or all of his job in another language – English.

E − Efy. The Academic with International Connections

Efy is an academic with international connections. She is a lecturer and researcher in any subject who uses her own language in her own country. She needs to submit proposals for the publication of academic papers in English, to make occasional conference presentations in English and to co-ordinate international research funding bids in English.

Efy, like Dan, needs a special EAP course, though to develop somewhat different skills − academic writing and presentation skills.

F − Flo. The Specialist English Student

Flo is a specialist English student. She is a student on an English degree course or a teacher training course specialising in English − *many or most of her class will be expected to become English teachers or translators or similar.*

Flo needs to develop a high (C1/C2 on the Common European Framework of Reference) level of English, a specific knowledge of how to use English in a classroom environment and *an understanding of educational principles, classroom practice and cultural knowledge (see Edge and Mann 2013)* for examples of practice with this type of learner.

Further Explanation of the Model

We can map the six learners above against the four dimensions of the model as follows. For the first dimension, English is only a central part of the learner's HE studies in the case of Flo; for the other five, it is an additional element. On the second dimension of whether the content is delivered in English, we see that Ana, Ben and Dan (who might be Ben's teacher) are clearly in an EMI situation. Cleo is clearly not in an EMI situation. Efy is usually not in an EMI situation but is plunged into an English-medium environment occasionally. Flo, who is on a specialist English course, possibly teacher training, may receive much of her instruction in English medium, but may be surrounded by colleagues who receive instruction in a local language, and may herself receive instruction in some subjects in the local language. On the third dimension of whether any English-medium instruction is in a majority English-speaking country, only Ana will study in such a context, though part of Efy's training might be to prepare for that context. On the fourth dimension of whether the learner is an HE student or teacher, we see that Dan and Efy are teachers while Ana, Ben, Cleo and Flo are students.

As stated above, the model is designed as a useful conceptual tool rather than a complete explanation, and many issues arise. For example, there is much similarity between the needs of Ana and Ben, and the divide between the two, if there is one at all, could be made on the basis of the location of their EMI study (thus suggesting a difference in the need for cultural or social training), or on the basis of the home base of the HE university (thereby suggesting a difference in the need for training in academic culture). We might also question the relevance of including a student versus teacher distinction in the model, but we feel that this is a useful addition as HE students are generally not required to teach in English nor to undertake non-teaching technical academic work in English. Also, we feel that this is useful to highlight the fact that increasing internationalisation of HE and growth in English-medium instruction has highlighted the need for English training of different types for HE staff as well as HE students.

Analysis of the Model and Implications for Policy and Practice

An obvious next question after distinguishing the six learner types (only four of which are students as opposed to HE staff) is to look at the relative size of each of the types. If we take the overall size of the English learner market as 30 to 50 million, and the number of international students (HE students studying in another country) as in the region of 2.5 million, then we can see that the number in the position of Ana is that subset of the 2.5 million which is both studying in a majority English-speaking country and in need of training in English (that is, not already having a sufficient mastery of the language, which many international students do indeed have). Thus the number of students in Ana's position might be something around or above one million. If we see Flo as usually a future English teacher, then we can estimate the number of teachers produced is what is needed to replenish a global English teacher pool of some ten million, and if we posit an average career lifespan of an English teacher as 20 years to take account of significant early departure from the profession, then some half-million English teacher trainees would be in each year of university study, or a population of two million in HE at any one time, given an average course duration of four years. It is more difficult to estimate the number of students in Ben's position – the modern EAP learners, studying via EMI in their own country. There is certainly rapid growth in this sector in East Asia, Europe and other parts, but it is from a low base and is a relatively recent phenomenon. We treat EMI in HE in regions such as Africa and South Asia as different. While HE EMI is widespread, the general perception is that HE students, having usually come from EMI secondary systems, do not need specific help with their English. The reality that we are left with is that the great majority of HE learners with an English learning need are those standard English learners like Cleo, who would appear to comprise as much as 90 per cent or more of the totality of English learners in global HE.

The implication of this is that what is driving the need for more English learning in universities worldwide is not the various elements of HE internationalisation itself, whether student mobility or EMI growth, but rather the more general globalisation of English. This leads HE students like Cleo, students of any discipline and in any country, whether with international mobility ambitions or not, to believe that they need to invest time in developing a competence in English. This is the student body that is largely driving the HE world's need for English teachers. It would, of course, be simplistic to think that this group of learners is monolithic. Some will expect their English learning to focus on particular skills, on particular semantic areas, some will want a more general approach which will allow them to travel and negotiate on a day-to-day basis, and some will want a qualification which gets them through some part of a job selection process in the public or private sector in their countries.

Considering the case of this standard English learner in global HE, the TIRF research report English at Work on English training for the 21st-century workforce highlights a number of trends that university authorities would do well to consider in catering for this predominating category of learner. We see a move away from the traditional harder skills such as formal presentation and letter writing and towards skills that resonate with 21st-century skills posited in Trilling and Fadel's seminal work 21st Century Skills (2009): collaboration, critical thinking, communication, creativity and cross-cultural understanding. There is a move towards specialisation and personalisation of ELT, the consolidation of online technologies into learning and teaching, and a rise in project-based learning and authentic materials. While different skills, content and learning outcomes will be appropriate in EAP as opposed to standard English contexts, the general trends of specialisation, integration of technology, and resources and methodology remain relevant. At a policy level, institutions need to take decisions around the appropriateness of making the attainment of certain English levels compulsory for certain groups of students or courses.

Regarding the particular case of English-medium instruction, we see that a key driver of change is the growing trend to offer EMI courses in various disciplines in traditionally non-English-speaking countries. This is a significant new dimension in international HE, which has until now been characterised largely by student mobility, especially towards English-speaking countries. EMI for non-native English-speaking home-country students will lead to new challenges for students and teachers; the solutions will be as much around school-based and lifelong ELT as around the traditional HE-based EAP solutions. However, institutional policy makers need guidance on the right circumstances for English-medium instruction and feasible ways of implementing EMI policies, including staff recruitment and training, and student selection.

As national systems strive to improve access to HE for wider socio-economic groups, the issue of access to English for those who might have had little opportunity to develop proficiency before university comes into sharper focus. While universities might traditionally see their role as teaching higher-level specialised English, there is an increasing demand for lower-level remedial teaching, which is effectively an attempt to make up for lower than anticipated learning outcomes from the secondary school system. Nor is there as yet any solid evidence that national policies to introduce English earlier, in primary school, have had any real positive effect. Equally, policy makers will want to consider the full range of languages that can contribute to multilingual tertiary education, and not be blindly drawn into English as a panacea for all. While any society is likely to need a proportion of technicians and taxi drivers who know English, we should question whether there should also remain a place for professionals – lawyers, engineers, accountants – who choose to operate at national or local level and perhaps do not need competence in the language that has become the lingua franca for international professional and academic exchange.

References

Edge, J and Mann, S (2013) Innovations in Pre-Service Education and Training for English Language Teachers. British Council from (www.teachingenglish.org.uk/publications/innovations-pre-service-education-training-english-language-teachers)

First European Survey on Language Competences: Final Report. European Commission (2102) from (http://ec.europa.eu/languages/eslc/docs/en/final-report-escl_en.pdf)

Fitzpatrick, A and O'Dowd, R (2012) *English at Work: An Analysis of Case Reports about English Language Training for the 21st Century Workforce.* The International Research Foundation (TIRF) from (www.tirfonline.org/wp-content/uploads/2012/04/TIRF_EnglishAtWork_OnePageSpread_2012.pdf)

Rixon, S (2013) Survey of policy and practice in primary English language teaching worldwide. British Council from (www.teachingenglish.org.uk/publications/british-council-survey-policy-practice-primary-english-language-teaching-worldwide)

Trilling, B and Fadel, C, (2009) 21st Century Skills: Learning for Life in Our Times. Jossey-Bass

Chapter 2.7

The Role of International Collaboration in Developing Skilled Knowledge Workers – The Case of Kumasi Polytechnic

Nicholas NN Nsowah-Nuamah and Patricia G Owusu-Darko

Introduction

Polytechnics in Ghana are faced with challenges that threaten to impede their capability to effectively carry out their mandate as accented in the Ghanaian government's Polytechnics Act (Act 745). These challenges include low institutional image, low staff motivation, uncertain academic progression for students and low employability of the polytechnic graduate. Polytechnics in Ghana are mandated to train tertiary-level skilled manpower for development. Higher educational technical institutions have fostered collaborations with several international institutions of higher learning, yielding a number of mutual benefits.

Kumasi Polytechnic, since November, 2010, has engaged several international institutions of higher education in several levels of collaboration inuring to mutual benefits. Other polytechnics in Ghana have also started involving themselves in such collaborations

Students, graduates, staff, the local community, international partners and the polytechnics have directly benefited from the collaborations via an enhanced image of the polytechnic, staff mentoring, staff capacity building, joint programme delivery and positive impact on the community. Heightened interest by potential employees and partners – both local and

Going Global: Knowledge-Based Economies for 21st Century Nations
ISBN: 978-1-78441-003-2

international – has also been reported, while staff interest in professional and academic development has also heightened. Polytechnics in Ghana have made giant strides within a short time, which shows that international collaboration is, therefore, critical to developing quality polytechnics like Kumasi that are able to carry out their mandate.

Collaborations used synonymously with partnerships denote a form of mutually beneficial relationship, in which both parties have specific responsibilities and privileges. The Polytechnics Act, 2007 (Act 745), Section 34 accents the role of collaborations in the functioning of Polytechnic Councils. Collaborations at several levels could be forged with both private and public educational institutions (foreign or local), businesses, policy makers and others to ensure that polytechnics are equipped to carry out their mandate of training a highly skilled technical workforce, as illustrated in Figure 1. Collaborations could be between institutions, faculties or individuals for staff capacity building and retention, joint research opportunities and project delivery.

Requirements for collaborations include the profile of each partner institution This involves matters of accreditation, quality-assurance systems, infrastructure, institutional policies and staff profile (qualifications, experience and expertise).

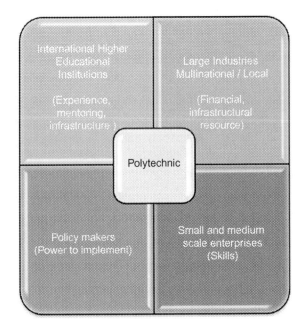

Figure 1: Collaboration matrix for polytechnics.

The Case of Ghanaian Polytechnics

The Polytechnics Act, 2007 (Act 745) of Ghana empowers Ghanaian poly-technics to train a highly skilled and competent workforce. In Section 4, sub-sections A and B, the objects of a polytechnic are to:

a) provide tertiary education in the fields of manufacturing, commerce, science and technology, applied social sciences, applied arts and any other field approved by the minister
b) provide opportunities for skills development, applied research and pub-lication of research findings.

Polytechnics in Ghana are therefore required to employ all available opportunities, resources, infrastructure and avenues to train skilled man-power for national development and to engage in applied research to solve specific problems. They are, therefore, expected to be involved in demand-driven activities that holistically impact national development through tertiary technical education and hands-on training in specific competencies for industry and commerce.

It is imperative to strategically furnish polytechnics financially and with appropriate infrastructure in order to develop staff capacity to enhance delivery of quality tertiary technical education that would ensure employ-ability of the graduates. This implies that the courses run at the polytech-nics must be dynamic and relevant to industry with value-added short courses, where applicable, to enhance the students' knowledge and impact the community. Figure 2 illustrates the ideal position of Ghanaian poly-technics to ensure the capability to carry out their mandate.

Current Position of Polytechnics in Ghana

The polytechnics in Ghana are faced with several challenges in the pursuit of their mandate. The main challenges are low institutional image, mini-mally motivated staff (leading to high staff turnover), uncertain academic progression of students and uncertain job placement for graduates, among others. The matrix of challenges can be seen in Figure 3.

The low institutional image of polytechnics stems from the fact that all polytechnics were previously post-secondary institutions that were hastily given elevated tertiary status in 1992 by the repealed Polytechnic Law 1992 (PNDC Law 321). The law mandated polytechnics to train middle-level personnel for the manpower needs of the country. The then post-secondary institutions were inadequately prepared in terms of human and infrastruc-ture resources to carry out the mandate. There had to be, as a matter of

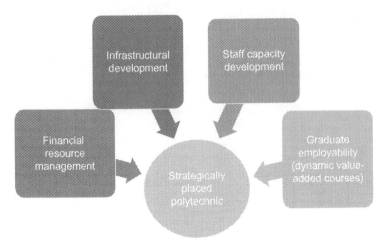

Figure 2: The ideal strategic position of polytechnics in Ghana.

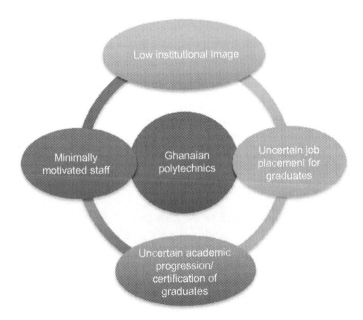

Figure 3: Matrix of challenges of polytechnics in Ghana.

urgency, a drastic staff development agenda coupled with the recruitment of new qualified personnel for certain positions to ensure that there was quality training and education for students who enrolled on the programmes. The staff turnover in polytechnics has been high due to the disparities in conditions of service between polytechnics and other tertiary institutions. Another major challenge of the polytechnics is the enrolment of students, as polytechnics have to compete with universities for prospective students. Since polytechnics offer Higher National Diplomas, they have ended up with students whose grades are marginal.

Students, after completing their Higher National Diploma (HND) at polytechnics, are uncertain about their academic progression, as the Technical Education Qualification framework is not clear. The academic progression from HND to Bachelor of Technology (BTech) to Master of Technology (MTech) and Doctor of Technology (DTech) is not a clear pathway and is impeded by the unwillingness of the National Council for Tertiary Education to allow polytechnics to run straight four-year programmes leading to a BTech qualification.

Job placements for polytechnic graduates is another challenge that polytechnics face. Employers are in a dilemma as to where to place the polytechnic graduate, whom they consider a poor cousin to the university graduate.

Collaboration as a Solution to Challenges of Polytechnics in Ghana

Collaboration can provide solutions to the challenges outlined above. The recipe for successfully attaining good collaboration can be seen in Figure 4.

Based on four major principles that drive the success of every partnership, collaboration must be mutually beneficial, sustainable and driven by strong commitment, trust and transparency from both partners. There

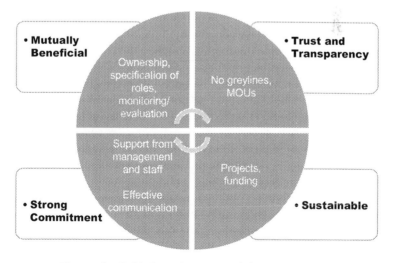

Figure 4: Guidelines for successful collaboration.

should be clarity of roles, responsibilities and privileges. A key requirement for successful collaboration is a team or an office dedicated to handling matters of collaboration and co-operation efficiently. Such a team forms the heartbeat of all institutional linkages. The team must be well resourced (both in personnel and infrastructure) to handle the volume of communication and daily workload. Staff in such an office must have a good understanding of cross-cultural issues, must be diligent and work tirelessly with elastic working hours and flexible deadlines. Initial activities that involve relationship building, and subsequently maintaining them, have serious cost implications. Activities should include staff exchange visits (foreign and local), the hosting of visitors (foreign and local), and the equipping of outfits to international office and communication standards.

The Benefits of Collaboration

The benefits of collaboration could be considered on four levels – to the partner institutions, to the staff, to the student or graduate and to the community (as can be seen in Figure 5).

Within the context of international collaborations, an appreciation of the strengths and cultures of partner institutions will ensure that

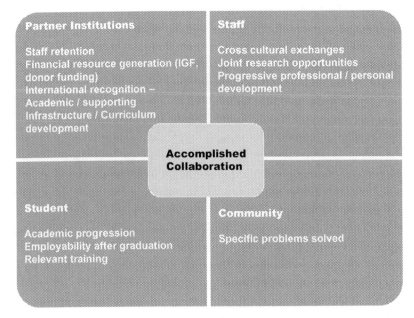

Figure 5: The benefits of collaboration.

polytechnics are able to impart technical and competency skills. Past collaborative projects have enabled partner institutions to exchange experiences in management, curricula development and delivery, assessment and quality assurance, and provide a healthy understanding of cross-cultural issues. International collaborations have resulted in human capacity building and the enhancement of infrastructure for the polytechnics and, for the partner institutions, an exchange of knowledge, ideas and methods, joint projects leading to joint authorship of manuscripts, cross-cultural exchanges and networks that last for long periods.

On the national front, the Council for Technical and Vocational Education and Training (COTVET), a body empowered by an Act of Parliament of Ghana to co-ordinate and oversee all aspects of technical and vocational education and training in the country, has mutually beneficial developmental partners such as the African Development Bank, Danish International Development Agency (DANIDA), Japan International Cooperation Agency (JICA) and the World Bank, with collaborating partners such as City and Guilds for skills development, the Mauritius Qualification Authority, the College of Haringey, Enfield, the North East London Tottenham Centre and John Hopkins University. These collaborations have positioned COTVET strategically as the supervisory body for the impartation of competency skills and cutting-edge technology in technical HE institutions including polytechnics.

Partners in the NUFFIC NPT 045 project (Netherlands organisation for international cooperation in higher education), a collaboration between higher education institutions in Ghana and the Netherlands, witnessed a number of mutual benefits. The polytechnics benefited by capacity building and infrastructure enhancement, senior and middle management were trained in leadership, some teaching staff were supported to pursue master's and PhD programmes, and computer laboratories were equipped with computers and accessories. The partners, meanwhile, gathered data for relevant research and had valuable cross-cultural experiences.

The Story of Kumasi Polytechnic

In compliance with Section 5 of the Polytechnics Act, under Powers of a Polytechnic (sub-section D), which states: 'A polytechnic may exercise powers that are incidental to the performance of the object and functions of a polytechnic,' Kumasi Polytechnic has identified certain partner institutions of higher learning in other parts of the world whose faculty, expertise, equipment and technology would enhance the quality of training given to the students. Since November 2010, the polytechnic has embarked on activities to foster relationships and collaborations with them, including staff exchange visits, the hosting of world-class professors, the sourcing of funds for scholarships and grants, joint proposals and projects. Table 1 summarises Kumasi Polytechnic's international collaborations and the corresponding benefits.

With the successful collaborations indicated in Table 1, the Kumasi Polytechnic is in discussions with more institutions to carry out project specific collaborations that would inure to the benefit of both partners. The Universities of Portsmouth and Dundee both in UK; Southern Polytechnic State University in the US, University of Johannesburg in South Africa, University of Port Haecourt in Nigeria and University of Koudougou in Burkina Faso are potential partners with whom discussions are being held.

Benefits to Kumasi Polytechnic

The staff exchange has exposed our faculty to modern technologies and techniques. The faculty is expected to benefit from global perspectives, which are necessary for good performance in numerous fields. Another benefit of collaborations with foreign institutions of higher learning is scholarship opportunities for staff development and capacity building, as can be seen in Figure 6. The cost of training a PhD student abroad is between US$15,000 and US$40,000 per academic year. This could be a drain on the scant financial resources of the polytechnic. With collaboration, Kumasi Polytechnic has increased staff capacity development dramatically. There was a 260 per cent increase in the numbers of staff pursuing their PhD abroad on scholarship in the 2010/11 and 2011/12 academic years (collaboration period), as compared to 2008/09 and 2009/10.

With the enhanced image of Kumasi Polytechnic gained via collaboration, there has been a significant increase in applications for employment and a subsequent recruitment of highly qualified staff (Figure 7), including expatriates. The polytechnic has a team of qualified, highly motivated staff, including 20 PhD holders and three professors – one on sabbatical from a highly respected university in Ghana and a full-time expatriate.

The collaboration has resulted in an increase in books and equipment at the polytechnic and has gone a long way to addressing the critical problem of equipment and teaching aid deficit.

Exchange visits of world-class professors to Kumasi Polytechnic have resulted in mentoring, staff motivation and the streamlining of academic activities. Among the benefits of these collaborative visits have been the revision of curricula, the drafting and presentation of proposals for funding, the definition of research and conference activities, and the creation of a basis for the start of a PhD programme at the polytechnic.

Table 1: Kumasi Polytechnic international collaborations.

Collaboration institutions	Nature of partnership	Benefits to Kumasi Polytechnic	Benefit to partner organisation
Glasgow Caledonian University, UK	Joint projects and joint curriculum development; staff/student exchange; staff capacity building	Donation of library books and laboratory equipment	Specific projects in different locations in Ghana; cross-cultural exposure
Hertfordshire University, UK	Joint projects; staff and student exchange, staff capacity building; curriculum development	Staff invited to witness international fashion projects	Exchange of good practice; international exposure, exchange of curricula
Hackney Community College, UK	Joint projects; staff capacity building; curriculum development	Capacity development of senior and middle management	Exchange of best practices; cross-cultural exchange
The Royal Environmental Health Institute of Scotland (REHIS)	Accredited centre for delivery of courses	Donation of training materials; income generation; impact to trainees	Extension of activities/training programmes of REHIS in Africa
Jiangsu University, China	Joint delivery of programmes; staff and student exchange; staff capacity building	Award of five PhD scholarships	Exchange of best practices; student exchange; cross-cultural exchange
Business College of Shanxi University (China)	Joint delivery of programmes; establishment of Chinese Language and Culture Centre; staff and student exchange Staff capacity building	Award of scholarship for Chinese language training; sending of Chinese language teachers to teach at Kumasi Polytechnic	Exchange of best practices; staff exchange; cross-cultural exchange; opportunity to introduce Chinese language to Ghanaians

Table 1: (*Continued*)

Collaboration institutions	Nature of partnership	Benefits to Kumasi Polytechnic	Benefit to partner organisation
Yangtze University, China	Joint delivery of programmes; staff and student exchange; staff capacity building	Award of five PhD scholarships	Exchange of best practices; cross-cultural exchange
Wuhan University of Technology, China	Joint delivery of programmes; student and staff exchange; staff capacity building	Award of two PhD scholarships	Exchange of best practices; cross-cultural exchange
Solbridge International College of Business (WOOSONG University), South Korea	Joint delivery of programmes;; student and staff exchange	Income generation from part of tuition fees	Exchange of best practices; cross-cultural exchange
University of Electronic Science and Technology of China	Staff capacity building; technology transfer	Award of two PhD scholarships	Exchange of best practices; cross-cultural exchange
South Connecticut State University, USA	Joint delivery of programmes; joint projects	Donation of library books	Exchange of best practices; cross-cultural exchange

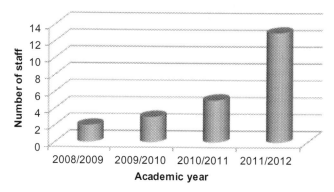

Figure 6: Members of staff pursuing PhDs abroad on scholarship over a four-year period (2008–2012).

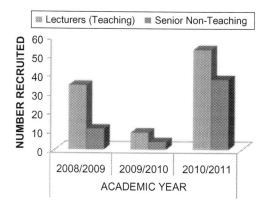

Figure 7: Staff recruitment over a three-year period (2008–2011).

These collaborations have exposed Kumasi Polytechnic to the outside world, and the polytechnic has been receiving a number of offers for collaborations with other institutions. In fact, the overall result of the colla-boration is an increase in image building. The collaborative programmes are targeting the entire West African sub-region and already the polytech-nic is receiving applications from students from the **Economic Community Of West African States** (ECOWAS) region. With its enhanced image, the first series of short courses organised by the polytechnic in the summer of 2012 was highly patronised by the public. The courses, ranging in duration from two days to four weeks, were well attended and led to an increase in internally generated funds.

Benefits to the Students

Students who enrol on collaborative programmes at Kumasi Polytechnic can be assured of completing the first degree in four years under a special two-plus-two arrangement, where the student studies for two years in Ghana and then continues to the partner institution in China, the USA or Korea to complete their studies. The students gain from the highly equipped and technologically advanced foreign institutions in the areas of engineering, science, technology and commerce. They are exposed to the state-of-the-art technology and hands-on training, thus enhancing their versatility and making them more employable in the job market. Through the collaborations, students in partner institutions could also benefit from cultural exchanges. The overall cost of having the entire training overseas is higher, so to make such training affordable and accessible to most students, the two-plus-two system is used.

Benefits to the Community

Kumasi Polytechnic is also a centre of excellence for running courses accredited by the Royal Environmental Health Institute of Scotland (REHIS), a food standards body with worldwide recognition. The polytechnic lecturers have been trained and accredited by REHIS and Kumasi Polytechnic has, therefore, been organising training (with high patronage) in food hygiene and safety, and food and health for small, medium and large-scale food handlers.

The collaboration with JICA, meanwhile, has resulted in the invention of a solar-powered wheelchair and a[1] fufu-pounding machine. Collaborative projects with some other international partner institutions have given rise to the Solar Dryer Project, the Ethanol Project and the incorporation of the Centre for Renewable Energy. These projects will benefit the farming and other rural communities in Ghana.

Benefits to the Partner Institutions

As can be seen in Table 1, the partner institutions also benefit in the areas of cross-cultural exposure, exchange of good practice, joint execution of projects and joint authorship of manuscripts. Available data and

---

1. Fufu is a local dish, which is manually pounded and this invention is a big relief for most communities in Ghana.

environments also provide a unique opportunity for academics to undertake projects and provide a good cross-cultural experience for members of staff who otherwise would not experience other countries.

Conclusion

The role of international collaboration in expanding the frontiers of acquiring knowledge in the face of global competition cannot be overemphasised. Through mutually beneficial collaborations, high-quality technical education and training can reach as many people as possible. The polytechnics will develop a highly skilled workforce, competent and ready for the demands of the job market – which is the mandate of the polytechnics. The polytechnics in Ghana have made giant strides as a result of international collaborations with overseas partners. Partner institutions have also benefited. Collaboration is critical to developing polytechnics like Kumasi Polytechnic in ensuring quality while carrying out their mandate.

References

COTVET (2004) TVET Policy, Accra
Polytechnics Act (2007) Act 745, Ghana Government
African Unit (2010) Good Practices in Educational Partnerships Guide. UK–Africa Higher and Further Education Partnerships.
COTVET (2011) Manual for Workplace Learning, Accra
Kumasi Polytechnic (2011) Statutes of Kumasi Polytechnic, Kumasi
Kumasi Polytechnic (2011b) Rector's 7th Congregation Report, Kumasi
Kumasi Polytechnic (2013) Rector's 8th Congregation Report, Kumasi
Kumasi Polytechnic's Memoranda of Understanding (MOUs) with partner institutions

Chapter 2.8

UK Occupational Competency and Academic Learning – An International Anathema?

Sue Parker

Introduction

Much has been written about the issue of graduate unemployment and the lack of graduate preparedness to join the labour market. This paper reviews the role of higher education institutions (HEIs) in preparing students for the labour market, the changing relationship between HEIs and industry in the area of skills development, and the mechanisms and structures required for international coherence. There is no doubt that more could be done to create new forms of higher education relevant to specific nations, but cultural traditions underpinning the format and delivery of HE and employment may make the use of international standards problematic. However, more could still be done to create flexible approaches to skills portability and mobility.

Are University Education and Higher Skills Development Compatible?

Few would disagree that higher education is the driver of economic development and is instrumental in global prosperity and productivity. The OECD reported in 2012 that without proper investment into higher education and skills, people 'languish on the margins of society,

Going Global: Knowledge-Based Economies for 21st Century Nations
ISBN: 978-1-78441-003-2

technological progress does not translate into economic growth and countries can no longer compete in an increasingly knowledge-based global society.' (p. 3)

HEIs play a critical role in developing and fostering talent. They provide an environment for creativity to flourish, they produce and accumulate human capital, new ideas, information and technology, and they provide cutting-edge research so that a nation can develop its competitive edge. Governments call on universities to facilitate the shift to a knowledge-based economy and technology to ensure productivity and prosperity in the global market. A forward-looking higher education system is, therefore, critical for preparing a competent workforce. However, the CBI's *Tomorrows Growth* report argues that relying alone on traditional university courses will not meet the growing demand for higher skills'[1]. The default route of an academic undergraduate degree is not suitable for young people with different talents who learn in different ways. In other words, HEIs should work hand in hand with the private sector to meet the demand for higher skills.

The shift of emphasis to talk about 'skills development' rather than 'technical and vocational education and training' (TVET) is helpful. In the late 20th century, the term vocational was hijacked and the acronym 'TVET'[2] emerged, becoming a proxy for non-academic, craft and technical-level training in many developed nations. It was primarily associated with a supply-led system, dictating the mode of learning and the pathways to be followed[3]. The focus of TVET on basic education led to its neglect and exclusion from the UN Millennium Development Goals.[4]

---

1. Skills and skills development have become 'buzzwords' meaning different things to different people and groups. Employers may refer to the 'right' skills. A skill is the learned ability to carry out activities to achieve a pre-determined result with minimum outlay – i.e., is an attribute possessed by an individual.
2. Technical and Vocational Education and Training is defined as '*Those aspects of the educational process involving, in addition to general education, the study of technologies and related sciences, and the acquisition of practical skills, attitudes, understanding and knowledge relating to occupants in various sectors of economic and social life*' (UNESCO, 1999).
3. Vocational education and training prepares individuals for specific trades, crafts and careers at various levels from trade, craft or technician or a professional position in, for example, engineering, accountancy, medicine, law or architecture. TVET is largely characterised by procedural knowledge – learning by doing – rather than declarative knowledge – typified by abstract and concepts – in other words, an understanding of how to do something without actually doing it.
4. Perhaps one reason for this is that TVET is characterised by procedural knowledge – learning by doing – rather than declarative knowledge – characterised by abstract and concepts – in other words, an understanding of how to do something without actually doing it.

The focus on skills development alters the relationship between HEI provision and the labour market. Skills development serves industry, focusing on specialist and soft skills needed by economies now and in the future.[5] It is normally based on national occupational standards (NOS)[6] or occupational definitions[7]. Skills development may also encompass professional education[8], bridging TVET and higher learning. HEIs often, of course, work closely with professional bodies and administer their examinations, but traditionally there has been limited involvement in the definition or use of occupational standards by professional bodies. Professional bodies define standards that are regulated and must be met in order for an individual to be admitted into a profession (which may include across borders). National occupational standards have many uses[9] but are rarely a requirement for entry into a job[10].

Anticipated changes to occupational structure in the UK means that by 2020 nearly half of all employment will be in highly skilled roles[11]. However, successfully delivering the skills for the 2020 knowledge economy will depend on producing the right number of graduates with the right

---

5. See also the 2012 World Bank initiative – Skills Toward Employment and Productivity (STEP) survey, which will generate new, internationally comparable data on adult workers' skills, covering cognitive, technical, behavioural and social skills.
6. NOS are defined by the UK Commission for Employment and Skills in the UK as the 'measurable performance outcomes an individual is expected to reach in a given occupation'. Other nations may have different names and definitions, but all are associated with competent performance in a given job role.
7. The most commonly used definition is the International Standard Classification of Occupations (ISCO) administered by the International Labour Organisation (ILO) www.ilo.org/public/english/bureau/stat/isco/isco88/ ISCO organises jobs into clearly defined groups according to the tasks and duties undertaken in each job. It is intended for use in a variety of client applications, includes the matching of job seekers with job vacancies, the management of short- or long-term migration of workers between countries, the preparation of national occupational standards and the development of training programmes and guidance. In principle, this should form the bedrock of any international standard for skills development or occupationally relevant qualifications.
8. A 'profession' may be defined as a vocation founded upon specialised training, bounded by codes of conduct and standards, with formal qualifications, examinations and assessment. This is normally regulated by a professional body, which admits successful candidates into that profession.
9. 115 uses have been identified in the UK http://clients.squareeye.net/uploads/dea/documents/uses_of_standard.pdf
10. The exception would be in a nation such as Australia, where national occupational skills standards form the basis of training packages defined and used by specific industries. In Scotland, a NOS unit directly forms a qualification unit.
11. The 2010 Report *Ambition 2020: World Class Skills and Jobs for the UK: Key Findings and Implications for Action.* UKCES, 2010.

knowledge, competencies and qualities. An effective balance needs to be found between delivering sufficient graduates with the right professional skills (such as engineers, statisticians and lawyers) to drive the economy and specialist skills to innovate (such as technologists, entrepreneurs) but still enable talented thinkers who wish to develop their wider intellectual capacity to do so.

The UK position is typical: nations at different stages of development show that where systems of education focus on producing largely academic graduates, governments and employers have to find ways to train them in skills post-graduation so that they can contribute in an increasingly competitive global marketplace.

As an example, in India, a recent report[12] concluded that 47 per cent of graduates are not employable for any industry role. Their lack of English-language knowledge and cognitive skills[13,14] were identified as major obstacles in job suitability[14]. China has rapidly expanded higher education, with around seven million graduating in 2013. However, where jobs are available, employers report that too many graduates have a poor attitude, unrealistic expectations and largely theoretical knowledge.[15] In 2012, although Canada continued to top the list of all OECD countries for skills, with 51 per cent of its adult population holding a post-secondary degree or diploma, one in four young people under the age of 30 with a university degree is currently employed full-time in a job that does not require that level of education[16].

In the developing world, Uganda has invested heavily in university education, but statistics indicate that although institutions produce 400,000 graduates annually, only 20 per cent gain meaningful jobs. The rest are unemployed or underemployed. Job creation has not gone hand in hand with skills development, creating a social and demographic challenge as more youth enter the labour market annually, but cannot be absorbed. Indonesia's policy is to produce as many graduates as possible, but it views their quality as of secondary importance. Many are, therefore, unprepared

---

12. Aspiring Minds Employability Report on Indian Graduates, September 2013.

13. Cognitive skills – the ability to process thoughts and new information.

14. For example, only 25 per cent of the graduating students could apply concepts to solve a real-world problem in the domain of finance and accounting but 50 per cent of graduates could answer theoretical questions based on the same concept. This shows that even though students have exposure to concepts, they really do not understand them or know how to apply them.

15. BBC China report by Martin Patience, 7 August 2013.

16. www5.statcan.gc.ca/subjectsujet/subthemeoustheme.action?pid = 2621&id = 2624&lang = eng&more = 0

to compete for employment in Indonesia; job vacancies for HEI graduates are low[17]. Malaysia also faces high graduate unemployment rates (26.7 per cent in 2009). Malaysia and the Philippines have an over-supply of graduates in some fields, leading to many who cannot find jobs in their specialisation. There is therefore an over-supply of nurses and information technologists in the Philippines, addressed in part by migration. Lack of work experience, particularly in the IT sector, limits graduate employment prospects.

Faced with these difficulties, many graduates end up underemployed or employed in areas for which they were not trained. Furthermore, if they wish to migrate to gain employment and use their skills at the right level elsewhere, they may find themselves being de-skilled and going into low-level jobs such as housemaids or carpenters, often with no training[18]. This trend is reflected across Asia.

So, provision of higher skills through state-supported HEIs may be falling short of what is required and there is widespread international evidence that education institutions are not providing alumni with the right skills for employment. Meeting the skills development challenge will require different routes into higher-skill roles, particularly technical pathways, for both young people and experienced workers. Employers may, therefore, attempt to fill gaps by providing in-house training. Although beneficial to those who receive it – since it is fully aligned to industry needs – rarely is employer training based on national occupational standards, and it can be narrowly focused, have limited impact in the wider economy and rarely attract formal recognition. Thus, the skills developed may have limited or no portability. Whether at the strategic or training delivery level, skills development needs to be undertaken in partnership with the state, with each party recognising the strengths and responsibilities of the other. It also points to a need for HEI programmes to focus more specifically on 'skilling' graduates.

How do Academic Standards and Occupational Standards Differ?

Based on competency,[19] NOS offer transferability between organisations with similar occupations and between occupations with similar skills

---

17. Indonesian Ministry of Manpower and Transmigration.
18. See page 7.
19. Behaviours that employees must have or acquire to achieve high levels of performance, as defined by CIPD, 2008.

requirements. Introduced into the UK in 1986, their overall purpose was to improve the match between vocational qualifications and the skills that employers required, and to help employers make sense of a confusing array of qualifications. NOS are now offered in over 80 nations and the numbers are growing.

In 1997, the National Council for Vocational Qualifications (NCVQ) in England reviewed the definition of knowledge and skills by industry sectors (i.e. in National Vocational Qualifications – NVQs) against those defined by higher education institutions. The reports concluded there were substantial gaps in the knowledge and skills specified in NVQs, which were substantially different to higher education qualifications. Although some assessment methods commonly used in higher education could conceivably generate evidence to assess competency in NVQs, they did not meet the criteria for NVQs. However, Roodhouse and Hemsworth (2004) mapped NOS against university qualifications and found subject areas where NOS had been used directly or indirectly, although by 2009 there was little evident synergy between HEI standards (including professional) and NOS.

Academic standards are distinguished from occupational standards since they follow a progressive accumulation of knowledge, understanding and skills, rather than a systematic description of occupational tasks, functions and associated competences. Across Europe, differences are evident in the objects of academic standardisation (duration of programmes, teaching content and methods) with countries granting varying autonomy to local authorities, training providers and teachers to design and undertake learning programmes. Evidence suggests that the diversity of national approaches to setting academic standards reflect cultural norms and, in particular, flexibility in the way in which objectives embedded in standards are achieved, despite some moves to a common approach through the European Higher Education Area designed to ensure more comparable, compatible and coherent systems of higher education in Europe. The only trends evident are that more countries are introducing outcome-based standards and are at the same time institutionalising the participation of social partners in standard-setting.

Although limited in scope, these trends are important as they underline the need for a common language bridging education/training and work, and for balanced participation in standard-setting for individual programmes, both of which are pre-conditions for increasing the relevance and credibility of qualifications. However, this is not the same as the development of international standards and may be the only realistic solution to internationalising skills in a situation characterised by rapid change in occupations and qualifications.

Enabling Frameworks or Enforcing Structures?

To address issues of skills development, portability and labour mobility, National Qualifications Frameworks (NQFs) and the associated systems and processes that support them are being developed in over 120 countries. Evident in every continent, they are outcome-based referencing structures introduced to encourage skills progression and to support economic goals. They are often blunt policy instruments for governments wishing for systems reform, including internal recognition of qualifications in a globalised labour market. Most NQFs define qualifications in terms of the knowledge and skills required, ranked according to a single hierarchy of levels. The majority of NQFs also include applied qualifications and measure competency; for example, in the workplace (sometimes defined as the product of skills + knowledge + attitudes and behaviours).

Although early NQFs (such as in the UK, New Zealand, Australia and Ireland) covered large, primarily vocational qualifications, driven by a need to improve market responsiveness, recent NQFs have been overarching, embracing all education and training within a single, integrated system. Some established NQFs, such as the New Zealand National Qualifications Framework (NZNQF), now include general and higher education. NZNQF was possibly the first integrated system. Integrated NQFs have fairly complex quality-assurance systems and assessment processes, but it is relatively easy to recognise and put value on previous learning, credit accumulation and transfer at all levels. Focusing on NQFs as enablers rather than enforcing structures has enabled the successful introduction of outcome-based qualifications with a greater emphasis on acquisition of skills in HEIs in the United Arab Emirates.

NQFs have also been referenced across borders – the European Qualifications Framework (EQF), the ASEAN Framework and the Arab Qualifications Framework (for the Gulf and MENA) enable transnational labour market mobility. There is, however, only limited evidence that NQFs achieve the economic goals, employability and improvements in labour market mobility expected of them[20], and this lies behind current moves to develop global recognition systems that simplify articulation processes.

Where they are based on bilateral or multilateral agreements, NQFs can provide referencing, especially when linked to 'mutual recognition schemes', developed at a global level. They are seen as crucial in supporting, for

---

20. See ILO research on NQFs: www.ilo.org/wcmsp5/groups/public/@ed_emp/@ifp_skills/documents/meetingdocument/wcms_126589.pdf

example, skills development for migrant workers.[21] One example is the 'Small States of the Commonwealth' NQF, which supports mobility between small, largely Pacific, nations. The new Indian Skills Qualifications Framework and the emerging Pakistan NQF will be of value for migrant workers who can have skills assessed before migrating, and on return to their home nation. There is therefore a specific emerging link between skills and job matching, and skills acquisition in a destination country. Migration is such an important phenomenon – for example, remittances represent 8.5 per cent of the wealth of the Philippines – that the role of HEIs in the development and implementation of NQFs and mutual recognition schemes must be reviewed in conjunction with the debate around underpinning international standards.

Do International Standards Help in Skills Matching for Migration?

Skills under-matching and de-skilling at all levels in the economy have been identified as obstacles to optimising the benefits of labour migration for development. However, skills under-matching does not automatically equate with de-skilling. New higher-level skills can be acquired that are in demand in the origin country or can be used to support reintegration (for example, project management, financial/business management skills, language skills). Despite its role in economic development, higher education rarely plays a role in migration and development[22] in countries of origin

---

21. *Global mutual recognition schemes: UNESCO's 6 Regional Conventions on the Recognition of Qualifications* (Africa, Arab States, Asia and Pacific, Latin America and the Caribbean, and two European conventions) and one inter-regional convention (Mediterranean Convention) are aimed at promoting mutual recognition of academic qualifications for academic purposes and diplomas for professional purposes. They are at different stages of development and implementation. They do not seem to adequately cover lower level skills, and may not even be keeping pace with new qualifications, new providers and the latest forms of education delivery. It is also not yet clear how they are facilitating cross-border skills mobility.

22. International migration in the development context relates both to people who have chosen to move of their own accord, and forced migrants who may ultimately end up contributing to both their country of resettlement and possibly their country of origin if it is ever safe to return. Development, meanwhile, is a dynamic process implying growth, advancement, empowerment and progress, with the goal of increasing human capabilities, enlarging the scope of human choices, and creating a safe and secure environment where citizens can live with dignity and equality. In the development process, it is important that people's productivity, creativity and choices are broadened, and that opportunities are created. Maximising the positive relationship between migration and development is especially relevant now, in this era of unprecedented mobility. www.iom.int/cms/en/sites/iom/home/what-we-do/migration–development-1.html

and destination. Several nations have adjusted their national higher education programmes to offer internationally recognised opportunities for pre-professional roles in sectors where there are skills shortages in higher-income countries, including hospitality, care-giving, nursing, teaching (India,[23] Philippines[24], Jamaica,[25] South Africa respectively). However, some of the schemes have had problems, largely because of misplaced expectations on the part of one or both countries.

If there are no national occupational standards, countries sourcing labour may train and certify worker competency against International Standard Classification of Occupation (ISCO) international standards for an employment visa. These include Mauritius–Canada/France, Senegal–France and Colombia–Spain[26]. In the Philippines, occupational standards could impact on remittances sent back to the origin country. Filipinos account for around 30 per cent of all seafarers globally, sending around US$300 million (12.9 billion pesos) a year in remittances. If the Portugal-based European Maritime Safety Agency found that Philippine training standards did not meet international SCTW standards, the loss of Filipino jobs in this sector would affect the 25 per cent of remittances received by the Philippines from seafarers.[27]

So, there are no commonly agreed frameworks or standards for international standards or recognition schemes for skills acquisition. The major challenge in skills development and qualification reform is, therefore, to develop a more inclusive, flexible, accessible and transparent system that does not undermine quality and credibility. With this in mind, the ILO's SKILLS-AP programme and HRD Korea[28] initiated in 2006 a project to recognise the newly acquired skills of migrant workers. This led to the development and endorsement of the Regional Model Competency Standards (RMCS) to guide skills assessment and recognition across the Asia–Pacific region.

---

23. In India, City and Guilds has signed an agreement with Manipal Education, one of India's largest education providers, to deliver training through IndiaSkills.
24. Japan–Philippines and Japan–Indonesia Economic Partnership Agreements.
25. A scheme training nurses in Jamaica for the Canadian market was halted in 2011, since three years after the scheme was launched the vast majority of those trained were still in Jamaica, having paid significant fees to be trained.
26. See papers presented to Global Forum on Migration Development www.gfmd.org/en/
27. Report from *Sun Star Manila*, December 04 2011.
28. www.ilo.org/asia/whatwedo/events/WCMS_099936/lang–en/index.htm.

Conclusions

Could or should, therefore, international occupational standards be used to define knowledge and performance requirements aligned to economic development goals in higher education programmes? Would this support movement of highly trained, intelligent human capital to where it is needed? Should different approaches be taken to internationalise skills development at all levels? Is intervention by industry needed in HEIs to marry competency with academic learning? Given most occupations have much the same performance criteria regardless of location, is this best achieved through international collaboration – and, if so, how?

This paper asks as many further questions as it answers. Autonomous HEIs develop degree programmes based on an academic approach, only loosely related to industry needs and occupational requirements. Emphasis on research, driven by national and international university rankings, may have a negative effect on competency-based degrees, which train people to do as well as to think. Although national occupational standards and national qualifications frameworks in principle provide mechanisms for HEIs to build competency-based programmes, there is limited synergy between so-called skills development routes and academic programmes that truly drive national productivity and global competitiveness. Equally, across the migration spectrum, migration policy frameworks should not only assure legality of status, but also include enablers, whereby migrants gain skills and experience that enable them to develop and progress socioeconomically, in both origin and receiving countries. Although applying occupational standards across nations to address specific training issues where it is essential there are international norms, such as in aviation or seafaring, human capital development largely benefits from bilateral agreements associated with specific labour mobility (such as nurses from the Philippines) or broad recognition agreements, rather than trying to manipulate a generic international standard to meet cultures or traditions in a given nation.

Given the problems of agreeing common standards, what is the role of higher education in skills development, skills matching and skills recognition? Within nations, and outside the complexity of migration, much still needs to be done. It is incumbent on HEIs as the creators of new knowledge and cutting-edge technologies to work with industry to ensure that human capital matches these. However, unless young people have had exposure to new and creative ways of learning and experimenting while still at school, insufficient skills-savvy human capital will materialise in the national system.

To address the system-wide skills deficit some nations, such as the UK (RPA)[29] and the Philippines[30], have raised the age of participation in learning, introducing new TVET or skills development routes into higher-level skills, including (in England) apprenticeships. University Technical Colleges (UTCs) have also been opened to encourage a positive choice of academic with practical learning[31] leading into practically focused higher education. There are also proposals for the re-introduction of a limited number of polytechnics (which still operate successfully in competitive countries such as New Zealand and Finland[32]) – to offer alternatives routes into higher education. Modern NQFs facilitate transferability across academic and skills routes – since the knowledge required at a given level is the same – but it is how knowledge is used which defines whether a qualification is academic or skills-based. Furthermore, graduates would benefit from taking diplomas and skill development programmes alongside their degrees to make them far more employment-ready, so blending pure academia and skills.

Although it may be impossible for cultural reasons to define common international standards, whether academic or occupational, the pressing need for skills portability and labour mobility remains. HEIs, working with employers and governments, must find ways to introduce and mutually recognise skills, informed by up-to-date national occupational standards, so crucial for economic development, national prosperity and competitiveness.

---

29. This is not the same as raising the school leaving age – young people may be in school, college or employment with training or an apprenticeship, www.education.gov.uk/childrenandyoungpeople/youngpeople/participation/rpa
30. The Enhanced Basic Education Act, 2013, www.gov.ph/2013/09/04/irr-republic-act-no-10533/
31. www.utcolleges.org/
32. Lessons can also be learned from Finland, which introduced a dual higher education system in the 1990s to stem rising unemployment and economic decline. The government set out to double participation in higher education and to transform and upgrade skills education. It amalgamated vocational colleges to create 22 polytechnics (*Ammattikorkeakoulut – AMK*) alongside 20 traditional universities. By 2000 there were 29 *AMKs* enrolling 58 per cent of all new higher education students, which focus on skills-based education and the training of 'high-quality experts in working life'. The four-year AMK courses lead to a bachelors-level degree, as opposed to the five-year master's offered at universities. They aid regional development, as many AMKs are owned by municipalities, and there is co-operation with small and medium-sized enterprises. According to a 2003 review by the OECD, the policy was 'remarkably successful'. AMKs offer about 150 degree programmes in seven broad sectors of study.

References

'Better Skills, Better Jobs, Better Lives, A Strategic Approach to Skills Policies', OECD May 2012.

Creating prosperity: the role of higher education in the UK's creative economy. EKOS Consultants on behalf of Universities UK, December 2010.

Graduate Employment in Asia, UNESCO, 2012.

Tomorrow's Growth: new routes to higher skills Confederation of British Industry, July 2013.

Hopkins, L and Levy, C, Shaping Up for Innovation: are we delivering the right skills for the 2020 knowledge economy?

The Work Foundation, University of Lancaster, September 2010.

Engaging the Private Sector in Skills Development, DfID Guidance Note, 2010.

Hartl, M, Technical and vocational education and training (TVET) and skills development for poverty reduction − do rural women benefit? International Fund for Agricultural Development, Italy, 2009.

The 2010 Report Ambition 2020: World Class Skills and Jobs for the UK: Key Findings and Implications for Action. UKCES, 2010.

Aspiring Minds Employability Report on Indian Graduates, September 2013.

Education at a Glance, OECD, 2013.

Promoting Inclusive Growth in Uganda, World Bank, February 2012

Education at a Glance, OECD, 2013.

Graduate Employment in Asia, UNESCO, 2012

Parker, S, Desk top study on international approaches to standards, UKCES, January 2009.

Higher-level vocational qualifications: Workshops: HVQs, SVQs and higher education, NCVQ, August 1997.

Higher-level vocational qualifications − case studies, NCVQ, August 1997.

Roodhouse, S and Hemsworh, D, A Higher Education Context for National Occupational Standards, University Vocational Awards Council, October 2004.

Parker, S, Review of National Occupational Standards − Outcomes of Stage 1 Consultation − prepared for UKCES as part of a wide-ranging review of the use, purpose and future of National Occupational Standards.

The dynamics of qualifications: defining and renewing occupational and educational standards, Cedefop, 2009 (www.ehea.info/).

Young, MFD (2003) 'National Qualifications Frameworks as a Global Phenomenon: a comparative perspective', Journal of Education and Work, Vol. 16, No. 3 (updated by Sue Parker − see reference below).

Parker, S, Qualifications for a world class, progressive, education and skills system, ANQAHE, December 2011.

Parker, S, ibid 2011 www.col.org/PublicationDocuments/pub_VUSSC_Transnational QualificationsFramework_April2010_web.pdf.

Parker, S, Beyond-the-Border Skills and Jobs for Human Development paper prepared for Roundtable 1.1, Global Forum for Migration Development, Mauritius, November 2012.

Appleton, S, Sives, A and Morgan, WJ, The impact of international teacher migration on schooling in developing countries — the case of Southern Africa, School of Economics, University of Nottingham, UK; School of Politics and Communication Studies, University of Liverpool.

SCTW— Standards of Training, Certification and Watching-keeping — the Institute of Maritime reports 113 signatories.

Holzmann, R and Pouget-Hirschegg, V (2011). Admission Schemes for Foreign Workers: A Labour Market Tool for National Economic Development, p. 8.

Vertovec, S, (2007) Circular Migration: the way forward in global policy? Institute of Migration, University of Oxford. (First appeared in 'Around the Globe', a publication of the Monash Institute for Study of Global Movements, Australia).

Parker, S (2012) Beyond-the-Border Skills and Jobs for Human Development paper prepared for Round Table 1.1, Global Forum for Migration Development, Mauritius.

A critical path: securing the future of higher education in England, Institute of Public Policy Research (IPPR) Commission on the Future of Higher Education, June 2013.

Chapter 2.9

The UK Higher Education Outward Mobility Programme: A National Strategy for Increasing the Proportion of UK Students Accessing International Opportunities

Joanna Newman

Introduction

Currently, just one UK student studies abroad for every 15 international students in the UK – and the UK lags behind Spain, France, Germany, Italy and Poland in accessing the European Commission's Erasmus funding for study or work placements. Financial, linguistic and non-recognition of qualifications are some of the barriers that deter students in the UK from gaining valuable international experience, with worrying implications for the cultural understanding and long-term employability of the country's graduates.

The UK Outward Student Mobility Strategy was launched in July 2013 and aims to boost the number of students gaining vital international experience from overseas study and work placements, allowing them to compete in the global race for jobs and skills. The strategy was developed following close consultation with the UK higher education sector and is funded by the UK government. The UK Higher Education International Unit (IU), which promotes and supports all UK higher education institutions and

Going Global: Knowledge-Based Economies for 21st Century Nations
Copyright © 2014 by Joanna Newman
All rights of reproduction in any form reserved
ISBN: 978-1-78441-003-2

universities in developing international opportunities, runs the Outward Mobility Programme on behalf of the sector.

This paper explores the background and drivers to the development of the strategy and outlines the strategic aims for the programme, how best practice will be shared and how the impact of a national strategy will be evaluated.

Why a National Strategy?

With the introduction of tuition fees in 1998, UK students taking a year abroad as part of their studies under the Erasmus programme did not have to pay fees to their home institution while overseas. In 2011, with the introduction of higher tuition fees for UK students, the UK government proposed the removal of this fee waiver for Erasmus[1] students. Universities and higher education institutions were concerned that the prospect of paying up to £9,000 per year would dissuade students from taking four-year degrees and have a negative effect on the country's already comparatively low take-up of study and work placements abroad. Universities contacted the UK Higher Education International Unit (IU) to raise their concerns, which were shared by the IU's Chair, Professor Colin Riordan, Vice-Chancellor of Cardiff University. The UK Higher Education IU flagged the concerns of the UK HE sector to government in a paper to the Rt Hon David Willetts, Minister for Universities and Science, with evidence from higher education and sector organisations on the importance of retaining the fee waiver. The minister recognised the serious concerns of the sector and agreed to maintain the Erasmus fee waiver for UK students, but he was also concerned by the wider issues around outward student mobility highlighted in the paper, and asked the IU to investigate further.

In response, the IU set up a Joint Steering Group on Outward Mobility and, within that, established expert groups to discuss the particular challenges facing outward student mobility and the take-up of overseas study and work abroad opportunities. Groups were set up to consider four topics: the implications of the fee waiver, the view of business and industry

---

1. Erasmus is the European Union's educational exchange programme for higher education students, teachers and institutions. It was introduced with the aim of increasing student mobility within Europe. It encourages student and staff mobility for work and study, and promotes transnational co-operation projects among universities across Europe. The scheme currently involves nine out of every ten European higher education establishments and supports co-operation between the universities of 33 countries.

on outward mobility, best practice in the UK and international best practice.

International Best Practice

As part of its work, the expert group on international best practice looked at other countries' models for promoting outward student mobility. It is evident that the challenge of increasing outward student mobility is not just confined to UK higher education. In the USA, the Institute of International Education initiated in 2009 the Get a Passport: Study Abroad programme to encourage US students to access overseas experience, working with universities to promote outward mobility through workshops, advice and an online information portal.

In Australia, as part of its Asia strategy, the Australian government has committed AUD $37 billion to promote outward mobility to Asia through student grants, including raising the maximum student loan for Asia placements to $7,500 (compared to the standard 2013 loan of $6,051) through its supplementary OS-HELP[2] programme.

Closer to home, Germany has an established outward mobility programme. The 'Go Out' campaign invested €72 million in 2010 in implementing a strategy that aims to get 50 per cent of graduates experiencing life abroad during their studies, and 20 per cent of students taking at least a full semester outside of Germany. With a programme of events and workshops, advice and guidance for universities, and an online information portal, it is the flagship strategy for promoting and increasing outward student mobility in higher education. In the UK, Scotland had already taken steps to promote outward student mobility by funding the Scotland Goes Global[3] initiative to promote outreach activities via the National Union of Students in Scotland and creating the Saltire Scholarship Outward Mobility Fund[4] to provide additional funding for mobility at university level.

---

2. OS-HELP is a Commonwealth government loan scheme to assist eligible undergraduate, Commonwealth-supported students to undertake part of their course of study overseas.
3. www.scotlandgoesglobal.co.uk
4. The Scottish government made up to £130,000 available through the Saltire Scholarship Outward Mobility Fund in 2012/13 to universities, colleges and student associations as part of a drive to increase the options available for students based in Scotland. This funding is in addition to standard student loans, giving students greater financial flexibility when studying or working overseas as part of their studies.

The View from UK Higher Education

In July 2012, the IU's Joint Steering Group conducted a sector-wide consultation[5] to inform its work and make evidence-based recommendations. The consultation responses highlighted several issues that need to be addressed in order to increase the proportion of students accessing outward mobility opportunities:

1. The diversity of institutions represents a particular challenge for outward student mobility. Universities have their individual strategies, and outward mobility is not prioritised equally across the higher education sector. Within universities, outward mobility is more highly valued by some subject disciplines, with participation low in others. This diversity, combined with the different policy contexts across the UK devolved administrations[6], presents a range of barriers to participation in study and work abroad.
2. While there are several scholarships available for study overseas and, of course, the Erasmus mobility programme for Europe, financial barriers do exist in UK higher education. Tuition fee and maintenance loans are only payable to students at UK institutions, and there are other financial constraints that leave many students unable to access flexible or shorter-term mobility opportunities. Family commitments, accommodation contracts and part-time work are just some of the cost implications for UK students and are particularly problematic for those students from a socially or economically disadvantaged background.
3. The sector is concerned that the lack of foreign language skills, or a lack of confidence in their language skills, prevents many UK students from applying for overseas study opportunities or work placements in non-English-speaking countries. It's not just language skills — the fall in language provision in schools is a concern, as the number of students with some language skills decreases with each year's intake[7].
4. While there are established procedures in place for a year or semester abroad, it is often difficult to include an accredited period of study or work abroad in practice. This may be due to curricula requirements or

---

5. *Sector-wide consultation on a UK strategy for outward student mobility: report on responses*, October 2012, UK Higher Education International Unit.
6. The United Kingdom is governed by Her Majesty's (HM) government on central issues such as the constitution, immigration, national security and tax, but Northern Ireland, Scotland and Wales have devolved governments which lead on areas such as health and social care, education, housing, the environment and planning. The devolved governments may have different policies from HM government and each other, depending on national priorities.
7. www.jcq.org.uk/examination-results/a-levels.

academic timetables. Where study abroad is available, there may be issues around recognising credit achieved in another institution. To widen participation in study and work abroad for under-represented groups, students must be able to access shorter or more flexible international opportunities, which may not be credit-bearing.

5. Many students find that their ability to make informed decisions about their opportunities for study or work abroad is hampered by the lack of consistent and accurate information online. With no single information point for study or work abroad in higher education, students are reliant on a range of sources to influence their decisions. These sources may often be conflicting, causing confusion and uncertainty. Respondents indicated that finance is not just an issue for students — higher education institutions' own international offices face their own resourcing challenges.

6. There was considerable support from the consultation responses for an outward student mobility strategy to co-ordinate UK higher education activity in study and work abroad, promote opportunities, conduct research and raise awareness of the benefits of overseas experience. Respondents indicated that a strategy would streamline data collection, co-ordinate evidence of good practice in UK higher education and promote the importance of outward mobility to students and academics.

Based on the feedback from the expert groups and following further discussion, research and consultation, Professor Riordan submitted a proposal to the International Education Advisory Forum in November 2012. Its central recommendation was a co-ordinated strategy for outward student mobility in UK higher education. The Minister for Universities and Science committed funding from the UK government's Department for Business, Innovation and Skills and the Higher Education Funding Council for England (HEFCE) to fund a dedicated team within the IU to develop and implement a UK Higher Education Outward Mobility Strategy.

How Will the Strategy have an Impact on Outward Student Mobility?

The Outward Student Mobility Strategy has now been established as part of the UK government's 2013 International Education Strategy. Following extensive consultation with key stakeholders, a high-level strategy for outward student mobility in the UK was launched in October 2013 and a range of strategic activities to build UK higher education's capacity in outward student mobility activity will be delivered over the next three years.

By increasing the proportion of students with international experience, the strategy's aims are to increase the number of UK graduates prepared for the global labour market and extend the UK's influence internationally. Initially funded until June 2016, it aims to promote international opportunities across the three cycles of higher education, not just at undergraduate level. It aims to widen participation in study and work abroad by addressing barriers to mobility. To achieve this, its objectives are:

1: To promote study and work abroad and raise awareness of how to access opportunities
Working with the higher education sector and other stakeholders including the British Council and the National Union of Students, the IU will co-ordinate a promotional campaign to raise awareness of the benefits of study and work abroad. To support this campaign, it will conduct research into the outcomes a student might expect to achieve from a period abroad and the benefits of international experience for employability. Qualitative evidence will contribute to the promotional messages and resources of the campaign, which can be used by institutions in their own outreach activities and international offices, and quantitative evidence will be used by UK higher education and devolved governments for strategic planning.

The campaign will also work to increase awareness of the importance of language competence by gathering evidence from graduates and employers of the value of language and intercultural skills gained from international experience, and then communicating this value to students by means of a distributed campaign in schools and higher education institutions. It will work with another publicly funded higher education programme, Routes into Languages, which conducts outreach activity with schools to promote language learning to distribute messages linked to the benefits of outward mobility.

2: Collect data on outward student mobility in the UK
The Outward Mobility Strategy is exploiting the full range of data sources, including the UK's Higher Education Statistics Agency (HESA) and the Organisation for Economic Co-operation and Development (OECD), to collate outward mobility statistics for the UK, establish baseline data and set specific targets for the programme. These targets will contribute to the Bologna Process target that, by 2020 there will be 20 per cent of European Higher Education Area graduates who have had a study or training period abroad.

The IU will track data and trends throughout the strategy's implementation, providing quantitative and qualitative data for use in UK government policy making and higher education strategic planning.

3: Define the range of outward student mobility opportunities

The strategy is not just setting a statistical baseline. The 2012 consultation indicates that there is a wide range of outward student mobility opportunities, not just the traditional semester or year abroad. The IU will work with UK higher education institutions to map the range of mobility opportunities available via international collaborations, including virtual links, and will explore good practice across the various types of outward mobility. The IU will publish an overview of the types of mobility UK students can access, from summer schools or volunteering to full scholarships overseas, including information on flexible opportunities and their potential outcomes.

4: Widen access to and participation in outward mobility

In conjunction with UK universities and other relevant organisations, the IU will explore ways to widen access to international opportunities for disadvantaged groups. This will include national-level discussions with the Office for Fair Access (OFFA), which promotes and safeguards fair access to higher education in the UK, and charitable institutions working with socially disadvantaged groups. It will also involve institutional-level discussions with university officers who conduct outreach activity aimed at widening access to higher education. As well as addressing financial barriers, it will promote the full range of flexible mobility opportunities identified in the mapping project to ensure that students who cannot access longer-term mobilities for other reasons (such as family commitments) can still gain some international experience.

5: Co-ordinate information on funding opportunities

By bringing information on existing funding sources together in one place, and linking it to advice and guidance on application processes, the strategy aims to support marketing activities for existing funded opportunities such as Erasmus and national or institutional scholarships. As well as official guidance, it will link to information about funding opportunities provided on student-facing platforms such as the British Council's UK Students Abroad portal (www.britishcouncil.org/uk-students-abroad) and www.thirdyearabroad.com/, ensuring that students, parents and academics can access everything they need to make a decision or application.

In addition to existing funding, the IU will identify and secure new scholarships, sponsorship funds and bursaries from higher education institutions overseas governments, business, industry and the third sector. It will also work with the UK government to explore the issue of non-portable loans[8], and their impact on outward mobility, as referenced in the new International Education Strategy for the UK[9], and propose potential solutions to funding barriers.

6: Build capacity in UK higher education to increase outward student mobility

The IU has established a Mobility Community of Practice as a forum for discussion and sharing information on best practice. The community has over 60 representatives and continues to grow. Its members include a diverse range of higher education institutions across the UK and other stakeholders in outward mobility activity, such as the British Council, the Association of UK Higher Education European Officers (HEURO) and British Universities Transatlantic Exchange Association (BUTEX). It also invites a network of external speakers to talk to the community, including experts on broader issues related to outward mobility, such as research or promotion, or international speakers presenting specific opportunities to the forum, such as individual countries or institutions.

To support its capacity-building work, the IU is developing a toolkit for higher education. As well as providing promotional resources and research evidence for a range of institutions to adapt to their individual requirements, the toolkit will also support the extension of study and work abroad in UK higher education by providing a range of advice and consultancy to individual institutions.

This will include guidance on existing and emerging approaches to quality assurance and accreditation, such as the Higher Education Achievement Record (HEAR) and the UK's Quality Assurance Agency (QAA) frameworks, to ensure students' international experiences are recognised by the home institution. By helping institutions to interpret and apply frameworks across different types and periods of mobility, the strategy aims to widen participation in study and work abroad.

7: Create an online information hub for outward student mobility

All information on outward mobility strategic activities, including promotional campaign resources, research reports, data and funding guidance, will feature on a new website for study and work abroad. The

---

8. A non-portable loan is a state-funded loan used to fund higher education tuition in an institution in the same country, and cannot be used to finance tuition in an overseas higher education institution

9. www.gov.uk/government/uploads/system/uploads/attachment_data/file/229844/bis-13-1081-international-education-global-growth-and-prosperity.pdf

website will lead users to relevant information and resources from stake-holders, including the British Council's UK Students Abroad portal, and act as the hub for outward student mobility activity in the UK.

How Can a Co-Ordinated Strategy Add Value to the UK Higher Education Sector?

The 2012 sector consultation and discussions at the Mobility Community of Practice demonstrated the wealth of valuable activity in outward student mobility that already takes place at an institutional and national level. The strategy does not set out to duplicate existing activity, but instead seeks to add value to UK higher education by:

- **Raising awareness of these activities in its promotional campaign.** By bringing together information on good practice in outward student mobility and sharing case studies of diverse mobility opportunities, it will channel sector expertise on outward student mobility into a national campaign, developing promotional messages and tools for use by a wide range of stakeholders.
- **Analysing existing data sources to develop a single statistical resource on outward student mobility.** As well as collating data on outward student mobility to set benchmarks and inform programme targets, it will review the available evidence of the value of outward student mobility to provide a complete picture for the sector.
- **Building new international relationships.** Through its activity to promote UK higher education overseas, the IU will continue to meet with a range of international government representatives and organisations to explore further mobility opportunities and promote these to the sector. It will provide support for universities in brokering and building new international partnerships, and establish reciprocal agreements with emerging markets on behalf of the sector.

Conclusions

The Outward Student Mobility Strategy represents a government commitment to promote and increase levels of outward mobility in the UK student population. It demonstrates the value that government places on UK graduates' international experience.

On an international level, it contributes to the government's corresponding aims of promoting UK higher education as a major export and increasing the numbers of overseas students coming to the UK to study by promoting the image of UK education overseas and providing ambassadors for the UK higher education sector. It will contribute to the UK's influence internationally by helping UK higher education establish reciprocal relationships with priority countries.

On a national level, the strategy will provide senior management of institutions with the information they need with regard to strategic planning for outward student mobility. It will support university international offices and sector organisations to extend their outward student mobility activities and increase the proportion of UK students gaining the international experience they need to make a difference on a global stage.

SECTION 3
HOW HAS INTERNATIONAL COLLABORATION CONTRIBUTED TO INTERNATIONALISING TERTIARY EDUCATION STRUCTURES AND SYSTEMS?

Chapter 3.1

Editors' Introduction to Section 3

In this final section we focus, as Martin Hall has said, on the ways that 'dimensions of teaching and research affect the ways in which individual institutions and systems of higher education are organised, and how current transitions are contributing to sustainability and new opportunities in the international sphere' (Pp. xv). The papers collected here arise, as in the other sections, from the Going Global conference in March 2013, and present us with a kaleidoscope of explorations and understandings of the theme as a whole from a variety of contexts and perspectives. The reader will therefore be enabled to develop a truly international picture of this global scene as a whole.

José Celso Freire Jnr and Leandro Tessler open this section with their paper exploring the 'Science without Borders' project — the project which, over four years, aims to provide the opportunities for academic staff and students in Brazilian science, technology, engineering, mathematics and medical faculties in universities to benefit from collaborative academic partnerships with international counterparts.

Lucky Tebalebo Moahi and Kgomotso Moahi explore the Botswana Education Hub. This is a student hub that aims to ensure that high-quality education, research and training are key to the country's economic diversification and social developments.

In the paper by Hans Pohl and Andrew Gottenberg, we are given a clear analysis of the internationalisation strategies in Swedish universities, and their underpinning rationales, while in Dorothea Rüland's papers there is an analysis of the German approach to transnational education (TNE). Kenneth Omeje's paper on Kenyan transnational education for peace gives

Going Global: Knowledge-Based Economies for 21st Century Nations
Copyright © 2014 by Mary Stiasny and Tim Gore
All rights of reproduction in any form reserved
ISBN: 978-1-78441-003-2

us a third national case study demonstrating the varied drivers for TNE, while Maryan Rab's paper is illustrative of the practice in Pakistan whereby TNE has enabled the development of international approaches to higher education.

Finally, in concluding this third section, Christopher Hill's paper about the University of Nottingham campus in Malaysia takes us away, in his words, 'from the international drive for numbers to ... the local need for education and seeks to discuss 'need' within a contextually and culturally relevant framework'. As he says, TNE is now 'a global phenomenon' and is a key contributor to the international education scene. His prediction is a fitting one to close this volume of readings:

> 'the movement and delivery of nationally linked programmes ... will continue to morph into intra-national education, with the ability to shape regional alliances, promote balanced exchange and redefine global values and education'.

Chapter 3.2

Beyond Science without Borders: Long-Term Co-Operation with Brazilian Higher Education Institutions

José Celso Freire Jnr and Leandro R Tessler

Introduction

At the end of 2011 the Brazilian government announced the Brazil Scientific Mobility Programme (BSMP, formerly called Science without Borders), its four-year plan to award 101,000 scholarships and promote international academic mobility in the STEM and medical science fields. The main objective of the programme is to provide Brazilian students and faculties with an opportunity to access up-to-date technology and innovation-based educational curricula abroad. Mainly focused on mobility, in its current form BSMP also intends to stimulate the internationalisation of Brazilian higher education institutions (HEIs).

Internationalisation in the Brazilian Higher Education System

Brazil has a very diversified higher education system. About six million undergraduate and 200,000 graduate students attend 2,500 institutions ranging from isolated vocational schools to research-intensive universities. No more than five per cent of undergraduate students are in research universities (INEP, 2011) and the whole system never had important internationalisation initiatives until the 1990s (Tessler, 2012). For most non-research-intensive HEIs, BSMP was the first official incentive to internationalise. As a result, they associate internationalisation with sending a few undergraduate students abroad for six or 12 months. Of course this process is not sustainable in the long term, unless the Brazilian government keeps injecting funds to cover tuition fees and living expenses abroad.

At the other end of the scale, the top universities have a tradition of international research co-operation but not of exchanging students. They are struggling to become important players in the international higher education arena. As a result, BMSP is for these institutions a chance to increase their international visibility by not only sending their students abroad but also by hosting international students and faculties. The best way to ensure this presence is by participating in international research projects.

Brazil Scientific Mobility Programme

In its original form BSMP was designed to provide international-quality technical training for Brazilian STEM and medical science students. It was later modified to include support for visiting researchers and to attract young talents. Currently, one of the objectives of the programme is: 'To promote the international insertion of Brazilian institutions by opening similar opportunities for foreign scientists and students' (Ciência Sem Fronteiras, 2013). However, out of the planned 101,000 scholarships only 2,000 are committed to foreign researchers and another 2,000 to foreign graduate students. In this context, the programme may be perceived as an extra source of revenue for many foreign host institutions, in the sense that they are providing a service to the Brazilian students they receive. Nevertheless, an important number of institutions are apparently interested in long-term co-operation, judging by the unprecedented number of organised and individual visits to Brazil over the past two years. These shall take this opportunity to deepen their involvement beyond the short-term objectives of BSMP and its completion by the end of 2015 (although there are some indications that this end will be postponed). Sustainable co-operation projects must be taken on when BSMP vanishes.

Co-operation: Undergraduate Programmes

Perhaps the most accessible way to develop sustainable co-operation with Brazilian HEIs is through joint undergraduate programmes in STEM areas. This type of co-operation does not forcibly involve research and can have different degrees of commitment. One must always bear in mind that, like anywhere in the world, most Brazilian STEM education takes place in non-research-intensive institutions. At this level, virtually any qualified Brazilian

HEI could be a partner. The rewards of undergraduate exchange are directed towards the students, who benefit by having contact with a different environment, culture and, in the case of Brazil, a rapidly expanding market. Projections predict that there will be a shortage of engineers (Uchoa, 2012), and therefore many relevant opportunities are foreseeable in the near future. In Brazil, the highly competitive admissions process of undergraduate students is based only on their performance in tests that are offered solely in Portuguese. The only practical way for a foreign student to have a Brazilian experience is by means of an exchange programme. Exchange in a rapidly developing country also contributes to educate global citizens. Effective exchange could be achieved in the following ways:

- Establishing exchange programmes with approximately balanced student flow. When BSMP ends there will be a strong decrease in the availability of funds to pay for tuition fees. In Brazil, the public institutions, which are generally the most prestigious from vocational schools to top universities, are not allowed to charge tuition fees from Brazilian or foreign students. To ensure sustainability, the best option is to establish bilateral student exchange agreements with tuition fee waivers at both ends. Because the Brazilian curricula are content-oriented and heavy in class hours, some effort will be needed to create an easy and transparent accreditation process. Hopefully, in the long term, Brazilian directors will understand that not only is it possible, but it is better to educate STEM students with less time in the classroom. One problem that cannot be overemphasised is the resistance of Brazilian universities to adopt English as a teaching language. With very few exceptions, all academic activities in Brazil at the undergraduate level are undertaken in Portuguese. It is expected that the prospect of becoming more attractive to foreign students will motivate some institutions to offer courses in English. It is very unlikely that an exchange programme will succeed if English does not become the language of at least a few basic courses. It is also important to bear in mind that a very large percentage of Brazilians are not fluent in English, and a disproportionately large percentage of BSMP undergraduate students chose Portugal or Spain as their study destination for linguistic reasons only. The government is trying to provide quick English education to mitigate the problem (MEC, 2013), but the degree of success of this endeavour is still to be seen.
- Some Brazilian institutions have a positive experience with double or joint degree programmes. An excellent example is the programme between six Brazilian universities and the French Écoles Centrales, which ran for more than a decade (Tessler and Pissolato Filho, 2013) and trained more than 500 engineers, combining the best on offer from both academic cultures. Establishing double degree programmes is not

straightforward and requires dedicated faculties on both sides. They are built based on mutual trust, and in general it is a consequence rather than the cause of co-operation. Nevertheless, institutions interested in opening new possibilities for their students must consider this possibility.

Co-operation: Research and Graduate Programmes

In 2011, Brazil ranked as the 13th country in the world in terms of number of scientific papers published (SCIMago, 2013). Its research-intensive universities are largely responsible for this result. Six Brazilian universities (UFMG, UFRGS, UFRJ, UNESP, Unicamp and USP) are among the top 500 of international rankings, and have well-established graduate programmes that comply with international standards. For these, as well as most of the federal and state universities and some confessional and not-for-profit private universities, BSMP is an opportunity to consolidate the internationalisation of their graduate and research programmes. There are the already-mentioned possibilities to bring foreign students and researchers within the BSMP, but alternative funding sources must be considered to guarantee the continuity of the projects in the future.

Brazil is a key global player in areas of health science such as tropical diseases and parasitology, and also relevant in physics, space science and agricultural sciences (Adams and King, 2009). Its universities have world-class research laboratories and infrastructure. Brazil also hosts the only synchrotron accelerator light source in Latin America, part of the National Centre for Research on Energy and Materials (www.cnpem.br), and also has centres for biotechnology, nanotechnology and bioethanol research. Access to these facilities is free of charge for researchers involved in academic projects and is based on the quality of submitted proposals.

International research projects can be funded by different agencies in Brazil:

- The federal government maintains the National Council for Scientific and Technological Development (CNPq; www.cnpq.br), which has agreements with 46 foreign agencies. Funding is open to all Brazilian institutions. The allocation of funds is conducted on merit. CNPq regularly issues calls for proposals to support international research.
- Some state governments have relevant funding agencies. The most important is the São Paulo Research Foundation (FAPESP; www. fapesp.br). FAPESP receives one per cent of state sales taxes (approximately R$1 billion or US$500 million in 2012) to foster research and innovation. It is very flexible as far as international agreements go and can have as partners universities, consortia of universities, agencies,

foundations or governments in a principle of fund matching. FAPESP regularly issues calls for proposals to support international research. The other active funding agencies are FAPEMIG (www.fapemig.br) in Minas Gerais, FAPERJ in Rio de Janeiro (www.faperj.br) and FAPERGS (www.fapergs.rs.gov.br) in Rio Grande do Sul.

Unlike the case of undergraduate education, language is not a problem for co-operation in STEM and medical sciences graduate programmes and research. English is spoken in the laboratories and graduate students are expected to publish their results in English as articles in international journals with high editorial standards. Some institutions are now starting to offer courses in English (UNESP, 2013).

It would be very beneficial for both Brazilian and foreign institutions to have a sustained exchange of researchers and students. Brazil is very friendly to visitors and is becoming an attractive place to undertake research. Its top universities still lack international faculty members, but there are many opportunities for young, foreign researchers to opt for a challenging but welcoming environment with excellent career prospects.

Conclusion

Due to its novelty and impact, BSMP helped to attract the attention of the international higher education community to Brazil. In a period of a world financial crisis hitting the HE sector, not only talented students are welcome, but also the tuition fees associated with them. However, this is only one aspect of the possibilities of co-operation with Brazilian HEIs. BSMP will close by the end of 2015, and institutions that believe in co-operation with Brazil must pursue different strategies to keep the momentum. The Brazilian HE system is very diverse. There is room for different levels of engagement, ranging from bilateral undergraduate student exchange programmes to large-scale research projects. Local culture is important: it must always be understood that public institutions do not charge tuition fees from exchange students and expect reciprocity in agreements.

Very few Brazilian institutions offer undergraduate programmes or courses in English; they must be convinced to do so if they intend to be relevant international players.

Research partnerships are perhaps the best way to ensure a future of co-operation. Brazilian science is growing continuously in size and in quality, and there are world-class facilities and people eager to establish international scientific co-operation. There are also readily available funds to support research projects.

Institutions that are willing to establish strategic partners in Brazil will be rewarded by the results of co-operation with one of the fastest-growing economies in the world.

References

Adams, J and King, C (2009) Global Research Report: Brazil (available at http://ip-science.thomsonreuters.com/), London:Thomson Reuters.

Ciência Sem Fronteiras (2013) www.cienciasemfronteiras.gov.br/web/csf/objetivos. (accessed 22 August 2013).

INEP (2011) Sinopse Estatística Da Educação Superior 2011. INEP (available at http://download.inep.gov.br/informacoes_estatisticas/sinopses_estatisticas/sinopses_educacao_superior/sinopse_educacao_superior_2011.zip).

MEC (2013) Inglês Sem Fronteiras. http://isf.mec.gov.br/ (accessed 25 August 2013).

SCIMago (2013) SCIMago Journal and Country Rank. www.scimagojr.com/countryrank.php (accessed 23 August 2013).

Tessler, LR and Pissolato Filho, J (2013) Institutional Perspective over Double Degree Programs in a Latin American Research University: the Case of Unicamp. In *Trends in International Joint and Double Degree Programs*, edited by Mathias Kuder and Daniel Obst (in press).

Tessler, LR (2012) 'The Internationalisation of Higher Education in Brazil.' In *Going Global: The Landscape for Policy Makers and Practitioners in Tertiary Education*, edited by Mary Stiasny and Tim Gore, Pp. 189–198. Bingley: Emerald Group Publishing Limited.

Uchoa, P (2012) 'Brazil's Rousseff Seeks US Help with Skills Shortage', BBC News. www.bbc.co.uk/news/world-us-canada-17642138 (accessed 26 August 2013).

UNESP (2013) International Courses at UNESP. www.unesp.br/portal#!/arex/novo8425/courses-in-english/ (accessed 23 August 2013).

Chapter 3.3

Education Cities and Hubs: What is their Contribution to Global, National and Local Community Agendas? A Case of the Education Hub in Botswana

Lucky T Moahi and Kgomotso H Moahi

Introduction

Knight (2011) described education cities or hubs as the third generation of cross-border education. Typically, the hubs are set up by countries that want to diversify their economies beyond the one or two activities and products they rely on. The Botswana Education Hub (BEH) is one of a number of hubs articulated in the Botswana Excellence Strategy for Economic Diversification and Sustainable Growth, and was established in 2008 to co-ordinate and lead Botswana in attracting high-calibre students, scholars and other education-sector investors. Unlike other hubs around the world, the BEH was conceptualised as a virtual hub. Its role would be to strengthen the capacity of existing local education providers, and attract new providers and international scholars and students to Botswana. A key component of the hub would be to encourage the development and enhancement of education and training in niche areas such as mining and energy, tourism, agriculture and livestock management. This paper describes the BEH, its activities since inception, and considers its contribution to the national agenda of economic diversification. The paper situates the establishment of BEH within the local and national agenda of Botswana, by providing a background to its establishment and what it hoped to achieve. It then considers

Going Global: Knowledge-Based Economies for 21st Century Nations
ISBN: 978-1-78441-003-2

how BEH aims to achieve internationalisation, the progress made and both the successes and challenges encountered. Finally, some recommendations are made regarding the future.

The Botswana Context

Botswana is an upper middle-income country in Southern Africa sharing borders with Namibia, South Africa, Zambia and Zimbabwe, with a population of two million people. Attainment of middle-income status is attributed to the discovery and subsequent exploitation of mineral deposits, mainly diamonds, leading to the significant growth of the economy at an average rate of just over eight per cent per annum by 2008 (Botswana government, 2009a). Education has been consistently allocated the largest share of the annual recurrent budget; for the financial year 2013/14 the Ministry of Education and Skills Development has been allocated 22.98 per cent (Ministry of Finance and Development Planning, 2013). This has been due to a deliberate policy of government to educate its citizens and empower them to deal with global challenges. A sizeable proportion of the education budget has gone into the importation of education services, particularly at the tertiary level.

The Botswana Education Hub was one of the hubs envisaged in the Botswana Excellence Strategy for Economic Diversification and Sustainable Growth in 2008 (Botswana government, 2008a). The strategy aimed to channel a diversification of the economy away from minerals, especially diamonds. A skilled and empowered population constitutes human capital and is recognised as being central to diversification. The strategy calls for the repositioning of the education system by reorienting tertiary education and vocational training to sharply focus on job-ready outcomes in order to serve a dynamic private-sector-led economy.

To this end, the Botswana Education Hub aims to make high-quality education, training and research key parts of the country's economic diversification and social development. The sector is to be built through strengthening the capacity of existing institutions and attracting new providers, both international and local, to establish ventures and attract international students and scholars. Among others, the BEH strategy focuses on business development projects in education and training for the niche areas in which Botswana has a competitive advantage, in order to enhance the country's skills. These niche areas as identified by the then Botswana Export Development and Investment Authority (BEDIA)-led study, include medical science and research, mining and energy, business, agriculture and livestock management, hospitality and tourism, conservation, and peace and justice. It is hoped this will attract investment and education providers to enter Botswana or start up therein.

Project or investment profiles within these identified niche areas that can make meaningful contributions to economic diversification have been developed. The profiles define the specific areas within each niche field that hold the greatest opportunity for investment and represent a comparative advantage or significant growth potential for Botswana.

The Education Context

Observations have been made that, despite Botswana's status as a middle-income country, the achievements in education and other sectors, while impressive, have not led to a skilled and empowered workforce, poised to take the country's economy to another level. Although education expenditure in Botswana is high at eight per cent of the GDP, and nearly universal and free primary education has been attained, the sector has not provided the skilled workforce required by the economy (Ezekwesili, 2012). Unemployment remains close to 20 per cent, and this includes hundreds of tertiary-education graduates who may or may not be absorbed into the nation's internship programme. Ezekwesili further states that the quality of education in Botswana is quite low, with the country lagging behind in mathematics and science education. This is something that has been acknowledged even within Botswana and is witnessed with the low enrolments in maths, science and technology-based programmes at various tertiary education levels. Indeed, the Botswana Excellence Strategy for Economic Diversification and Sustainable Growth identified the challenge of poor-quality education at all levels, learner performance in mathematics and science and skills mismatch as a hindrance to economic diversification (John, et al., 2008).

Knight (2011a) describes education hubs as a third generation of cross-border activities in a more globalised world, and as the most recent developments relating to internationalisation in the area of education. She posits that there are a variety of factors driving efforts towards the establishment of education hubs, including the modernisation of domestic tertiary education and the need for trained workforce. Knight also observes that, given higher education is preoccupied with competitiveness and rankings, it is not clear whether plans by countries to develop education hubs 'is a fad, the latest branding strategy or, in fact, an innovation worthy of investment'. (2011a: 222) For Botswana though, the education hub is seen as a way to enhance and develop the human capital required for economic diversification.

The establishment of the BEH in 2008 coincided with the adoption of the Tertiary Education Policy: Towards a Knowledge Society, which also aims to increase and raise Botswana's human-resource capacity. It presents a comprehensive set of policy recommendations for the Botswana tertiary education system, further provides guidance on the direction of tertiary education over two decades and is a milestone in the development of Botswana towards a knowledge society (Botswana government, 2008b).

Along with the Tertiary Education Policy, the National Human Resource Development Strategy also gives impetus to the development of Botswana as an education hub. The Botswana government (2009b) recognised that, in spite of the economic transformation largely attributed to minerals, continued reliance on natural resources was in the long term neither desirable nor sustainable. The strategy signalled a different way of planning manpower development that would focus on the needs of the economy in terms of manpower, in order to avoid the prevailing scenario of an education system that was producing graduates without the skills required by the economy.

The Botswana Education Hub: Role, Scope and Mandate

Knight (2011b) notes that there are three types of hubs: student, talent and knowledge/innovation hubs. The BEH, as a student hub, aims to make high-quality education, training and research key parts of the country's economic diversification and social development. This is to be achieved through a number of strategic themes:

- support the educational development of Botswana's priority stakeholders
- build a competitive education sector
- establish an education hub co-ordinating unit for Botswana
- promote Botswana as an education hub.

These themes would be operationalised as follows:

- Strengthening the capacity of existing institutions and promoting access. John et al. (2012) note that in developing the Botswana Excellence Strategy, poor quality of education at all levels was identified as a challenge for economic diversification, as well as a mismatch between training and industry requirements, leading to unemployed graduates. Also, large numbers of students were sponsored at great cost abroad for tertiary education due to limited places locally.
- The role of BEH was to attract international students, academics and investors or partners in education, through marketing the sector as well as removing barriers to development.

- It was also the intention of the BEH to facilitate production of high-level skills for the other five economic hubs, and so promote economic diversification.
- Finally, was to foster business development projects in education for niche areas where Botswana has a competitive advantage, to enhance skills in these areas and attract investment and education providers.

Clearly, the scope of activity for the BEH is wide and all-encompassing.

Current Activities of the Botswana Education Hub

The local and national agenda in Botswana is clearly that of diversifying the economy through the development and leveraging of human capital. Further, the recognised importance of education has resulted in a growing demand for education, particularly at the tertiary level. The existing local institutions have not been able to absorb all the numbers and the government's budget has not been able to cope with having to send students abroad. Given the mandate of the hub, it is safe to state that much has been achieved during the five years that it has been in existence.

One of the responsibilities of the hub was the implementation of the Botswana International University of Science and Technology (a new national university). After a series of false starts, the university enrolled its first cohort of students in August 2012 and the campus development is in progress. This development will not only contribute to increased access to tertiary education but also increased focus on research and education in the identified areas of operation of the other hubs – agriculture, diamond, health, innovation and transport. Another development in the public tertiary-education sector is the continued expansion of programmes in science and technology as well as health and medicine at the University of Botswana. Also, the technical and vocational education and training sector has been undergoing revitalisation to increase capacity.

As more opportunities for tertiary-education participation increase in the private education sector, the government has extended sponsorship to students admitted into such institutions, thereby contributing to increased tertiary participation from 11.4 per cent in 2008 to 16.4 per cent in 2012 (Tertiary Education Council, 2012).

An initiative of the BEH in relation to internationalisation is the Study in Botswana programme. This initiative involves a reduction in the number of students sponsored for education and training abroad while growing local capacity, even for foreign students. A marketing consultative committee made up of representatives of tertiary institutions and convened by the BEH is in place. Marketing missions to the region involving both public and private tertiary education has resulted in a steady inflow of international students into Botswana. The number of international students has increased from 295 in 2010/11 to 1,219 in 2012/13 with a resultant inflow of revenue from tuition fees and other costs amounting to just over BWP65 million (about US$7.5 million).

The BEH promotes partnerships between local tertiary institutions and reputable ones from abroad. Thus both public and private higher education institutions continue to enter into partnerships for the purpose of diversifying programme offerings, students and faculty exchanges. In some instances, the hub has played a critical role in the establishment of such partnerships, while in other cases, such as the University of Botswana (UB), there has been independent activity to develop partnerships and staff and student exchanges. UB now has more than 100 partnerships with tertiary institutions across the world, although only about 65 are actually active according to the International Education and Partnerships office. The partnerships involve faculty and student exchanges, collaborative research and twinning programmes across various disciplines. Other public institutions like the new Botswana International University of Science and Technology, the Botswana College of Agriculture and the Botswana Accountancy College have also entered into partnerships. In the private sector, Botho University recently signed a Memorandum of Understanding with Ohio University in the USA to cover curriculum issues, and Gaborone Institute of Professional Studies (GIPS) has partnered with Middlesex University in the UK to offer a twinning programme. GIPS has also acquired a plot of land for Middlesex University to establish a branch campus in Botswana.

Through a consultancy – Leadership Education and Development (2010) – the BEH has developed investment profiles, which serve as pre-feasibility information for each of the nine niche areas of medical science and research, agriculture and livestock management, hospitality and tourism, conservation and environment, veterinary science, mining and energy, business and management, peace and justice, and democracy, governance and economic management. In support of these, a package of investment incentives has also been developed. The BEH is working with the Botswana Investment and Trade Centre (BITC), the national investment promotion agency, to complete a value proposition, and prioritise the business profiles as investment opportunities.

In line with the ideal of establishing centres of excellence, a major objective of the BEH is the internationalisation of the education and training system in order to attract international students, scholars and researchers. Modest progress is being made towards achieving internationalisation by way of increased participation of private tertiary-education providers collaborating with others from abroad or setting up on their own. Examples include Ba Isago University College offering franchise programmes to the University of South Africa; Botho University (which developed out of NIIT of India) collaborating with the Open University and Teesside University in the UK on undergraduate and master's programmes in computing; ABM University College franchising with the Chartered Institute of Purchasing and Supply and the Chartered Institute of Management Accountants, among others; while Limkokwing University of Malaysia has established a branch campus in Botswana. Among the public tertiary institutions, Botswana Accountancy College offers programmes of some UK institutions such as Sunderland and Derby universities; and Botswana College of Open and Distance Learning (soon to transform into an Open University) offers the bachelor's and master's degree programmes of Amity University and the Indira Ghandi National Open University of India. The Botswana Tertiary Education Council (TEC), through the relevant legislation and regulations, has put in place systems for registration, accreditation and quality assurance for both public and private tertiary institutions.

At the basic education level, the BEH co-ordinates an initiative called 'Adopt-a-School', intended to involve corporate and other organisations as well as individuals in the provision of education. Through this initiative a corporate organisation would typically adopt a school or a number of schools in a particular area and provide specialised facilities such as libraries, ICT or other teacher support materials for innovation in teaching and learning.

Challenges

The implementation of the education hub has encountered a number of challenges: the scope of the hub from pre-primary to higher education and lifelong learning presents a challenge of focus; this is exacerbated by resource constraints. While the hub has grown from a one-person office to a complement of five professional staff over the past two years, this still falls short of the envisaged nine senior staff positions and up to 22 professional project and administrative staff indicated in the Strategy and Business Plan.

Some of the challenges facing the Study in Botswana initiative include ensuring that the right calibre of institutions is set up in Botswana. As Mpotokwane (2012:22) indicates '... short-term gains from having an initial explosion of regional students on our shores are nothing in comparison to the long term loss of reputation that may be suffered from substandard institutions.' Other challenges include the provision of student accommodation and the ability to attract quality staff and students through a more liberal and efficient work and study permit system.

There is a school of thought that transnational education, a component of internationalisation of education, involving new entrants into African higher education, might siphon off students and resources from national universities (Guttenplan, 2012). In Botswana this may not be an immediate challenge as such entrant numbers tend to be small and, in any case, competition is encouraged so as to achieve value for money while producing the much-needed skills for economic diversification.

For the hub to deliver, there is a need for relationships to be developed with all stakeholders in the education sector. Although moves have been made in this direction, lack of clear understanding of the purpose and objectives of the hub on the part of some stakeholders has made this a somewhat uphill battle. Some existing institutions providing education and training do not seem to appreciate nor understand what the hub really stands for and aims to achieve.

BEH is also required to work closely with the other hubs to create a cluster of business innovation and activity to transform Botswana's economy. At this point it seems the other hubs are all working independently. However, there are some efforts by the Botswana National Strategy Office to rationalise the cluster arrangements.

Botswana Education Hub – The Way Forward

The Botswana Education Hub Strategy and Business Plan 2009–2016 is now at its mid-term point and there is a need for a review of the performance of the hub against the targets or indicators set for internationalisation.

The Study in Botswana programme, in particular, is beginning to yield results by way of increased numbers of international students and the resultant inflow of modest revenue into the economy. To sustain such growth will depend on the ability of the tertiary institutions to attract and retain high-quality staff for teaching and research as well as to maintain international standards in their programme offerings. In this regard the BEH and TEC are in the process of conducting a survey of the local tertiary institutions so as to inform further marketing and promotion of the Study in Botswana programme. The collection of data on international students and the associated costs also need to be streamlined and systematic for full appreciation of the amount of value of exported education services.

On the whole, any review of the performance of the BEH will necessarily look at whether the current resource allocation – human and financial – is adequate for the delivery of the mandate to make high-quality education, training and research key parts of Botswana's economic diversification and social development. This is especially critical in view of the fact that, while the hub is mandated to address the needs of the entire education system from early childhood to tertiary, in reality a lot more focus has been on tertiary education by promoting investment at this level and partnerships with foreign universities as well as marketing local institutions in the region to attract international students. Even then, data collection on such internationalisation efforts, particularly transnational education, needs to be put in place to inform any academic, economic, and human resource development impact.

Conclusion

The Botswana Education Hub is an attempt at developing the education sector in Botswana in order to develop the requisite manpower to take the country beyond an economy dominated by natural resources and diamonds. In its five years of existence, the hub has made some strides, but challenges still abound. In particular, the model adopted by Botswana of having a virtual hub and creating it as a unit within the Ministry of Education with no dedicated resources of its own to carry through its mandate has presented a number of challenges, as pointed out in the paper. Of primary concern though, is the scope that the hub is to cover, and the fact that, in its current form, limited resources impact negatively on its ability to cover the entire spectrum of the education sector. Thus at present, most of its activities have focused on tertiary education when other sectors also demand attention – this will have to be addressed and resolved. There is a need for closer collaboration and interaction with all players in the education sector to facilitate the development of Botswana into an education hub. Concerted effort has to be expended on interesting potential education providers to invest in Botswana and to partner with existing institutions in order to help enhance quality and capacity. This, in turn, will make the task of marketing Botswana as a destination of choice for students, researchers and scholars that much easier. Now that the hub has been in place for five years, there is a need to take a hard look at the strategy for making Botswana an education hub with a view to determining what is achievable and what may not be, and therefore what to do next.

On the whole. there is great potential for the hub to contribute at the individual level to the development of citizens with a multicultural outlook, the skills and ability to work in global settings, at the national level to the diversification of the economy and at global level to the development of graduates able to criss-cross the globe seamlessly.

References

Botswana government (2008a) *Botswana Excellence: A Strategy for Economic Diversification and Sustainable Growth*. National Strategy Office.
Botswana government (2008b) *Tertiary Education Policy: Towards a Knowledge Society*. Ministry of Education and Skills Development.

Botswana government (2009a) *National Development Plan 10: 2009/10−2015/2016*. Government Printer, Gaborone.

Botswana government (2009b) *National Human Resource Development Strategy 2009−2022*. Ministry of Education and Skills Development.

Ezekwesili, O (2012) *Achieving Knowledge-Based Education in a Natural Resource Dependent Economy*. 12th Annual University of Botswana Gala Dinner, 2012, Gaborone.

Guttenplan, DD (2012). Local Options Help Slow Africa's Brain Drain. *The New York Times*. From http://nytimes.com/2012/01/02/world/africa/02iht-educlede02.html

John, BP, Wilmorth, D and Mokopakgosi, B (2014). *Botswana Country Hub: Africa's First Education Hub*, in Knight, J (Editor), International Education Hubs: Student, Talent, Knowledge-Innovation Models. Springer Netherlands.

Knight, J (2011a) 'Education Hubs: a Fad, a Brand, an Innovation?' *Journal of Studies in International Education* 15(3) Pp. 221−240, retrieved from http://quic. queens u.ca/resources/training/files/Education%20%Hubs%20A%20Fad,%20a% 20Brand,%20an20Innovation.pdf 06/09/2012.

Knight, J (2011b) *Three Types of Education Hubs: Student, Talent and Knowledge − Are Indicators Useful or Feasible?* in The Observatory on Borderless Education, University of Toronto OISE.

Leadership Education and Development (2010) *Technical Report for the Botswana Education Hub*. Ministry of Education and Skills Development.

Maiketso, JT (2009) *Prospects for the Establishment of an Educational Hub: The Case of Botswana*. Botswana Institute of Development Policy Analysis, Gaborone.

Ministry of Finance and Development Planning (2013) *2013 Budget Speech*. Government Printer, Gaborone.

Mpotokwane, P (2012) 'Building Botswana's brand strength through harnessing national talent', *Weekend Post*,Saturday 6−12 October 2012.

Performance Growth Consultants and Learning Cities International (2009) *Botswana Education Hub Strategy and Business Plan*. Ministry of Education and Skills Development.

Tertiary Education Council (2012) *Annual Report 2011/12*. Tertiary Education Council, Gaborone.

Chapter 3.4

Strategic Internationalisation in Sweden – Activities and Rationales

Hans Pohl and Andreas Göthenberg

Introduction

> 'The establishment of a world-class university requires, above
> all, strong leadership, a bold vision of the institution's mission
> and goals, and a clearly articulated strategic plan to translate
> the vision into concrete targets and programmes.' Salmi
> (2009:9)

Which are your top-priority internationalisation projects? This question
was answered in 2012 by the university presidents/vice-chancellors or their
immediate staff at 20 different Swedish higher education institutions
(HEIs). The answer was in the format of an application for co-funding and
thus offered not only a wish list.

The aim of this study is twofold. One aim is to discuss the internationalisation strategies of Swedish universities in 2012, based on the 31 applications in the Strategic Grants for Internationalisation programme. Even
though this is just a single case study, the results might be of interest to
HEIs and other actors when they develop their internationalisation strategies or programmes. It might also contribute to a better understanding of
current trends in this highly dynamic field. The second aim is to contribute
to the growing literature discussing the internationalisation of higher
education and in particular to the literature discussing frameworks for how
to study and describe this process in a structured manner. These type of

Going Global: Knowledge-Based Economies for 21st Century Nations
ISBN: 978-1-78441-003-2

frameworks are not only of academic interest, but are also useful for people trying to support and manage internationalisation endeavours on the institutional, national or even supra-national level.

International relations are and always have been inherent in higher education and research (Smeby and Trondal, 2005). However, internationalisation of HEIs exhibits a growing trend (cf. The Royal Society, 2011), with globalisation as the main driver. Within the concept of globalisation lies increased international competition as well as increased international collaboration (cf. McKelvey and Holmén, 2009). A global market develops, which leads to students and firms having international references and requirements. Partly due to globalisation, individualisation and marketisation follow (Frölich, 2006). Among other things, these trends challenge the leadership of the HEIs and lead to changes in management structure (Sporn, 2007).

Internationalisation Activities and Rationales

One aim of this study is to develop a framework of internationalisation activities and rationales. This framework might serve when comparing different internationalisation approaches (as in the present case) but it can also be used for the management of internationalisation of HEIs. According to Bartell (2003), internationalisation is far from a clearly defined and understood concept. Given the growing importance of internationalisation in contributing to HEIs' accomplishment of their missions, there is a need for a framework to facilitate a structured approach. 'Internationalisation of higher education can be understood as [...] a defining feature of all universities, encompassing organisational change, curriculum innovation, staff development and student mobility, for the purposes of achieving excellence in teaching and research.' (Rudzki, 1995:421) In line with this definition, this study considers internationalisation as a tool to better achieve the HEIs' missions.

The framework for the empirical analysis is based on Knight (2007), which in turn refers to previous literature (e.g. Knight, 2005, 2004, 2003, 1999; Knight and de Wit, 1995). However, the framework was modified with the aim of:

- making a specific framework that focuses on the institutional level
- adding activities and rationales devoted attention to in 2012
- reducing the overlap within and between sets of activities and rationales.

Particular attention is often given to distance education or e-learning as a means of serving an international audience (Stokes, 2011; Wildavsky et al., 2011). To make this type of education more visible in the framework, an activity has been added: cross-border distance education. Other activities that evoke much discussion are various forms of branch campuses (Altbach, 2007; Altbach et al., 2009), thus leading to the addition of offshoring and branch campuses as an activity.

The service mission or 'third mission' of the HEI is relatively invisible among the academic rationales proposed by Knight (2007). One such rationale, which receives much attention, is innovation and how universities can contribute to it (cf. Gibbons et al., 1994; Nowotny et al., 2001). Another similar rationale related to knowledge production, innovation and some of the predominantly national rationales is global or 'grand' challenges, such as climate change (The Royal Society, 2011). Therefore, innovation and grand challenges have been added to the list of rationales.

Given the strong interdependencies between activities and rationales, it is difficult to make a clear-cut distinction. A number of activities and rationales have been removed or merged in order to enhance the focus on institutional aspects and reduce overlap. Another method of reducing overlap and increasing the framework's clarity is the introduction of a revised hierarchical structure. Depending on the intended use of the framework, this hierarchy could be further refined with a third level of activities and rationales. The activities and rationales in the proposed framework are exhibited in Figure 2 and Figure 3 below in the *Analysis – strategic internationalisation in Sweden 2012* section.

Universities in Sweden and the Role of STINT

In 2012, there were 47 HEIs in Sweden, of which 36 universities were entitled to award licentiates and PhDs. In 2010, the Higher Education Act was amended to introduce application and tuition fees for citizens outside the European Economic Area and Switzerland. HEIs were required to charge tuition fees to these students covering the full costs (Swedish National Agency for Higher Education, 2011).

STINT, the Swedish Foundation for International Cooperation in Research and Higher Education, was set up as an endowed independent foundation by an act of the Swedish Parliament in 1994. The mission of the foundation is to enhance the quality and competence of Swedish higher education and research through international co-operation.

Empirical Data and Methodology

A study of university leadership positions in terms of internationalisation revealed them to be quite interested, although weak in terms of resources, actual management power and ambition to drive institutional change (Göthenberg et al., 2012). In the light of this, the Strategic Grants for Internationalisation programme was launched by STINT. Its aim was to contribute to the renewal and development of internationalisation strategies at university level and the following four project selection criteria were determined:

A. The anticipated contribution of the university's activities to strategic internationalisation.
B. The level of renewal in regard to internationalisation in the project and/ or forms of international cooperation and potential of the project.
C. The university leadership's commitment to and involvement in the implementation.
D. The project proposal's planning and approval, such as quality and level of clarity in the project plan, plus the anticipated benefit in relation to the size of the investment.

Among the formal requirements was 50 per cent co-funding and each university president/vice-chancellor was allowed to submit up to two applications. Project duration was restricted to two years and granted funding of the project was limited to SEK1 million (approximately €115,000). The first call was published in December 2011 and closed at the end of March 2012. Out of 47 theoretically eligible universities, 20 submitted a total of 31 applications.

The main difficulty relating to the mapping of the applications against the framework was that the rationales and activities were more or less explicitly described in the applications. A guiding principle in this study was to include only those activities and rationales explicitly mentioned in the proposal.

Empirical data comes from the applications in STINT's first call for proposals in the Strategic Grants for Internationalisation programme. Applications respond to the call text and the postulated selection criteria, and are thus not a true reflection of what the university leadership considers most important. An initial check involved comparing the criteria with the activities and rationales used for the analysis. This check indicated no direct correlation. However, one definite bias introduced by the call requirements involved the budget and time restrictions, which exclude larger or longer initiatives. A further potential bias comes from the sampling method, and there is a risk that a certain type of university will have responded to the call. However, any bias was considered to be small, especially as a large number of eligible universities responded and showed great variety of size, age, profile and location.

Finally, as in all externally (co-)funded calls, there is a risk that projects are proposed just because there is additional funding available. There is a delicate balancing act for a funding organisation between funding projects which would not otherwise have been carried out and funding those of core interest to the applicants (cf. Nelson, 1959).

Analysis – Strategic Internationalisation in Sweden 2012

Almost one third of the received applications addressed internationalisation at home, with activities mainly targeting the better management of international students, including initiatives to involve international students in improving the routines. The cross-border projects were largely aimed at establishing, reinforcing or using networks (cf. Figure 1).

Sometimes internationalisation is considered to be international students and not much more. The activity 'International students: Inbound' was also most frequently mentioned among the applications (cf. Figure 2). Another typical, simplified conceptualisation of internationalisation is to reduce it to international collaboration between HEIs. This simplification was also partly supported by the data. A lot less attention is normally given to internal activities to strengthen capacity for managing internationalisation. However, according to the applications, almost 50 per cent included such activities.

Among the rationales, seven out of ten applications mentioned international branding, profile and status (cf. Figure 3). The second most mentioned rationale was student and staff development, while the third was knowledge production.

The applications differ a lot in terms of ambitions and scope, even though most of them have approximately the same budget volume. As

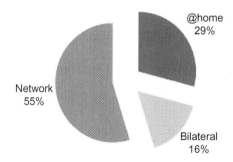

Figure 1: Types of internationalisation projects.

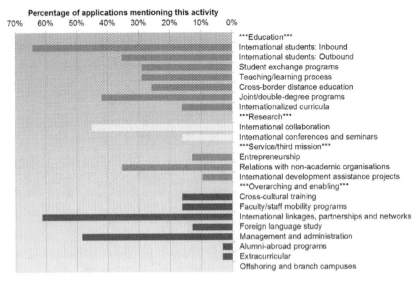

Percentage of applications mentioning this activity

70% 60% 50% 40% 30% 20% 10% 0%

Education
International students: Inbound
International students: Outbound
Student exchange programs
Teaching/learning process
Cross-border distance education
Joint/double-degree programs
Internationalized curricula
Research
International collaboration
International conferences and seminars
Service/third mission
Entrepreneurship
Relations with non-academic organisations
International development assistance projects
Overarching and enabling
Cross-cultural training
Faculty/staff mobility programs
International linkages, partnerships and networks
Foreign language study
Management and administration
Alumni-abroad programs
Extracurricular
Offshoring and branch campuses

Figure 2: Internationalisation activities.

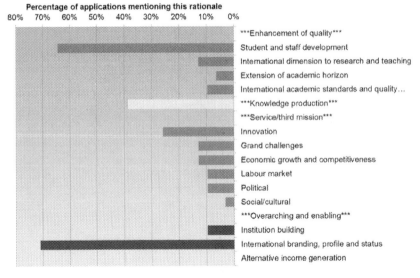

Percentage of applications mentioning this rationale

80% 70% 60% 50% 40% 30% 20% 10% 0%

Enhancement of quality
Student and staff development
International dimension to research and teaching
Extension of academic horizon
International academic standards and quality...
Knowledge production
Service/third mission
Innovation
Grand challenges
Economic growth and competitiveness
Labour market
Political
Social/cultural
Overarching and enabling
Institution building
International branding, profile and status
Alternative income generation

Figure 3: Internationalisation rationales.

shown in the histograms of Figure 4 and Figure 5, three to five activities and two or three rationales were typically mentioned in an application.

Finally, an attempt was made to investigate whether the university size (and in most cases the related age: an old university is normally a large

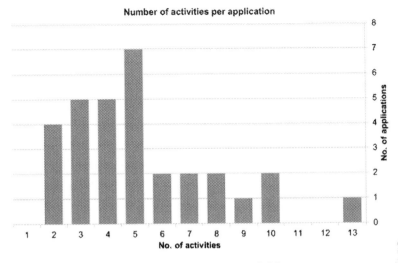

Figure 4: Histogram — activities.

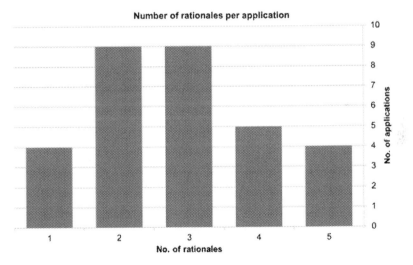

Figure 5: Histogram — rationales.

university) correlates to certain activities or rationales. The applicants were divided into three groups based on their staff numbers (cf. Table 1).

As Figure 6 and Figure 7 indicate, there does not appear to be a systematic correlation between size and activities or rationales. The only clear difference is the absence of applications from medium-sized universities

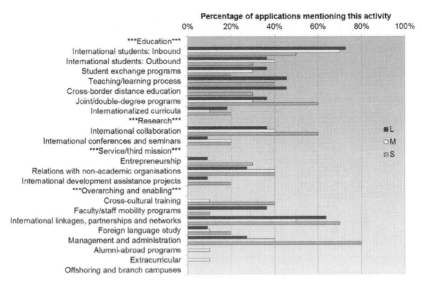

Figure 6: Activities in relation to university size.

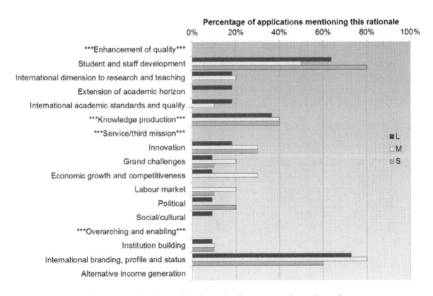

Figure 7: Rationales in relation to university size.

mentioning activities relating to the teaching/learning process and cross-border distance education programmes. Another potentially systematic difference is the higher level of interest in management and administration among the smaller organisations.

Table 1: Group sizes.

Size*	Group label	Number of applications
Above 3,000	L (large)	11
1,000–3,000	M (medium)	10
Below 1,000	S (small)	10

*Size is presented based on the FTE number of teaching and research staff (Source: Swedish National Agency for Higher Education 2011)

Discussion – Activities and Rationales in Theory and Practice

Data indicates that the top priority for several university presidents/vice-chancellors is the internationalisation of education. Given that international collaboration is natural in most research domains, there may be a greater need for the university leadership to engage in educational issues. It could be argued that research collaborations are largely organised according to a bottom-up process, whereas educational collaborations need more support from the leadership at the university.

The most common rationale mentioned in the applications was branding. This is in line with Knight (2007), where branding was positioned as one of the institutional rationales of emerging importance. Contributing to the interest in branding was probably the ongoing change towards more competition for funding and the new and more difficult situation regarding attracting international students. Branding is important in the market for international students and there is, consequently, a link between the domination of educational activities and branding rationales.

Innovation, i.e. various measures to ensure the implementation and use of new concepts and ideas emanating from research, was a relatively common rationale. The involvement of firms in internationalisation efforts is interesting and challenging, especially as it introduces intellectual property issues. The structure of Swedish industry, with a few large multinational firms carrying out the majority of research and development, may be one contributing factor to this rationale.

In general, the applications did not mention many rationales behind internationalisation. One explanation is that the writers of the applications may have considered it obvious that internationalisation is 'good'. However, consistent with the perspective used in this study (that internationalisation is just one tool to improve fulfilment of universities' missions), there is clearly a need to explain why a certain activity is proposed.

Offshoring and branch campuses are the cause of much discussion but, according to the study, are of limited interest in Sweden. One explanation might be that the modest volume allowed for in the project applications made it impossible to accommodate such endeavours.

There was no significant correlation between size and the type of internationalisation proposed. One potential difference indicated was that the smaller universities address the improvement of management and administration of international affairs to a greater extent.

The framework in Knight (2007) consists of 32 activities (when clustering all organisational strategies into one activity) and 30 rationales. It aims to cover the national, sector and institutional levels. The modified framework proposed in this paper has 20 activities and 15 rationales and a hierarchy linked to the mission of the university. It only covers the institutional level and incorporates a few new activities and rationales that were high on the agenda in 2012. Considering the fact that this is just a single case study, there is clearly room for further research. Apart from simply repeating this study with other sets of data, there are a wide range of opportunities to test the framework for other purposes. How do such lists of activities and rationales support the management of strategic internationalisation from an institutional perspective, for example?

Conclusions

This paper addresses strategic internationalisation at HEIs with the aims to:

- study the higher education leaderships' agendas for internationalisation
- develop a framework for description and analysis of internationalisation at institutional level.

Empirical data was taken from the response to a call for applications addressing university presidents/vice-chancellors in Sweden.

In relation to the first aim, the higher education leaderships' agendas for internationalisation were studied using the theoretical framework. Analysis of the 31 applications revealed very diverse approaches to internationalisation. Internationalisation of higher education was frequently addressed, with international students and joint/dual degree programmes as common types of activities. Internationalisation of research was mentioned in a smaller number of applications and it is argued that the internationalisation of education might need more top-down involvement than the internationalisation of research.

International branding and profile was the single most-mentioned rationale among the applications. This is in line with one of the emerging trends proposed in previous literature. Student and staff development was also very frequently mentioned and it might be of interest in future modifications of the framework to split these rationales into more narrowly defined ones in order to increase the information value.

In relation to the second aim, a framework with activities and rationales for internationalisation was developed based on previous literature. The tests of the modified framework indicate that it has some advantages:

- being more compact, it is easier to use
- it is updated to reflect current trends in internationalisation
- it reduces the overlap both within the sets of activities and rationales and between the sets.

However, it is also argued that the value of the framework depends very much on the purpose of its intended use.

Finally, with reference to Salmi (2009), a few indications of bold visions and strong leadership could be traced in the data. Still, the rather modest ambitions exhibited in most applications underline the fact that university management is approaching internationalisation with realistic and relatively short-term goals.

References

Altbach, PG (2007) Globalization and the university: realities in an unequal world. In Forest, JJF and Altbach, PG (eds) *International Handbook of Higher Education Part One: Global Themes and Contemporary Challenges* (Pp. 121–139). Springer, Amsterdam, Netherlands.

Altbach, PG, Reisberg, L and Rumbley, LE (2009) *Trends in Global Higher Education: Tracking an Academic Revolution*. Boston College Center for International Higher Education, Chestnut Hill, USA.

Bartell, M (2003) Internationalization of universities: A university culture-based framework. *Higher Education*, 45, Pp. 43–70.

Frölich, N (2006) Still academic and national – Internationalisation in Norwegian research and higher education. *Higher Education*, 52, Pp. 405–420.

Gibbons, M, Limoges, C, Nowotny, H, Schwartzman, S, Scott, P and Trow, M (1994) *The new production of knowledge*, SAGE publications Ltd, London, UK.

Göthenberg, A, Pohl, H and Adler, N (2012) 'Strategic measures for competitive internationalization of higher education and research'. Paper at Institutional Management in Higher Education, OECD, Paris, France.

Knight, J (1999) Internationalisation of Higher Education. In Knight, J and de Wit, H (eds) *Quality and Internationalisation in Higher Education* (Pp. 13–28). OECD, Paris, France.

Knight, J (2003) Updating the Definition of Internationalization. *International Higher Education*, 33, Pp. 2–3.

Knight, J (2004) 'Internationalization Remodeled: Definition, Approaches, and Rationales'. *Journal of Studies in International Education* 8(1), Pp. 5–31.

Knight, J (2005) 'An Internationalization Model: Responding to New Realities and Challenges'. In de Wit, H, Jaramillo, IC, Gacel-Ávila, J and Knight, J (eds) *Higher Education in Latin America: The International Dimension* (Pp. 31–68). World Bank Publications, Washington DC, USA.

Knight, J (2007) 'Internationalization: Concepts, Complexities and Challenges'. In Forest, JJF and Altbach, PG (eds) *International Handbook of Higher Education Part One: Global Themes and Contemporary Challenges* (Pp. 207–227). Springer, Amsterdam, Netherlands.

Knight, J and de Wit, H. (1995) 'Strategies for internationalisation of higher education: historical and conceptual perspectives'. In de Wit, H (Ed.) *Strategies for internationalisation of higher education: A comparative study of Australia, Canada, Europe and the United States of America* (Pp. 5–32). European Association for International Education (EAIE), Amsterdam, Netherlands.

McKelvey, M and Holmén, M (2009) *Learning to Compete in European Universities: From Social Institution to Knowledge Business*. Edward Elgar Publishing Ltd, Cheltenham, UK.

Nelson, RR (1959) The Simple Economics of Basic Scientific Research. *Journal of Political Economy*, 67, 3, Pp. 297–306.

Nowotny, H, Scott, P and Gibbons, M (2001) *Re-thinking Science: knowledge and the public in an age of uncertainty*. Blackwell Publishers Ltd, Cambridge, UK.

Rudzki, REJ (1995) 'The application of a strategic management model to the internationalization of higher education institutions'. *Higher Education*, 29, Pp. 421–441.

Salmi, J (2009) *The Challenge of Establishing World-Class Universities*. The World Bank, Washington DC, USA.

Smeby, J-C and Trondal, J (2005) 'Globalisation or Europeanisation? International contact among university staff'. *Higher Education*, 49, Pp. 449–466.

Sporn, B (2007) 'Governance and administration: Organizational and structural trends'. In Forest, JJF and Altbach, PG (eds) *International Handbook of Higher Education Part One: Global Themes and Contemporary Challenges* (Pp. 141–157). Springer, Amsterdam, Netherlands.

Stokes, P (2011) 'What Online Learning Can Teach Us about Higher Education'. In Wildawsky, B, Kelly, AP and Carey, K (eds) *Reinventing Higher Education: the Promise of Innovation* (Pp. 197–224). Harvard Education Press, Cambridge, USA.

Swedish National Agency for Higher Education (2011) *Swedish Universities & University Colleges — Short Version of Annual Report 2011*, 2011:15 R, Högskoleverket, Stockholm, Sweden.

The Royal Society (2011) *Knowledge, networks and nations: Global scientific collaboration in the 21st century*. RS Policy document 03/11, The Royal Society, London, UK.

Wildawsky, B, Kelly, AP and Carey, K (2011) *Reinventing Higher Education: the Promise of Innovation*. Harvard Education Press, Cambridge, USA.

Chapter 3.5

Transnational Education – The German Approach

Dorothea Rüland

Introduction

Transnational education (TNE), a comparatively recent phenomenon, has undergone rapid development over the past decade. It has become one of the most vibrant fields of higher education internationalisation through international collaboration. With an increasing number of countries engaged as providers and hosts of TNE, the range of approaches, motivations and forms of TNE is widening as well, calling for a discussion of the objectives, potentials and possible risks. This paper aims to analyse the German approach to TNE and discuss its features, challenges, opportunities and impacts within the context of global development.

Definition, Development and Motivation of TNE

TNE is one of several terms used to describe a group of activities that have been part of the internationalisation process of higher education (HE) for about 25 years. As the organisation of German universities for the internationalisation of the German higher education system and the main funding body for the engagement of German higher education institutions (HEIs) abroad, the German Academic Exchange Service (DAAD) embraces a definition of transnational education that takes into account the predominant character of German engagement so far and emphasises academic responsibility: 'Transnational education (TNE) refers to universities, courses and

Going Global: Knowledge-Based Economies for 21st Century Nations
Copyright © 2014 by Dorothea Rüland
All rights of reproduction in any form reserved
ISBN: 978-1-78441-003-2

individual study modules that are offered abroad essentially for students from the respective country or region, while the main academic responsibility lies with a university in another country. Academic responsibility first of all refers to contents (curricula), but typically embraces at least some of the following elements as well: German faculty, degrees awarded and quality assurance conducted by the German university.[1]

The development of TNE began in the late 1980s, when Australian, British and American universities pioneered offering the first degree courses outside their own countries. Germany entered the field about a decade later. Between 1990 and 2011, the number of tertiary students enrolled outside their country of citizenship more than tripled from 1.3 to 4.3 million. The vast majority of these were hosted by OECD countries, especially the USA, the UK, Germany, France and Australia.[2] The worldwide demand for international study places is forecasted to rise even further to 5.8 million by 2020.[3] This increase in demand begins to overstretch capacities in host countries, especially in the most popular destinations for international students.

In this context − a growing interest of HEIs in internationalisation on the one hand and the growing demand for HE on an international level on the other hand − TNE creates a win-win situation. HEIs from providing countries are motivated to engage in TNE by their objectives to increase their visibility on the international level, to gain the loyalty of well-qualified students, junior researchers and alumni and to collaborate with universities in other countries. Host countries (especially emerging economies and developing countries) benefit from TNE as they face difficulties in providing sufficient numbers of university places and/or need to improve the quality of courses, teaching, research and university administration.

Germany as a TNE Provider

Since 2001 the DAAD has funded more than 70 TNE projects, with more than 10,000 graduates to date and more than 20,000 students enrolled at the moment. With a largely state-funded HE system based on an understanding of education as a common good and public task, and without a tradition of approaching HE entrepreneurially, the situation of German

---

1. DAAD position paper *Transnationale Bildung*, translation to be published in spring 2014 (www.daad.de/tnb)
2. Cf. OECD: Education Indicators in Focus − 2013/05 (July), p. 2
3. Cf. Böhm e.a., *Vision 2020. Forecasting international student mobility − a UK perspective*, 2004, p. 32

HEIs as TNE providers differs from that of other countries. This difference also shows in the financial support granted by the German government, which in fact has facilitated the emergence of Germany as a major TNE provider. The motivations for encouraging the ventures of German HEIs abroad differ between the three main government funders:

- The Federal Ministry of Education and Research (BMBF) funds the TNE endeavours of German universities as part of the internationalisation of German HE. By offering their study courses on the international higher education market, German HEIs are expected to demonstrate their competitiveness and create 'beacons' abroad as intersections for co-operation in research and teaching.
- The Federal Foreign Office supports TNE following a 'soft power' approach in order to enhance the image of Germany in other countries. HE is seen here as a vehicle to transport knowledge about Germany, heighten familiarity with German culture and create a supportive climate for scientific, political and business contacts. Funding for certain TNE projects (especially for scholarships) or a number of bi-cultural German–Arabic master's courses in Jordan, Egypt and Lebanon, for example, is granted as an element of superordinate regional politics.
- For the Federal Ministry for Economic Co-operation and Development (BMZ), TNE is an instrument to assist capacity building and foster cross-cultural dialogue between developing and advanced countries. In this political field, TNE forms part of a broader strategy to use education for economic and social advancement. The BMZ therefore provides funding for projects with TNE components in a variety of programmes.

The German TNE model is characterised by a partnership approach.[4] The offers of German HEIs are shaped by academic specialisation and a practical orientation with the objective of employability. More than half of the DAAD-funded TNE projects are in the engineering sciences, which have a high reputation but are also cost-intensive. Three prevalent models of German TNE activity have emerged:

- German courses abroad (in particular in MENA, Eastern Europe and Asia) are the basic model: a German university runs one (or several) of its courses (bachelor's, master's or doctorate) at a partner university abroad. As a rule, the partner is largely responsible for providing the infrastructure as well as the staff for some of the basic teaching.

---

4. Cf. Clausen, A, Schindler-Kovats, B and Stalf, N, 'Transnational Education, Made in Germany' In: *Journal of the European Higher Education Area* 4/2011, Pp. 1–20.

- Universities abroad with German backing are established according to the host country's higher education legislation or on the basis of a special status. A special legal status is most likely to be granted in the case of politically triggered projects that have a model function in the respective host country. Seven 'bi-national' universities are currently funded by the DAAD: German–Jordanian University (GJU)/Amman, German–Kazakh University (DKU)/Almaty, German University Cairo (GUC), German University of Technology (GUtech)/Muscat, Sino–German University (CDH) at Tongji-University Shanghai, Turkish–German University (TDU)/Istanbul and Vietnamese–German University (VGU)/Ho-Chi-Minh-City.
- An affiliated or branch campus is a branch of a German university abroad and thus, unlike bi-national universities, a foreign education institution in the respective educational landscape. The parent university bears full responsibility for teaching and administration. The degrees awarded are those of the German university.[5] Four branch campuses are supported by the DAAD: Al Gouna/Egypt (TU Berlin), GIST–TUM Asia Singapur (TU Munich), FAU Busan (U Erlangen-Nürnberg) and Heidelberg Center Santiago de Chile.

Other forms of TNE provision, such as validation, franchising and distance learning, have not played a significant role in Germany so far.

Impact of TNE: Ten Keywords

The variety of approaches, models and motivations on the providing as well as on the receiving side also applies to the impact. For German HEIs, an engagement in TNE activities is seen in the context of internationalisation:

- German teaching staff gain valuable international experience, e.g. as flying faculty in TNE degree courses offered at the foreign partner institution
- The transnational context gives essential impulses and enables the development and testing of new teaching models, new curricula and innovative study modules
- The home campus intensifies its connection to the globalised HE environment: The presence of international students from TNE courses at partner institutions, who pass a part of their studies or an internship in Germany and arrive there already identifying with the institution

---

5. Cf. DAAD position paper 'Transnationale Bildung'

providing their study course, enriches the student body and adds to the international flair of the university

- The home institution's administration is challenged to adapt the possibilities and regulations for the mutual recognition of credits or course achievements and to facilitate the mobility of academic staff who temporarily teach at the partner institution abroad
- German researchers and companies get in touch with highly motivated junior staff and future international partners through TNE

Even though the impact is difficult to measure, it is quite obvious from the experiences so far that TNE is able to develop transformative power, especially in the host countries, which in return gives additional motivation to the participating universities and investors in order to engage in these activities.

There is a wide range of social, economic, education-related, even political and legal aspects to consider through which TNE activities may and very often do have an impact in host countries. Notwithstanding the differences, the main points to consider when talking about the sustainable impact of TNE from the perspective of the German partnership approach can be summarised under ten keywords, which all have to be taken into account even though some of them overlap or are interconnected.

1. Modernisation

In many host countries, the need to modernise the domestic system of higher education in order to keep up with the development of the global knowledge society is often a major motivation for permitting or even supporting the activities of foreign education providers. TNE is seen as a vehicle for introducing and establishing new models into existing HE environments, ranging from alternative teaching methods and innovative curricula to new ways of organising study courses or entire institutions. TNE is expected to effectively contribute to raising the local level of education to international standards and strengthen the integration of host countries in a globalised world.

2. Access to international HE

With the number of study places available to international students in the main target countries for student mobility threatening to fall behind demand, TNE presents a viable alternative for the enhancement of access to international HE. For students who cannot afford to go abroad or, for cultural reasons, are hindered from leaving home in order to pursue HE, the presence of transnational study offers in their home countries can open up educational options which otherwise would be completely out of reach. In addition, TNE reduces the risk of brain drain by providing an international study experience and international degrees 'at home' without the need to physically move to another country. In this way, TNE effectively supports the democratisation of education and upward social mobility through education in host countries.

3. **Capacity building**
By importing study courses and institutional structures from other countries, especially in partnerships between local and foreign HEIs, host countries profit from TNE by developing better conditions for enhancing knowledge and skills locally, introducing more effective methods of management and stimulating a greater flexibility of administrative procedures. In a mid- and long-term perspective, TNE study offers can act as an effective tool to strengthen a host country's ability to compete on the market and present its attractiveness as a place of investment.

4. **Quantity**
Developing and newly industrialised countries, in particular, struggle with the challenge of having to modernise and at the same time rapidly expand their HE systems. More and better study opportunities are required to fulfil these countries' aspirations to participate and integrate in a knowledge-based global economy, in order to provide adequate qualification opportunities for future generations and thus enable more young people to choose a self-determined way of life.

5. **Quality**
Through their content, curricula and teaching methods, TNE provision transfers knowledge as well as know-how from providing countries to host countries. In the case of German HEIs engaging in TNE, this transfer goes along with specific concepts of HE, like the Humboldtian idea of the university as uniting research and teaching or the concept of practice-orientation realised in universities of applied sciences. An orientation on German concepts of adequate quality and mechanisms of quality management can imply that study courses are accredited in Germany or required to undergo the internal approval procedures of their home institutions, but it can also mean that German universities develop and implement complete quality control systems for their TNE endeavours.

6. **Awareness of current issues**
A further aspect to consider when assessing the impact of TNE is the degree to which its educational offers reflect broader themes and issues. HE today is called upon to produce graduates with the necessary skills

and knowledge that will enable them to find solutions to the challenges resulting from industrialisation and globalisation. Green engineering, sustainability and the characteristics of open societies are just a few examples of topics that need to be addressed in order to safeguard and improve the quality of life and support transformation processes in a socially responsible way. The special strengths of German universities in engineering and environmental sciences resulted in a variety of study courses dedicated to the solution of challenges that are increasingly felt to affect the safety and wellbeing of countries and people all over the world. By transferring these courses to other countries, German HEIs also transport new perspectives, alternative approaches and specialist knowledge on issues transcending national borders and create links for host countries to enter into international discourses.

7. Academic values

As a by-product of transferring their study programmes, TNE providers at the same time transport their specific academic culture and values. For German HEIs concepts like university autonomy and academic self-management, the ideal of encouraging the creative and critical thinking of students for the advancement of research and development, and student self-government as a form of participation in academic life, form part of their self-image as education providers. With reference to their TNE engagement, this self-image of German HEIs finds expression in the Code of Conduct for Higher Education Project Abroad adopted in May 2013 by the members of the German Rectors' Conference (HRK), following a joint initiative of HRK and DAAD.[6] Put into practice in transnational study offers, these values are apt to shape and support the formation of a knowledge-based society; they strengthen the location as an outstanding centre of education and science, and produce responsible graduates.

8. Interconnectedness

A characteristic of the German HE system reflected in many TNE activities of German universities and universities of applied sciences is a high level of collaboration between science and industry in research, but also in academic training. German universities often integrate mandatory industry internships in their curricula and maintain close links with companies and potential employers to be able to adapt their teaching content to actual professional requirements and impart

---

6. Cf. www.hrk.de/resolutions-publications/resolutions/resolution/convention/code-of-conduct-for-german-higher-education-projects-abroad/

real-life working experience to their students. In their teaching and research, they foster the perception of education as part of a broader societal, political and economic context. In this way, they support the institutional and individual integration of higher education and university graduates into a globalised world and bridge the gap between education and the labour market.

9. **Intercultural competence**

International experience and intercultural skills, once the privilege of a minority of students who could afford to pursue part or their entire education abroad, is increasingly seen not as an exceptional asset, but as an indispensable component of a complete education that enables graduates to work and interact successfully in a working environment characterised by globalisation. TNE opens additional avenues for a much larger proportion of students to gain international experience. In the study courses offered abroad by German universities with or without local partners, exposure to teaching staff from Germany or with a German background and integrated stays in Germany for studies or internships, often supported by German language training throughout the study course, provide international experience and convey different ways of teaching and learning.

10. **Economic impact**

The potential impact of TNE activity on the economy of host countries reaches far beyond its immediate monetary effects, such as revenue realised by tuition fees or the living expenses of students spent at the location of branch campuses. The skills and competences imparted to students, the expertise imported into the host country from abroad, as well as the collaborations and networks with partners inside and outside university in both countries, all operate within the host country's economic environment. Study courses offered abroad by German HEIs mirror the work-oriented understanding of education and knowledge, which typically characterise the engineering sciences in German HE in particular. Thus, German TNE study offers ensure good job prospects for their students and at the same time enhance the employability of the local workforce, contribute to the host country's competitiveness as a place of investment and create opportunities for an intensification of trade relations with the sending country.

Future Prospects of TNE

It was shown that the profiles, motivations, forms and impacts of TNE are multifarious. This is also true for the future development of TNE. At some locations, TNE could well turn out to be a transitional stage on the way towards national HE systems that are on a par with international standards, sustained by former host countries from their own resources. In other places, educational hubs or multi-national universities will establish themselves as lasting phenomena of a globalised HE world. For funding organisations such as the DAAD it is important to accompany future trends in TNE in a way that enables a further sustainable development of newly established and up and coming educational institutions. Core challenges are in the field of quality assurance, international compatibility of HE legislation and the further development of TNE ventures, which by their nature focus on teaching, into HEIs engaging in research. These challenges can only be mastered with the intensive dialogue of all stakeholders, which is what the DAAD embodies by tradition and conviction. We also support all efforts for an orientation of TNE on common academic values as they are illustrated on a national level by the German Code of Conduct for German Higher Education Projects Abroad, initiated by the DAAD and the German Rectors' Conference, and on an international level by the Declaration of the Higher Education Summit in the UK's G8 Presidency Year, held in London in May 2013.

Chapter 3.6

Transnational 'Education-for-Peace' in the Era of International Terrorism: Capacitating Universities as Drivers of Attitudinal Change in Volatile Transitional Societies

Kenneth Omeje

Introduction

The aim of this paper is to propose a framework for developing flexible capacity-building projects that can support the global anti-terrorism campaign in various developing countries, in particular countries considered to be highly vulnerable to international terrorism. The study places methodological emphasis on the *raison d'être* and processes of developing and mainstreaming functional values, skills and attitudinal patterns of transnational peace education into the curricula of university degree programmes among a cohort of participating regional universities, working in partnership with a lead Western university.

The 2001 9/11 attacks on the World Trade Center in New York and the American Defense Headquarters popularly known as the Pentagon in Washington DC, and the subsequent global war on terror launched by the ex-President George W Bush administration are some of the prominent reminders that international terrorism is a contemporary global reality. It is a threat that affects many developed and developing countries alike and one

Going Global: Knowledge-Based Economies for 21st Century Nations
Copyright © 2014 by Kenneth Omeje
All rights of reproduction in any form reserved
ISBN: 978-1-78441-003-2

that has also practically changed the way different communities live and perceive each other in a rapidly globalising world.

Akin to a hydra-headed monster, it is apparent that no one solution could easily stamp out the threat of terrorism. It is a multi-faceted threat that requires a multi-track remedial framework. The American government and their allies in the global anti-terrorism campaign have continued to use two contrasting approaches, namely the military 'hard-power' approach supported by robust intelligence networks, and the more diplomatic aid-oriented, development provisioning 'soft-power' approach. Both approaches have delivered mixed results and they both have their challenges and externalities.

Peace education is concerned with educating people for and about all aspects of peace, which for the purpose of this project should be given a profound transnational focus. Transnational Education-for-Peace (TEfP) is essentially seen as the practically applied side of transnational peace education. TEfP is considered important under the present international dispensation to help mitigate the perennial cycle of violence associated with international terrorism. TEfP is a type of education that promotes peace and tolerance in a globalised multicultural setting, and seeks to understand and transform hatred, suspicion and violence. The UN General Assembly proclaimed 2001–2010 'The International Decade for a Culture of Peace and Non-violence for the Children of the World', but it is apparent that international terrorism has not abated in the present decade. The UN General Assembly Declaration and Programme of Action of September 1999 defined a culture of peace as: '... all the values, attitudes and forms of behaviour that reflect respect for life, for human dignity and for all human rights; the rejection of violence in all its forms and commitment to the principles of freedom, justice, solidarity, tolerance and understanding between people.'

The idea of TEfP proposed in this paper is only a complementary measure to all other constructive intervention initiatives led by governmental, inter-governmental and non-governmental organisations. In fact, there are, for instance, a growing multiplicity of peace-oriented NGOs and university-level educational programmes in many of the developing countries of Africa (in particular, countries in the Arab Maghreb and Sahel) and the Middle East, regions considered as the soft underbelly of international terrorism. I use the stereotypical classification of Africa and the Middle East as soft underbelly of international terrorism in a typically journalistic sense because empirical evidence has shown that there are sections of the American, British, French, Dutch and Spanish societies that are just as vulnerable to terrorist indoctrinations and activities as some of the most stereotyped developing countries.

Be that as it may, the key emphasis in any projects arising from this study is on the need to flexibly mainstream education-for-peace within the framework of transnationality in a scalable and sustainable way. Organisationally, the type of transnational education proposed in this study is different from the conventional pattern of 'higher education study programmes, or sets of studies or educational services (including distance education) in which the learners are located in a country (usually in the developing world) different from the one where the awarding institution is based (usually in the developed world)' (ESU, 2011). The proposal for transnationality is more in the content of the education offered than in its organisational structure and origin, albeit a considerable measure of international and regional collaboration and partnership would be useful.

Background to the Proposed TEfP Project: Education-for-Peace in the Context of Post-Conflict Societies in Africa

The background to this project proposal is a raft of externally funded education-for-peace projects I have helped to develop and implement since 2004 at both the University of Bradford in the UK and the United States International University in Nairobi, Kenya. These projects have taken place in war- or violence-affected countries and regions like Sierra Leone, Liberia, Northern Uganda, the *Democratic Republic of the Congo* (DRC) and Kenya. The projects have been variously funded by the British Council, the Westminster Foundation for Democracy and the Allan and Nesta Ferguson Trust.

In post-war Sierra Leone, the capacity-building project aimed to promote peace education, human rights and democratic governance community policing (2004–2008). In post-war Liberia, on the other hand, the project aimed to re-invent higher education for conflict transformation and peace-building (2006–2008). The rationale was that in the post-war dispensation, Sierra Leone and Liberian universities and security forces (mostly the police) should be capacitated to play functional roles in:

1. Building peace by initiating or participating in various national and community-based peace-building projects (for example, security-sector reforms; disarmament; demobilisation; rehabilitation and reintegration of rebels, child soldiers and ex-combatants; confidence-building measures between the civilian populations and security forces, etc.).
2. Ensuring peaceful resolution or transformation of conflicts as they arise.

Besides universities, the police forces were targeted for these capacity-building projects because of their alleged violations of human rights, their apparent lack of knowledge of human-rights principles, and what many see as their ambiguous role with regard to democratic activities and in civil wars and violent conflicts in the two countries.

We sought to achieve the capacity-building project goals by:

- Developing a new study programme in two Liberian universities: the University of Liberia in Monrovia and Cuttington University in Gbanga (Diploma and BA degree programmes in Peace and Conflict Resolution) and three Sierra Leonean universities: Fourah Bay College, University of Sierra Leone (Diploma/BA degree courses in Peace and Conflict Studies), Njala University College (Diploma and MA degrees in Peace and Development Studies) and Milton Maggai College of Education and Technology (Diploma/BA degree in Peace Education).
- The curriculum development and review workshops (CDRWs), as we often called them, emphasised an integrative blend of both the global/international and the local/regional realities, as well as the 'theory–praxis' nexus in terms of the pedagogical content of the education-for-peace curricula.
- Strengthening existing courses in cognate disciplines (such as Political Science, Sociology, History/African Studies, Psychology and Law) to teach practical modules and topics in peace, conflict, security and conflict resolution.
- Involvement of the West Yorkshire Police in England in the development/review of community policing strategies in the Sierra Leone Police (SLP) and Liberian National Police (LNP). We also facilitated the establishment of a staff development visit of selected SLP and LNP officers to the Bishopgarth West Yorkshire Police Training and Development Centre.
- Organising specialised training workshops on the core values and pedagogy of education-for-peace for lecturers in the social sciences, humanities and law. In Liberia, instructors and senior officers of the LNP were invited to these workshops while in Sierra Leone we organised a series of parallel workshops for instructors in the SLP training school.
- Provision of resource materials, mostly relevant textbooks to support teaching, research and learning in the beneficiary institutions and police academies.
- Short-term staff development visits between the University of Bradford and the two Liberian universities to promote curriculum participation and learning.
- Promoting collaborative research and publications among lecturers in participating universities. A number of relevant university-level papers were published through these various projects. Newsletters and periodicals were also published to document and disseminate the achievements, best practices and challenges of the projects.

In the DRC, emphasis has been placed on capacitating universities for peace building and conflict transformation, notably the University of Kinshasa (2006–2008) and the University of Lubumbashi (2006–2012). In Kenya and Northern Uganda, I have worked with the United States International University in Nairobi and Gulu University in Gulu, Northern Uganda (2009–2012) in various areas of capacity-building. The capacity-building projects that I have co-ordinated at the partner universities in the DRC, Kenya and Northern Uganda have had two key objectives:

- to develop the institutional and collaborative capacities of the partner universities to play applied functional roles in conflict and development intervention
- to expand and strengthen the employability skills and opportunities of undergraduate and graduate students in the cognate fields of study.

Funded by the British Council EPA/DelPHE grant schemes, these projects were developed against the background of multi-faceted and inter-locking conflicts and wars that have blighted the African Great Lakes region for over the past two decades (see Omeje and Hepner, 2013 eds.); poor capacity for practical conflict and development intervention in existing higher education curricula; and the traditional inclination of higher education partnerships in Africa towards vertical co-operation with Western institutions, with the result that collaboration within the region is highly limited.

To help address some of the capacity deficits, various project activities were developed and implemented, including:

- The review and strengthening of the Peace, Conflict and Development Studies curricula of the three partner universities using the operational frameworks of 12 different collaborative and individual university-based workshops. Some new practical modules and training programmes (e.g. student work placement/internships, study visits to relevant organisations and community-service schemes) were developed or, in some cases, strengthened at different levels (BA, MA and PhD).
- Regional co-operation and inter-university faculty exchange visits between partner institutions to promote curriculum participation in teaching, research, students' counselling/thesis supervision, seminars and publication. Under this collaborative initiative, lecturers were cross-posted between different partner universities over a limited period of one to two weeks in each cycle.
- A research and publication opportunity/skill acquisition programme for project partners leading to the production of a relevant edited book project that can be used in research/teaching in the area of peace, conflict

and development studies in the African Great Lakes Region (AGLR) and beyond. The book is titled *Conflict and Peacebuilding in the African Great Lakes Region* (Indiana University Press, 2013) and the volume editors were Kenneth Omeje and Tricia Redeker Hepner.

- The provision of a limited number of relevant textbooks in Peace, Conflict and Development Studies for the comparatively under-resourced partner institutions (University of Lubumbashi and Gulu University).
- Career counselling services for students using both internal and external professional counsellors. At Gulu University, career counselling was complemented by community outreach programmes to, among other things, inspire war-affected schoolchildren and provide practical training in post-conflict counselling/victim rehabilitation for students of Development Studies and Conflict Transformation.
- The production of an annual project newsletter for the dissemination of information about project activities, challenges and opportunities for higher education partnerships in the region. The annual newsletters are distributed in both hard copy and electronic formats.

International Terrorism and Transnational Education-for-Peace: The Proposed Project's Content and Context

In terms of substantive content and pedagogical goals, the TEfP proposed in this study should focus on generating and acquiring the knowledge, skills and attitudes aimed at non-violent alternatives to positive behavioural change, institutional reconstruction and societal transformation. The content and context of the education provided should harmoniously integrate both the local and transnational imperatives to focus on what Reardon (1988:38) calls 'educating people for international responsibility'.

Broadly, this proposed project could flexibly aim to adapt some of the best practices from the various education-for-peace programmes that presently exist in different post-conflict societies of Africa and the Middle East, including:

- developing new study programmes and general education modules in interactive inter-regional curriculum development/review workshops, emphasising an integrative blend of the international and the local/regional realities, as well as the theory–praxis nexus
- strengthening existing courses in cognate disciplines (e.g. Political Science, Sociology, History/Area Studies, Psychology and Law) to teach practical modules and topics in peace, conflict, security, development and conflict resolution

- organising specialised training workshops on the core values and pedagogy of education-for-peace for lecturers in the participating disciplines
- the provision of resource materials, mostly relevant textbooks, to support teaching, research and learning in the beneficiary institutions
- short-term inter-university staff exchange visits to promote curriculum participation and learning
- promoting collaborative research and publications among lecturers in participating universities
- developing context-specific community outreach and internship programmes with a primary focus on improving university–community relations, peace building, community development and students' employability skills
- the opportunity for independent context-specific programmes that address the special-capacity needs of each participating institution.

Arising from the various UN declarations are a number of thematic areas essential for developing academic and practical training programmes of TEfP, including (see Kok, 2009):

- peace education (especially education for the non-violent resolution of conflicts)
- sustainable development (mainly involving the systematic eradication of poverty, the reduction of inequalities and environmental sustainability)
- human rights education (especially civil and democratic rights, rights/protection of minority groups, religious and cultural rights)
- gender equality
- democratic participation
- the promotion of understanding, tolerance and solidarity among peoples, vulnerable groups and migrants within a state and among states
- the rejection of all forms of violence at all levels – local, regional and international – promoting creative strategies and partnerships for discouraging and ending violence
- context-specific and research-based understanding of the historical, economic and cultural structures that underpin [the potential] violence in various societies, and working towards their peaceful deconstruction.

Finally, a project of this nature must recognise the peculiar socio-cultural circumstances, educational traditions and governance structures of the different participating universities and countries, which will obviously have implications on issues of curriculum reform, new course approval and accreditation, etc. Consequently, universities, like states, are sovereign institutions and are often suspicious of external donor-driven projects capable of compromising their sovereignties. These sensitive issues should be transparently discussed with stakeholders and participants in the project workshops with a view to figuring out the best ways of managing and navigating through them.

References

ESU (2011) *Transnational Education*, European Students Union policy paper, www. esu-online.org/news/article/6064/82/

Kok, H (2009) *What is a Culture of Peace?* USAK Centre for Eurasian Studies. www.turkishweekly.net/columnist/3193/what-is-a-culture-of-peace.html

Omeje, K and Hepner, TR (eds.) (2013) *Conflict and Peacebuilding in the African Great Lakes Region.* Indiana University Press.

Reardon, AB (1988) *Comprehensive Peace Education: Educating for Global Responsibility.* New York: Teachers College Press.

United Nations General Assembly (1999) *Declaration and Programme of Action on a Culture of Peace.* The definition is extrapolated from Resolution 53/243 adopted by the UN General Assembly, New York.

Chapter 3.7

Transnational Education – Building and Enhancing Capacity Through International Collaborations

Maryam Rab

> 'Transnational higher education (TNE) is defined as any higher education provision (including distance education programmes) available in more than one country. Students are studying in a country (host country) different from the one in which the awarding institution is based (home country).'
>
> (UNESCO, 2000)

Introduction

Transnational education (TNE) is an innovative idea that has taken root over the past decade or so in higher education as an initiative to support international education, quality assurance, teaching and learning strategies, and distance education in less-developed countries. Its primary objective is to build knowledge and enhance people and institutions in some capacity in foreign countries. The general connotation attached to the concept of capacity-building reflects that higher education through TNE is venturing not only into domains of sustainable development locally but also indigenous solutions that have a long-term impact on geographical and cultural boundaries. Though terms like 'borderless', 'cross-border' or 'global educations' are being used in order to streamline strategies to train human resource in developing countries, the effectiveness of all such initiatives might as well be assumed as questionable due to the lack of clarity in regulatory frameworks designed for such programmes at a national level in

Going Global: Knowledge-Based Economies for 21st Century Nations
Copyright © 2014 by Maryam Rab
All rights of reproduction in any form reserved
ISBN: 978-1-78441-003-2

less-developed countries. The result of this flooding of international programmes in the absence or scarcity of well-thought-out strategies raises questions such as what value do they add to existing local programmes, what is the level of quality, who maintains the standards and what is the impact on the existing national system of higher education? That is where the role of universities can provide counter-argument to achieve the trust of all stakeholders engaged in delivering or seeking TNE.

Universities and Internationalisation

In today's global world, the role of universities is rapidly changing. There is a need to understand that internationalisation of higher and further education is not a stop gap arrangement but it is a need which is long term. Graduates now need to have degrees that are not only globally marketable, but that must ensure some form of employability as well. Over the past decade, the explosion of higher education providers all over the world has raised concerns regarding the establishment of quality-assurance agencies and regulatory systems in governing the growing number of TNE programmes in Asian countries such as China, Malaysia, Thailand, Singapore, India and Hong Kong. Less-developed countries such as Pakistan and Bangladesh have concerns beyond the above-mentioned issues because in these countries TNE is emerging as a parallel system of education, in the not-so-strong or mainstreamed national systems created for higher education. However, it is also important to understand that for most TNE providers, South Asia was an unprepared market compared to Europe, which had some frameworks and codes of practice for such ventures initially. Subsequently, South Asian countries have managed to cover the existing gaps. Since most of the TNE vendors have already explored the European market and its code of practice, developing countries like Pakistan presented fairly easy markets in the absence of national codes of practice and frameworks. In most developing countries, a decade ago there were hardly any policies covering issues related to TNE. However, the recent pursuit for regional centres of education in the South Asia inevitably led to the growth of an accountable and transparent environment, especially when dealing with TNE providers. In this context, it is only fair to mention that the colonial and post-colonial mindset has had a bullish effect on the TNE market.

Pakistan and Transnational Education

The case is presented around the key areas of building local capacity through international collaborations in Pakistani universities and also the quality of such initiatives and who is responsible for maintaining them. I use the British Council's definition of TNE appropriate in the context of Fatima Jinnah Women University (FJWU), as it simply states: '... education provision from one country offered in another.' (British Council, 2008)

The road to internationalisation has not been smooth for Pakistan or other developing countries in South Asia. The resistance to change and the challenge of maintaining standards are among the most common issues. At the same time, the lack of recognition by the clientele makes it difficult to identify good transnational education from bad. General issues perceived in this domain can be the instances of unregulated higher education provision, with offshore campuses and franchised degrees quoted as a valid example here. Most of the local population accessing such services are at risk of being short-changed if the quality of these franchised programmes are not monitored and evaluated through some standardised procedures. There are issues of 'degree mills' as well, which might be interested in increasing their revenues and also reducing the income of local institutions. There is no denying the fact that universities, more than ever before, need qualifications and programmes that provide their graduates with skills and employment. In Pakistan, there is a sudden mushrooming of transnational programmes, especially in higher education. The country's higher education system and institutions are still grappling with the issues of standards and quality of indigenous degrees, and the introduction of international programmes make the issue multi-layered. In light of the above-mentioned argument, the most significant point supporting this new kind of TNE is (and should be) directly linked with its financial affordability and appropriateness to the local context and culture. It also brings to light the issue of quality assurance and management of all such programmes.

FJWU and International Partnerships

First, I would like to present the concept of international partnerships and how such collaborations were developed into more structured programme for the first government-funded women's university – Fatima Jinnah Women University (FJWU) – since its inception in 1998. It is important to keep in mind the fact that the past decade is perceived as a golden period in higher education in Pakistan. One of the main reasons behind this is the funds injection in universities (HEC, 2005–2006), which resulted in a strengthening of the capacity of the existing human resources on the one hand and existing facilities in universities on the other. During this period, this publicly funded women's institution made an effort to make such initiatives a part of its mainstream programme. TNE, in this instance, was taken as a framework and used to further streamline the objectives and vision of the FJWU. A good example is one of the earlier agreements signed between a US university and FJWU to initiate a course on cultural communication on both sites simultaneously through videoconferencing in 2004. It was a small step towards internationalisation of both the Pakistani and the US universities. Knight (2004) refers to it as 'internationalisation at home' and 'internationalisation abroad', and the internal committees and boards of both universities accredited the degree programmes. It also introduced TNE in a new form, leading to knowledge exchange and knowledge generation. The US classroom and the Pakistani classroom generated discussions, which was a giant leap for a young university like FJWU and a distant US university in the state of Nebraska. The objective of internationalisation was achieved with information exchange, team teaching between US and Pakistani faculties and a course accredited by both partner universities. Subsequently, two other brief, small partnerships focused on staff mobility and capacity building but the visibility of the impact in the form of a review of existing teaching and learning practices or improvements in any other areas was not visible. The next significant partnership, which can be categorised as the first formal TNE in 2005, was an MPhil degree titled Higher Education Leadership and Management (HELM), funded by the British Council and the Higher Education Commission of Pakistan. In the late 1990s, TNE frameworks existed in the UK, and the University of London had an external programme along with some other UK universities who had offshore campuses in countries like China, Hong Kong and Malaysia. The financial burden of all such programmes was much higher than local programmes, even then. However, in this instance, since the UK institution was a University of London affiliate, no conventional form of TNE, such as accreditation, dual degree or franchise was acceptable to the UK partner. As mentioned above, the only available option of external programmes was unaffordable for the female population of FJWU and peripheral areas. In the last year of the three-year project, a part-time modular research degree was initiated after developing a scheme of studies and training the human resource by the staff of the Institute of Education, University of London. The pilot of the degree seeking programme began in 2007, but the initial response was not very encouraging, which can be attributed to reasons such as resistance to change, recognition of qualification and so on. The programme, since its initiation, has been subject to quality-assurance practices. However, the challenges of local marketing and recognition still arise after five years and three intakes. The focus on maintaining standards and quality is visible though the work presented at the end of each module. Another significant feature of the programme is that it is designed for women aspiring to be in senior management and leadership positions. Interestingly, this is the only programme that is sustainable, even after the project funding and programme life has ended.

The feedback of the individuals who are involved in these two collaborations has been positive (Rab, 2007). There is no denying the fact that it does widen the choices of learning opportunities for individuals aspiring to go further as global citizens of the world community. It shows the potential of a great source of motivation and competition for the local (national) programmes, as well as a desire to improve their quality and maintain standards during the career-building years of individuals.

The most recent project under the TNE regime at FJWU was initiated in September 2012. It aimed to develop a certification course with its UK partner university in one year. The purpose was to prepare national human resources to adapt the course contents and cascade them to other staff members. The same will be extended to other public-sector universities as an induction course for all faculty members aspiring to become university staff or at any other institution of higher learning. The certification in teaching and learning, and leadership and management in higher education was achieved in 12 months. A group of 14 members of the staff were trained and mentored in London. The feedback of the programme highlights the acknowledgement of the gaps and the role this project has played in enhancing capacities.

The point interwoven with the issue of capacity-building though international programmes is the emerging debate on TNE, and the positive and negative effects the initiative has on national policies and systems in education. As a result, the rise of transnational education and the subsequent expansion of capacity-building opportunities in developing nations such as Pakistan have led government and education commissions to establish a framework of standardisation of the deliverables in the area of education, generally, and higher education specifically. It has also pushed them to develop better access strategies for target audiences and facilitate access to higher education. In addition to this, there is an effort to enhance the quality of local education systems by increasing the variety and relevance of degree programmes offered in the country. But a country like Pakistan, being a developing nation, faces huge educational challenges due to the lack of required investment in the field of education. Simultaneously, it also faces a lack of resources and training opportunities to improve and increase the capabilities of academics and educational institutions. There are thousands of Pakistanis who travel abroad each year for higher education to countries with large Asian international student populations, such as those in Europe, North America, China and Australia. As an example, UK statistics reflect that the intake of students of Asian origin is in the thousands (HESA, 2008). The investment in foreign education is seen as an opportunity for better employability and enhanced knowledge and skills. When these students return, they are not only equipped with the best education in the world, but also with a unique understanding of how to excel in an increasingly globalised world. There has been an increase in the types of programmes offered under TNE; however, there is a need to emphasise the practicality of the knowledge gained through these collaborations. More opportunities to make apprenticeships the norm and increase vocational training options along with the development of entrepreneurial skills during transnational education exchanges can give the country long-term benefits. TNE has also reduced the cost for all such students who need not travel abroad, as the same qualification is available for them in the comfort of their home country. However, there are no mapping or scoping studies available to either support or reject these claims in Pakistan. Hence, it becomes one of the reasons that there is a lack of policies to support the growth of TNE unlike its neighbours like India and China. In the given context, the value and standard of all such programmes becomes debatable for its stakeholders, especially government-sector institutions.

Conclusion

To conclude, it is fair to say that TNE is still in its nascent stage in most developing countries; we have to let the traffic flow from West to East and vice versa, but the need to develop structures simultaneously is evident in order for progress to occur in the field of TNE. All TNE providers and seekers need to have in-built systems of monitoring and evaluation and sub-standard institutions and degree programmes need to be eliminated from national institutions and international offshore campuses. All such strategic actions can help countries strengthen their institutions locally. The strategies need to be supported with the development of the policies, processes, skills and knowledge which contributes to the achievement of national development goals. The conclusion drawn from the experiences of FJWU reflects that TNE programmes can be moulded for the greater good of developing countries and can achieve its objectives if monitored consistently. The adaptation process of TNE programmes can give optimum output; for example, the teaching and learning modules will be more affective if they have local examples and situations which can be used for critical analysis If these programmes are redesigned keeping in view the local cultural values and norms they be widely acceptable. It is understandable that in developed countries TNE has reached the stage/phase where these programmes and institutions are in a position to examine existing their practices and evaluate real impact. Unfortunately, with limited resources and expensive evaluation products, Pakistani public sector higher education cannot afford much experimentation in this area and has to make do with the limited options available for assessing all such programmes.

References

British Council (2008) 'Education UK Partnerships: Transnational Education', British Council. February 2008.

Council of Europe/UNESCO (2000) Code of Good Practice in the Provision of Transnational Education. Council of Europe/UNESCO, Paris, 2000.

ENQA (2007) ENQA Report of Standards and Guidelines for Quality Assurance in the European Higher Education Area, 2nd edition. Helsinki, ENQA.

Higher Education Statistics Agency (2008) Statistics on International Students in UK Universities 2008.

Knight, J (2003) *Internationalization remodeled: responding to new realities and challenges*. Higher Education in a Globalized Society

Knight, J (2004) Internationalization remodeled: Definition, approaches, and rationales. *Journal of Studies in International Education*, Vol. 8, No. 1, Pp. 5–31.

OBHE (2004) Mapping Borderless Higher Education. Observatory on Borderless Higher Education (www.obhe.ac.uk)

Bennett, P, Bergan, S, Cassar, D, Hamilton, M, Soinila, M, Sursock, A, … Uvalic-Trumbic, S and Williams, P (2010) Quality Assurance in Transnational Higher Education. ENQA Workshop Helsinki Finland, 2010.

Rab, M (2007) Professional Development in Higher Education: Three International Links Schemes and their Role in Capacity-building of a University. Unpublished Thesis. Institute of Education, University of London.

Chapter 3.8

Re-Defining TNE: The Challenges and Opportunities of Internationalisation

Christopher Hill

Introduction — Defining TNE

A re-definition of transnational education (TNE) moves the debate away from the international drive for numbers to include the local need for education and seeks to discuss 'need' within a contextually and culturally relevant framework. It also provides balance to the historical understanding of the development and growth of TNE, which has often failed to take into account the impact, legacy and perception of the 'foreign' programmes within the local. It is precisely this element of the debate that is central to the strategic agenda of more developed nations but often not considered by those in the early stages of educational progress, usually to their detriment.

Transnational education, or cross-border education, is characterised by mobility of higher education students, programmes, providers and resources across national jurisdiction/borders and represents an area of tremendous potential. It is therefore one that requires considerable scrutiny. While the definition of TNE is easily established, a fundamental understanding is not always as apparent. TNE is often seen as a destination, a solution, a completion, and yet it is more accurately viewed as a journey, a process, a mechanism for development. This paper explores the need to re-define TNE, from a local and global perspective, to ensure more sustainable and relevant partnerships are entered into, a more transparent and relevant system of development and management is supported, and the value of global education is protected.

Going Global: Knowledge-Based Economies for 21st Century Nations
Copyright © 2014 by Christopher Hill
All rights of reproduction in any form reserved
ISBN: 978-1-78441-003-2

The Impact of TNE

TNE can bring significant value to a host nation and provide substantial rewards. Malaysia, in particular, is looking to support economic growth by increasing the number of international students studying in Malaysia from the current circa 90,000 to 200,000 by the year 2020. While this will result in an estimated £1.2 billion increase in revenue, there are additional factors to consider in addition to financial developments, such as the issue of brand and reputation. In supporting TNE programmes and delivery, through initiatives such as EduCity, Malaysia is rapidly gaining global recognition as a home for TNE and an attractive destination and location for foreign investment and engagement.

Education, particularly in the developing world, is of such importance to individuals and societies that those institutions providing it must accept responsibility to ensure that what is delivered is relevant, quality-assured and contextually embedded. The social aspect of the student experience, the ways in which programmes are marketed, society and community engagement is developed and local integration is pursued are all susceptible to, and require, adaption to fit with the country in which the provision is offered. TNE cannot be treated as a business initiative without attention to process and experience, and is not simply an abstract concept, but instead has form, identity and legacy. It is precisely this dimension that needs re-evaluating in light of the continued proliferation of the medium.

To what extent are institutions responsible for supporting the development of global values? Should their role be in defining or defending these values? As global patterns of education shift, questions of access and mobility become central and the necessity to better understand the value of education, its reach, impact and legacy upon development become paramount. The increasingly global nature of education requires that universities address issues such as curriculum development, student experience and the nature of global citizenry to ensure that students develop during their studies and can articulate these experiences upon graduation. TNE should not simply be about the delivery of degree programmes abroad, but should address the larger questions of mobility, internationalisation and development.

According to a 2013 UK government report: '... in 2011/12 there were 570,000 higher education students studying for a UK higher education qualification at institutions abroad or via distance learning, with 124 UK institutions offering accreditation for these courses. In 2011/12, there were also nearly 8,000 international students studying at alternative providers via distance learning.' QAA reports indicate 35 UK universities with active collaborative arrangements in India (2009), 471 TNE programmes in operation in Singapore (2011), 72 UK institutions operating a total of 260 collaborative links with 107 Malaysian partners (2009) and 70 UK institutions with provision in China reporting 275 distinct relationships with 186 separate Chinese institutions. The total number of students studying in China through UK TNE was recorded by the survey as 33,874. In addition, there were 5,392 students studying in the UK, having transferred from a partner institution in China (2013). While data is still incomplete as to experience and legacy, 'it is estimated that the demand for transnational higher education in Asian countries (excluding China) will reach nearly 500,000 students by 2020. This presents both a challenge and an opportunity for those universities who are key transnational providers in the region' (Miliszewska 2008, 79). We can take this argument one step further and assert that the challenges are likewise all too real for the host country. The introduction of foreign-based education due to demand, necessity or the desire to internationalise and build capacity through collaboration and competition is only part of the equation. There are also issues of perceived value and quality, dependence and identity that must be addressed. TNE does not take place within a vacuum, but can seemingly either address gaps in local provision, or highlight them for all to see.

TNE's Wider Impact

The origin of this paper began with a two-year research project looking at TNE practices and policies between the UK and Malaysia (Fernandez-Chung et al., 2011). There was considerable scope for this project, given both the strong historical ties between the two countries in question and the plethora of TNE programmes on offer within Malaysia. The project aim was to better understand the mechanisms for collaboration, delivery and communication between TNE partners and, while this was achieved, it also became a research discussion as to impact, value and relevance, and developed a series of questions, not considered in the original project proposal, around the inherent value of TNE, the potential for damage, as well as progress and the ultimate role of international education for global development. The research project, and subsequent findings, provided a discussion and analysis of Malaysia's TNE journey, from necessity to outreach, and argued for a more systematic understanding that takes into account power distribution and aims rather than viewing TNE simply as an abstract concept.

TNE is often seen as 'the answer' for developing nations, with little consideration given as to what exactly was 'the question'. TNE is a process rather than a product and while there are considerable advantages to the inclusion, development and integration of TNE programmes within a national framework, there is also potential for confusion, distrust and concern over credibility. Malaysia provides us with an excellent case study, having moved through various stages of TNE — from necessity to

development to strategic alignment and export – and there is value in looking regionally, as well as nationally, to gain a clearer picture of impact and
value, and gain a broader understanding of the nature of TNE. This
broader understanding will promote the necessity for a re-definition of the
role of the international within the national debate.

Coping Mechanisms

Whether driven by necessity or design, the opening of borders for the delivery of TNE programmes is a common feature for developing nations.
There is much to be gained for the host nation – in terms of access to international education, revenue, partnership and development – while for the
foreign provider there are new markets to explore, revenue streams to
develop and a possible internationalisation of the core through new activity. In the absence of a global governing body to regulate TNE, national
agencies and ministries constitute the gatekeepers. The drive to partner
with top-ranking universities is frequently at odds with the unequal partnership this relies upon. TNE is often about power imbalance between
those who have and those who want. This creates dependency, which in
turn creates challenges and problems. TNE has the potential to support
long-lasting sustainable internal capacity-building and development, and
also has the potential to provide a quick-fix to the question of becoming
internationally recognised, relevant and valued.

A recent British Council report, *The Shape of Things to Come*, provides a
valuable insight into the inner workings of TNE and the lessons for success
and sustainability by highlighting that, 'unsurprisingly, the most active/long
standing host countries for TNE are generally those with the most robust
QA systems in place. Malaysia recognises TNE as being 'part' of the
Malaysian higher education system, and all IBCs are monitored and accredited by the Malaysian Qualifications Agency.' This reality in Malaysia is
the result of a process of engagement and development over the past 50
years. TNE originally filled a very real need within the country as, 'at the
time of Independence, opportunities for higher education in Malaysia were
limited as there were no public universities in the country. Private higher
education institutions (PrHEIs), however, were already present as tutorial
centres for transnational programmes that were geared toward selected
skills and professional qualifications. After Independence, PrHEIs in the
country continued to grow over time, in response to market forces from
within and without the country' (Tham, 2010). Through an adapting process of regulation, Malaysia has successfully responded to, and harnessed,
TNE to support strategic development. The initial dependency on the
'other' evolved into a perception in the 'other' as better and further

developed into the 'other' becoming an intrinsic element of the centre. This was achieved over time and is a result of a redistribution of the initial power imbalance discussed above. While the specifics of the Malaysian case are not applicable to all, their story should be of interest to developing nations looking to attract and embed TNE within local provision.

Shifting Landscapes

TNE can no longer be viewed as a product moving solely from West to East. Increasingly, we are seeing internal regional movement and traditional hosts of TNE becoming exporters. With these new developments must also come new definitions, understanding and contextual markers. The traditional English language, Western-centric offering has evolved, been adapted in places and must subsequently be viewed in a new light.

China's decision to develop offshore campuses in Laos and Malaysia clearly reflects a new level of competition in the international arena and a growth in their national approach to education. In China's case, it is not merely the fact that offshore campuses are being considered and developed; it is the sheer size and level of commitment of the projects in question that demonstrate an absolute confidence in the endeavour and an awareness of the value and importance of this aspect of educational growth.

Chinese institutions currently operate two offshore programmes in Laos: Soochow University began offering programmes in Vientiane in 2012 and is moving towards the establishment of two branch campuses in the city, which will reportedly target 5,000 students; while Kunming University of Science and Technology operates an offshore programme based on the Laotian campus of Thailand's Dhurakij Pundit University, thus engaging in multi-partner collaborative delivery. China's activity in Laos and Malaysia can be seen as a result of China's current long-term education reform and development plan (2010–2020), which includes a clear statement as to China's interest in promoting its 'educational institutions overseas to enhance the international exchange of education, extensive international co-operation and education services' (ICEF 2013). In 2011, Xiamen University announced its intention to open a campus in Malaysia that makes a statement in both intent and design. The plans are for a 60-hectare (150-acre) site near Kuala Lumpur that will target 10,000 students and require an estimated start-up cost of almost US$100 million.

Al-Azhar University in Cairo has likewise recently announced plans to open a campus in Malaysia in 2014 with student recruitment targets of 10,000. The rationale behind this move is connected to the recognition of Malaysia as both an Islamic country and an education hub. With increasing activity of this nature, questions of saturation and integration will need to be addressed. The realisation that 'here a hub, there a hub, everywhere a hub hub' is a model rife with complications will force a need to reassess the distribution, purpose and nature of TNE as both a concept but also as a global reality. As the export of education becomes multilateral, multi-purpose and multi-directional, we begin to see the evolution of learning methods and teaching practices and the reduction in dependence on the 'traditional' Western approach, thus freeing up the next wave of TNE itself.

Future Developments

The proliferation of the hub model and the subsequent collective identity of the foreign within the local is an area of international education that requires further analysis and discussion. Within the arena of global learning, the hub represents many things and is, in many ways, about movement: the movement of students, of staff, of learning styles, of curriculum, of identity, of education. Should the aim be to carbon copy the home model for export or to contextualise teaching and develop the home model accordingly? Are we seeking to localise the international or internationalise the local? A closer examination of the hub model provides an opportunity to not only appreciate the international, but also to better understand that which we do on a local scale in terms of integration and learning support.

The development of the hub model, not uniquely that of the branch campus, represents the next wave of TNE development and "while government TNE strategy documents are lacking, the establishment of international education cities and zones represents a major commitment to develop TNE in some countries. In Qatar, for example, the Qatar Foundation has responsibility for the development of the country's Education City, which is home to ten international branch campuses. South Korea is developing the Songdo Global University Campus 40 in the Incheon Free Economic Zone." (The Shape of Things to Come Report, p26). The hub model can be adapted and controlled nationally to address specific demands, attract chosen partners and demonstrate the shift in power from those who have to those who want.

Conclusions

TNE has become a global phenomenon and a fundamental aspect of international education. It drives engagement, encourages mobility, promotes access, supports national development and is at the top of many developing nation's wish lists. The call for a re-definition and re-evaluation of TNE is precisely to address such issues. It should be clearly noted that TNE is a mechanism, or vehicle, for partnership and development, not a guarantor of success in this area. As universities increasingly embed and promote internationalisation strategies, evolving markets and student mobility patterns, such as the 2007 36 per cent to 42 per cent increase in mobile East Asian students studying within their region (ICEF 2012), rather than traditional one-to-one relationships, drive engagement. It is therefore essential that TNE is seen for what it is, warts and all, understood, harnessed and better managed to support the global development of education. Regional, rather than international or global movement presents opportunities for a geographical or ideological hegemony of ideas, and the evolution of the hub model provides relevant and sustainable focal points for this to take shape.

As TNE continues to evolve, it will move from the national to the supra-national and back to the national, having redefined local and foreign education along the way. Adam (2001) argues that "national autonomy and sovereignty in the domain of higher education (and tertiary education) have never before been challenged on such a scale." The movement and delivery of nationally linked programmes has already begun to blur and will continue to morph into intra-national education with the ability to shape regional alliances, promote balanced exchange and redefine global values and education.

References

Brandenburg, U and De Wit, H (2011) The End of Internationalization *International Higher Education* No. 62, Winter 2011 pp. 15–17.

Coleman, D (2003) Quality Assurance in Transnational Education. *Journal of Studies in International Education*, 7(4) pp. 354–378.

GATE (Global Alliance for Transnational Education): Demand for transnational education in the Asia Pacific. *Global Alliance for Transnational Education*, Washington (2000).

Hill, C, Kee-Cheok, C, Yin-Ching, L and Fernandez-Chung, R (2013) TNE – transnational education or tensions between national and external? A case study of Malaysia, *Studies in Higher Education* Published online: 14 Jan 2013.

Huang, F (2007) Internationalization of Higher Education in the Developing and Emerging Countries: A Focus on Transnational Higher Education in Asia, *Journal of Studies in International Education 11(3/4)*: 421–432

Knight, J (2011) Five Myths about Internationalization *International Higher Education* No. 62, Winter 2011 pp. 14–15.

Miliszewska, I (2008) *Transnational Education Programs: Student Reflections on a Fully-Online Versus a Hybrid Model*, in Hybrid Learning and Education, Fong, J, Kwan, R and Wang, FL (eds). (Springer Berlin Heidelberg) pp. 79–90.

Smith, K (2010) Assuring quality in transnational higher education: a matter of collaboration or control? *Studies in Higher Education*. 35 (7). pp. 793–806.

Tham, SY (2010) Trade in Higher Education Services in Malaysia: Key Policy Challenges. *Higher Education Policy* 23: 99–122.

Reports

Adam, S (2001) *Transnational Education Project Report and Recommendations.* Report commissioned by the Confederation of European Union Rectors' Conferences. Malmö, Sweden.

Transnational Education Policies and Practices: A Study of Selected Malaysian and United Kingdom Higher Education Institutions. A Report prepared for the Ministry of Higher Education, Malaysia 2011. (R. M. Fernandez-Chung, C, Hill, L, Yin Ching, C, Kee Cheok).

International Education: Global Growth and Prosperity. HM Government Report, July 2013.

The Shape of Things to Come. The evolution of transnational education: data, definitions, opportunities and impacts analysis. British Council, Going Global 2013.

QAA Review Report. Review of UK transnational education in China 2012, May 2013.

QAA Overview Report. Audit of overseas provision, Singapore, July 2011.

QAA Overview Report. Audit of overseas provision, India, July 2009.

Quality Update International, Issue 87, May 2013.

Web Resources

ICEF Monitor Review. *China to expand transnational education footprint with first off-shore campuses* (07 Aug 2013) http://monitor.icef.com/2013/08/china-to-expand-transnational-education-footprint-with-first-offshore-campuses/

ICEF Monitor Review. *A more complex marketplace taking shape in 2012* (16 Jan 2012) http://monitor.icef.com/2012/01/a-more-complex-marketplace-taking-shape-for-2012/

Chronicle of Higher Education. *China plans to build the biggest branch campus in the world, but will it succeed?* (14 Feb 2013) http://chronicle.com/blogs/worldwise/china-plans-to-build-the-biggest-branch-campus-in-the-world-but-will-it-succeed/31585

Conclusion

Jo Beall

Director, Education and Society, British Council

We have in this book the insight, experience, analysis and vision of over 1,000 global leaders in tertiary education, from 16 countries across five continents. The knowledge and variety of perspectives gathered between these covers form a tangible example of the interchange of scholarship and experience that is at the book's heart – a network of enlightenment made vibrant by our digital age. As the UK's cultural-relations organisation, the British Council is dedicated to promoting dialogue and co-operation in a variety of ways, the forum of Going Global, with its focus on tertiary education, being one. Going Global builds on the British Council's network, which includes government leaders, national agencies, academia and industry, to explore how cross-border co-operation in the field can help shape a better world. Yet we do this with an acute awareness of Professor Homi Bhabha's admonition in his introduction to the 2012 Going Global conference, that as we make our way through this 'tracery of intersecting global journeys', we should be wary of being bewitched by the 'magical thinking of globalisation'. We should not be blind to the deep inequalities of the distribution of knowledge, and in how knowledge is used, across the world – disparities which persist despite the wonders of new technology. An awareness that the apparent smoothness of communication in a digital age can disguise ongoing issues of inequality characterises many of the studies in this book.

The three key themes of Going Global 2013 have been explored here with thoughtfulness and perception. The preceding chapters take important strides forward in examining international collaboration in research and

Going Global: Knowledge-Based Economies for 21st Century Nations
Copyright © 2014 by Jo Beall
All rights of reproduction in any form reserved
ISBN: 978-1-78441-003-2

innovation; in looking at the development of highly skilled workers to enable their engagement in a knowledge economy; and in investigating how collaboration across borders can contribute to *truly* internationalising tertiary education structures and systems. It is clear, both from discussions at Going Global 2013 and in the studies published here, that – as we face the challenges of the 21st century – higher education is the foundation of economic diversification, the way to global prosperity and the key to improved prospects of global harmony. International collaboration – the strengthening and extending of a worldwide network of knowledge, experience and research – is the backbone of all three Going Global themes. Whatever a country's objectives and circumstances, from Qatar to Botswana, such collaboration can benefit economy, infrastructure and wider political engagement. By investing in the skills, people, research and systems needed to support a thriving global knowledge economy, we will ensure prosperous, innovative, interconnected and wise societies.

The consideration of these three themes has identified clear messages. The preceding chapters have revealed that the role of international collaboration is absolutely critical to peace and prosperity in our global world. International research links, innovative communications technologies, and cross-sectorial partnerships are crucial in meeting 21st-century challenges. We have learned how governments, employers and educational institutions are responding to the challenges of skills shortages and youth unemployment. Different contributors highlight the importance of integrating the needs of commerce and industry with what education systems can deliver, and many recognise the key role of the humanities and social sciences in this respect: it is a study of the humanities that imparts crucial language skills, intercultural fluency, critical thinking, and analytical ability. This is evident in the 'Culture at Work' research commissioned by Booz Allen and the British Council, which points to the business value of intercultural skills in the workplace, and suggests how policy makers and education providers can do more to develop such skills. It is evident in 'The Shape of Things to Come 2', new research by the British Council that highlights the importance of transnational education for international growth, and offers evidence of trends and best practices in the field. And we have seen how international tertiary education systems and structures are becoming more diverse as we move into the 21st century. This is an important step if we are to dispel the danger of being deluded by 'the magical thinking of globalisation' into ignoring world inequalities. Higher education systems must bring local and international contexts together if they are to make a difference in the world. With all this new technology at our fingertips, we should be looking at hybrid models of education, those that integrate online and face-to-face learning. Higher education has to be more flexible and innovative if it is to progress and reach ever-greater numbers across the world.

The impetus towards greater international collaboration carries over into Going Global 2014, which will be held in Miami, USA, a city that provides a bridge between Latin, Central and North America, and reflects the future of the region. The themes of the conference will be inclusion, innovation and impact. Innovation drives economic prosperity and growth. It cannot be contained within national borders. Countries aiming to develop strong local talent pools to fuel innovation must not only provide high-quality tertiary education, but need to be open to international collaboration. In turn, people with specialised skills and knowledge are internationally mobile. Nor can innovation be contained within individual sectors or disciplines; instead it feeds and catalyses across traditional divisions. Meeting the challenges of innovation, therefore, requires inclusion – widespread participation of citizens, the building of links between disciplines and different economic sectors, and transnational collaboration. Universities and colleges are central to these agendas, and an effectively internationalised higher education sector can deliver a global impact that goes well beyond traditional research and teaching roles.

This sort of multidisciplinary, cross-cultural, international collaboration in education goes to the heart of what the British Council is all about. With nearly 80 years' experience in international education, and offices in over 100 countries, the British Council has the range of contacts, has engendered the trust, created the opportunities, and developed a knowledge and expertise that make possible such ventures as the Going Global conferences, convening world leaders in tertiary education. We would like to thank sincerely all the authors who have contributed to this publication, as well as our International Steering Committee for their continuous support in developing and delivering the conferences. Our particular gratitude goes to the editors, Tim Gore and Dr Mary Stiasny, for the time and dedication they have put into delivering a publication of genuine value and interest to the international education community.

The British Council remains committed to tertiary education as a critical component of national and personal prosperity, of institutional and international collaboration, and of citizens' development, wisdom and well-being. The debate generated by Going Global 2013 and the ideas presented here will further stimulate our programmes and strategies. We have a long road ahead of us, as we equip higher education systems to meet the challenges of the 21st century. We owe it to our young people – who in many cases face an uncertain future – to develop systems, institutions and networks that enable them to participate in an internationalised economy and to contribute to a shared future as responsible and talented global citizens.

About the Authors

Abdul Sattar Al-Taie

Dr Abdul Sattar Al-Taie is the start-up director of the Qatar National Research Fund (QNRF) www.qnrf.org, where he currently serves as its Executive Director. He holds PhD in Chemical Engineering from the Imperial College London, as well as an MSc in Advanced Chemical Engineering and BSc (honours) in Chemical Engineering and Chemical Technology in addition to DIC and A.C.G.I; all from imperial College.

Prior to his formative work with QNRF, Dr Abdul Sattar Al-Taie held a number of key positions in Iraq with the Ministry of Oil, the Iraqi Atomic Energy Commission and the Ministry of Industry and Minerals and was a key player in a number of strategic projects and S&T initiatives in Iraq. He also taught in a number of universities in Iraq and supervised a number of PhD and MSc students.

Dr Al-Taie has received numerous awards, commendations and decorations in his career, including the Jabir Bin Hayyan Medal, the Reconstruction Medal and the prestigious Science Medal of the Republic of Iraq.

Alexander Bedny

Dr Bedny graduated from Lobachevsky State University of Nizhni Novgorod, Russia, and Roskilde University, Denmark (2001). He holds the scientific degree of Candidate of Science in Sociology awarded by Lobachevsky State University of Nizhni Novgorod (2005). He is Vice-Rector for International Affairs, Dean Faculty for International Students, and Head Centre for Student Innovation Entrepreneurship at Lobachevsky State University of Nizhni Novgorod − National Research University.

His research interests lie in the field of sociology, university management, and in particular in the organisation of university knowledge transfer, innovation and entrepreneurship ecosystem. He has 40 scientific and methodological publications. He has managed a number of international projects and programmes addressing the issues of higher education management, including several European Tempus projects (such as "Becoming an Entrepreneurial University", "Achieving Bologna through Total Quality Management", "University Knowledge Transfer for Sustainable Growth"), and US-Russian EURECA (Enhancing University Research and

Entrepreneurial Capacity) Programme. He is a member of Deans and European Academics Network (DEAN).

Alexander Grudzinskiy

Prof. Dr Sc. Alexander Grudzinskiy graduated from Lomonosov Moscow State University (1977). He has the scientific degrees of Doctor of Science in Sociology awarded by Saint Petersburg State University (2005) and Candidate of Science in Physics and Mathematics awarded by Dorodnicyn Computing Centre of Russian Academy of Science (1985). He is First Vice-Rector, Dean Faculty of Management and Entrepreneurship at Lobachevsky State University of Nizhni Novgorod – National Research University.

His research field is the sociology of management, university management, knowledge transfer. He has more than 170 scientific papers published. He has led a number of international projects in the field of university management under European Union Tempus Programme (such as "Becoming an Entrepreneurial University", "Achieving Bologna through Total Quality Management", "University Knowledge Transfer for Sustainable Growth") and American foundations (including "EURECA – Enhancing University Research and Entrepreneurial Capacity"). He is a member of Deans and European Academics Network (DEAN).

Andreas Göthenberg

Andreas Göthenberg was appointed Executive Director of STINT as of September 1, 2009. He received his MSc and PhD degrees from KTH Royal Institute of Technology, Stockholm, Sweden, in 1996 and 2003, respectively. From 2006 until 2009 he was a Science and Technology Attaché at the Embassy of Sweden in Tokyo, Japan. Previous to that he was working as a Center Manager and Senior Researcher in China, setting up joint research and education centers for KTH Royal Institute of Technology at Zhejiang University and Fudan University.

He has been a Research Fellow at Tokyo Institute of Technology and is currently an Adjunct Associate Professor at the Chinese University of Hong Kong. He has also been with Texas Instruments Inc., Dallas, Texas, U.S.A., and is a Senior Member of the Institute of Electrical and Electronics Engineers, Inc. (IEEE).

Christopher Hill

Dr Christopher Hill is the Director, Research Training and Academic Development and Knowledge Without Borders Network Convenor at The

University of Nottingham Malaysia Campus, where he has been based since 2008. Dr Hill's research interests include transnational education and its impact in SE Asia, the development of international education and the student experience in the global arena. Dr Hill has published and presented in the field of international education; organised and delivered conferences, workshops, training and lectures around the world and has led on funded projects to develop research capacity and internationalise HE systems in Iraq and Thailand.

Dorothea Rüland

Dr Dorothea Rüland studied German Literature, History and Musicology at the University of Freiburg.She has been Secretary General of the German Academic Exchange Service (DAAD) since October 2010. Before coming back to DAAD, she was Director of the Center for International Cooperation at the Free University Berlin for two years.

During her time in DAAD from 1980–2008, Rüland was responsible for several regions of the world. In 2004 she was assigned Deputy Secretary General of the DAAD. From 1999 until 2004 she was in charge of diverse DAAD activities in Asia, Africa and Latin America; from 1994 to 1999 she was head of the office in Indonesia. She is a member of several national and international associations and administrative boards.

Gerald Wangenge-Ouma

Gerald Wangenge-Ouma is the Director for Institutional Planning at the University of Pretoria in South Africa. He was previously an Associate Professor of Higher Education Studies at the University of the Western Cape, also in South Africa. His primary research areas of interest include higher education finance, higher education and development and higher education policy. Wangenge-Ouma is the author of numerous papers, many of which appear in leading journals such as *Higher Education, Oxford Review of Education, European Journal of Education, Higher Education Policy*, among others. Wangenge-Ouma received his PhD in Higher Education Studies from the University of Cape Town.

Hannah Ellis

Hannah studied German and Spanish at Exeter University with an integral year abroad in León, Spain. After several years working in London, she then interned at the Directorate General for Interpretation at the European Commission in Brussels, where she worked to promote language learning across Europe. Through this placement, she came into contact with the

StudyPortals team, and went on to intern in their Eindhoven (Netherlands) office in the summer of 2013. During this time, she analysed 25,000 international exchange student reviews in order to discover what truly motivates international study. She is currently studying for a Master's degree in Linguistics at the University of Oxford.

Hans Pohl

Hans Pohl is programme director at STINT, the Swedish Foundation for International Cooperation in Research and Higher Education. STINT's mission is to internationalise Swedish higher education and research. As a programme director at STINT, Pohl develops the portfolio of instruments and evaluates the impact of STINT's investments. Previous positions include analyst at Sweden's Innovation Agency (VINNOVA), engineering consultant at Grontmij AB, Science Officer at the Swedish Office of Science and Technology in Bonn/Berlin and area manager at ABB Switchgear. In 2010, he was awarded his PhD from Chalmers University of Technology with a thesis about innovation management and policy.

Ian Willis

Dr Ian Willis is Head of the Educational Development Division and formerly Director of Studies for the Postgraduate Certificate in Learning and Teaching at the University of Liverpool.

He has been involved in a number of international consultancy projects to enhance learning and teaching including work in Syria, Canada, Ghana, Tanzania and Malawi. Currently he is leading on a British Council-funded project to help build capacity in medical education in the Punjab. He was part of the team that developed the University's online professional doctorate in higher education and he now leads the programme's Learning and Teaching research cluster.

Jo Beall

Jo Beall joined the British Council and the Executive Board in July 2011 as Director, Education and Society, reporting to the CEO. Jo was formerly Deputy Vice-Chancellor, University of Cape Town with responsibility for academic matters, social responsiveness and external relations and the University's international strategy.

A graduate of the London School of Economics, Jo was formerly Professor of Development Studies in the LSE's International Development Department, which she directed between 2004 and 2007. During her academic career Jo has published numerous books and academic articles in the areas of gender and social policy, urban governance and development, cities and conflict and state fragility. She has worked in Africa, Asia and Latin America, undertaking significant research projects and advisory work in Afghanistan, India, Pakistan and South Africa. Her move to the British Council signals her commitment to education as a force for global good. Jo serves on the British Academy's Area Panel for South Asia, the Council of Overseas Development Institute, and the Higher Education Funding Council for England's Research Excellence Framework Panel for Anthropology and Development.

Joanna Newman

Joanna Newman MBE is Director of the UK Higher Education International Unit (IU). She represents the higher education sector on national and international platforms.

After receiving the Parkes PhD studentship at the University of Southampton and an Institute of Commonwealth Studies fellowship at the University of London, Joanna taught history at University College London and Warwick University before joining the British Library as Head of Higher Education. She is an Honorary Research Fellow at the University of Southampton and a Fellow of the Royal Society of Arts. Joanna was awarded an MBE in the 2014 New Year's Honours for services to the promotion of higher education internationally, particularly in Brazil.

John Knagg

John Knagg is Head of Research and Consultancy for English with the British Council, having worked in English language education all his career in Europe, Middle East, East Asia and Latin America. He designed and oversees the British Council's research partnership schemes and has been responsible for the British Council portfolio of publications and convenor of the panel of judges for the ELT Innovations Awards.

He is Chair of Accreditation UK – the quality assurance programme for English language teaching institutions in UK – and a member of the editorial panel of the English Language Teaching Journal of Oxford University Press.

Jonathan Ledger

Jonathan is the Managing Director of the Proskills UK Group. Jonathan is responsible for the strategic and operational interaction at all employer levels, local, regional and national Government agencies, understanding employer skills needs, occupational standard, training course and qualifications design, through to implementation of skills solutions for process and manufacturing industries.

Jonathan is the driver of partnerships with international Government agencies, British Council and skills bodies supporting the development and delivery of international qualification systems and skills solutions. He is currently working with a number of partners on initiatives from initial scoping through to operational delivery across the globe.

José Celso Freire Junior

Prof. José Celso Freire Junior is an Electrical Engineer graduated from Federal University of Rio de Janeiro (UFRJ). He has a Master's degree in Computer Science from University of São Paulo (USP) and a PhD degree in Computer Science from Université de Grenoble I (Joseph Fourier University), France. He is an Associate Professor at São Paulo State University, UNESP in Brazil and its Head of International Relations. He is also the President of FAUBAI – Association of Brazilian Higher Education Institutions Officers for International Relations, and as such has participated as a panellist to several international events like Going Global, NAFSA and EAIE.

Kenneth Omeje

Kenneth Omeje is Visiting Senior Research Fellow at the John and Elnora Ferguson Centre for African Studies (JEFCAS), University of Bradford and Professor of International Relations at the United States International University in Nairobi, Kenya. He holds a PhD in Peace Studies from the University of Bradford. He is a Fellow of the West Africa Institute (WAI) in Praia, Cape Verde and a member of the Scientific Committee of the United Nations-mandated University for Peace (UPEACE) Africa Programme in Addis Ababa, Ethiopia. He is a well-published scholar with specialist interest in peace education, conflict and peace building in Sub-Saharan Africa.

Kgomotso H Moahi

Kgomotso H. Moahi is currently Dean of the Faculty of Humanities at the University of Botswana. She has served at the University of Botswana as a lecturer in information studies, and carried out research on information use in Botswana, health information systems, indigenous knowledge systems and information management. As a dean, she has also taken an interest in higher education matters, including internationalisation of education and the role of education in development.

Leandro R Tessler

Physicist (UFRGS, 1982), MSc (Unicamp, 1985), PhD (Tel Aviv University, 1989). Joined Instituto de Física of Unicamp in 1991, where he is Associate Professor since 1999. He was a CNRS post-doc at ISMRa, Caen and Visiting researcher at Ecole Polytechnique, Palaiseau and University of Wisconsin – Madison. Author or co-author of more than 50 research papers, three book chapters and many articles about higher education in newspapers. Prof. Tessler was Dean of Admissions and Director of International Relations at Unicamp. He is a frequent consultant for the Ministry of Education. Research interests include access, affirmative action, internationalisation of higher education and rare-earth doped nanostructured semiconductors.

Lucky T Moahi

Lucky T Moahi is currently Coordinator of the Education Hub at Ministry of Education and Skills Development, Botswana. He has extensive experience as a science educator and administrator and in curriculum development. Mr Moahi has served in a variety of government sectors and ministries. He first served in the Ministry of Education as a teacher and later, administrator; he was instrumental in the establishment of a new Ministry of Communications, Science and Technology as a Deputy Permanent Secretary; he also served in the Ministry of Labour and Home Affairs coordinating matters of labour, immigration, national registration and internship programme for higher education graduates.

Martin Hall

Professor Martin Hall is a historical archaeologist and strategic leader. He took up his present role of Vice-Chancellor of the University of Salford in August 2009. Professor Hall joined Salford from the University of Cape Town where he was Deputy Vice-Chancellor for six years. He has a career that has spanned both political change and transformation in South Africa and new directions in archaeology over the past four decades. He has written extensively on South African history, culture and higher education policy.

Professor Hall's current areas of focus include open access and innovation, inequality and its consequences and post-conflict mitigation and mediation. He writes weekly on these and other issues at www.salford.ac.uk/vc

Dr Mary Stiasny

Mary Stiasny joined the Institute of Education from the British Council as Pro Director Learning and Teaching and International Strategy, in July

2007. In September 2013 she moved to the University of London where she is Pro-Vice Chancellor (International) and CEO of the University of London International Programmes.

Previously Mary has worked as a secondary school teacher and then moved to Goldsmiths College, University of London as a teacher trainer. She joined Oxford Brookes University as Deputy Head of the School of Education and was subsequently Head of the School of Education and Training at the University of Greenwich, followed by four years as the British Council's Director of Education and Training. She has written and spoken extensively about internationalism in education, with experience of leading the recruitment of overseas students to the UK, as well as developing international partnerships.

Mary has been a member of the UK UNESCO Education Committee, and a Director of the UK UNESCO National Commission, and is currently a Trustee of the Council for Education in the Commonwealth. In 2013 she was appointed OBE for services to higher education.

Maryam Rab

Dr Maryam Rab has worked in the public service sector for the last 17 years in different capacities. She has a Master's degree in Education Management from King's College London and a Doctorate in Education from the Institute of Education from University of London UK. She was Registrar in the first women's University in Pakistan for 60 years.

Mary started her career as an English language teacher in 1994 and later moved into higher education management. She designed, planned and initiated an MPhil programme in Higher Education and Leadership in Fatima Jinnah Women University for women professionals in Education. She has also worked with USAID, DfID, World Bank and UN agencies on various education projects. Her research focus is women and leadership, quality assurance, international collaborations and partnerships in higher education. At present she is working as Director Research Evaluation and Monitoring Unit (REMU) at British Council, Pakistan.

Nicholas NN Nsowah-Nuamah

Prof. Nicholas N. N. Nsowah-Nuamah is the Rector of Kumasi Polytechnic in Ghana. He was a Full Professor of Statistics at the Institute of Statistical Social and Economic Research (ISSER), University of Ghana. He was the Deputy Government Statistician and Acting Government Statistician at the Ghana Statistical Service. He has been the Chairman of the Regent University College of Science and Technology in Ghana since 2004.

He founded three Associations, namely Ghana Statistical Association (GSA), Ghana Association of Statistics Students (GASS), Ghana Association of Statistics Students Alumni (GASSA). Currently, he is the Interim President of GSA and the Chief Patron of GASS and GASSA.

Prof. Nsowah-Nuamah has consulted for a number of international organisations including Department for International Development (DFID), FAO, UNICEF, Economic Commission for West African Sub-region (ECOWAS), MICRO International, Educational Assessment and Research Centre (EARC), World Vision, ILO, HelpAge Ghana, FRR Limited of the United Kingdom, World Bank.

He has written more than ten books and a lot of refereed papers in reputable journals. He has presented papers in several international conferences and workshops.

Patricia G Owusu-Darko

Dr Patricia G. Owusu-Darko is the Director for International Affairs and Institutional Linkages of Kumasi Polytechnic. She is a Senior Lecturer in Food Science at Faculty of Applied Science in Kumasi Polytechnic.

She is a resource person for Root and Tuber Improvement and Marketing Programme (RTIMP) of the Ministry of Food and Agriculture (MOFA), Centre for Biodiversity Utilization and Development (CBUD) of Kwame Nkrumah University of Science and Technology (KNUST), Ministry of Social Welfare, Nestle (Ghana) and the Ghana Tourism Authority.

She is a reviewer for the following journals: *International Journal of Technology and Management Research, Food Control, Journal of Food Chemistry and the Sunyani Polytechnic Lecture Series.* She has attended several national and international conferences.

Peter Darroch

Peter Darroch is currently SciVal Consultant (United Kingdom and Ireland) at Elsevier BV. Peter completed his PhD in Molecular Signalling at the University of Strathclyde in 2002, following his first degree in Physiology at University St. Andrews. He subsequently spent four years as a researcher in both the United States and United Kingdom publishing several articles and conference proceedings.

In 2006 Peter left academic research and held several positions in the Healthcare industry before joining Elsevier in 2011. As SciVal Consultant, Peter works with Universities and Governments using SciVal to help institutions manage research information inform planning and Strategy and so drive successful research.

Rebecca Hughes

Professor Rebecca Hughes is joining the British Council after a career working extensively in international Higher Education and English language and linguistics. Rebecca's experience of trans-national Higher Education includes being the first Pro-Vice-Chancellor for Internationalisation at The University of Sheffield and, at the University of Nottingham, running a Department delivering UK degrees and English language support services in Malaysia and China.

Professor Hughes has published widely on her personal research interest of spoken language and given presentations on this topic at a number of international conferences. She regularly contributes to debates surrounding the globalised higher education system in forums such as the OECD where she brings the combination of a 20-year career working in University internationalisation and Applied Linguistics expertise to issues of academic capacity-building and language policy.

Her other recent roles have included Chair of the White Rose Advisory Group on East Asian Studies, Chair of the Worldwide Universities Network (WUN) Global Challenge on Higher Education and Research, and member of the board of governors of the Institute for Managers in Higher Education, Higher Education and Skills Division at the OECD.

Sue Parker

Sue is Global Director for Skills, GEMS Education Solutions. She works on global strategic skills reform programmes, develops GEMS skills capacity; builds skills partnerships with employers and major providers to enable quick entry into markets and helps organisations re-focus their skills business.

Sue was Expert, Qualifications Policy and Qualifications Framework for the National Qualifications Authority, UAE. Before moving abroad, Sue ran a highly successful SME providing consultancy and interim management for public and private sector clients. The work focused on the UK and Europe with short periods in the Middle East and Asia. Sue's early career included university lecturing, polytechnic accreditation, strategic consultancy with KPMG, Principal of two FE Colleges and senior management with Edexcel.

Tim Gore OBE

Tim Gore is Director, Global Networks, and Communities for the University of London International Programmes which is a unique and historic system of distance and flexible learning with 54,000 students in over 180 countries. Tim's main role is the development of the networks and communities of stakeholders that are crucial to reputation and brand of the international programmes.

As such he oversees planning and implementation of worldwide communications and marketing campaigns; the development of a global network of over 130 independent institutions; relationships with in-country stakeholders such as regulators and employers; and the alumni network. Tim is a regular speaker on university international strategy; reputation and risk; transnational education; online delivery; MOOCs and student experience. Tim has previously held senior leadership positions with the University of Greenwich and the British Council. In 2008 Tim was appointed OBE for services to the British Council.

Yussra Jamjoom

Dr Yussra Jamjoom holds a PhD from Institute of Education University of London, a leading research institution in educational studies. She also holds a Master's degree in Information Management from Marymount University, Washington DC and a second Master degree in Assistive Technology from George Mason University, Washington DC. She holds a Bachelor degree in Accounting from King Abdulaziz University, Kingdom of Saudi Arabia.

Dr Jamjoom served as the Vice-Dean of University of Business and Technology (Female Section) in Jeddah, Saudi Arabia. Dr Jamjoom also worked at Saudi Embassy of United States in Washington DC. Dr Jamjoom's research interests include higher education policy, national skills development, graduates' employablity, student development, globalisation in higher education and cultural identity.